Theology without Borders

Theology without Borders

An Introduction to Global Conversations

William A. Dyrness
and Oscar García-Johnson

Baker Academic
a division of Baker Publishing Group
Grand Rapids, Michigan

© 2015 by William A. Dyrness and Oscar García-Johnson

Published by Baker Academic
a division of Baker Publishing Group
PO Box 6287, Grand Rapids, MI 49516-6287
www.bakeracademic.com

Printed in the United States of America

Library of Congress Cataloging-in-Publication Data

Dyrness, William A.
    Theology without borders : an introduction to global conversations / William A. Dyrness
and Oscar García-Johnson.
        pages cm
    Includes bibliographical references and index.
    ISBN 978-0-8010-4932-3 (pbk.)
    1. Theology. 2. Christianity and culture. 3. Globalization—Religious aspects—
Christianity. I. Title.
BR118.D98 2015
230—dc23   2015023237

Contents

Preface

Not long ago Oscar was invited to speak at a conference on evangelism in the city of Suzuka, Japan. The host church in Suzuka consisted of Sansei and Nisei families whose primary languages were Spanish and Portuguese.[1] The founding couple of this church, Peruvians by birth, migrated with their parents to Japan as adolescents and met while attending a Brazilian Pentecostal church in Suzuka. Over the course of time, they married and were called into ministry. In order to serve both the immigrant populations and their Japanese neighbors, they decided to plant a multilingual/multicultural church where services (and, where necessary, translation) would be in Japanese, Spanish, and Portuguese. To their surprise, young Japanese eager to make their way in a globalizing world were drawn to the church in increasing numbers.

Clearly such boundary-crossing hybrids and other forms of cultural mixing and matching are becoming increasingly common. While mainline and traditional denominational churches are declining in North America (and have almost disappeared in Europe), immigrant and ethnic churches of all kinds are proliferating. So it is not simply that the center of Christianity has shifted to the South (and East) as Andrew Walls argued a generation ago, but that the *character* of this church is undergoing massive transition: it has gone ethnic, even transnational. And accompanying this change in character is a geopolitical transformation that is equally significant: the church doesn't necessarily depend on the economic and cultural resources of the West for its advance.

---

1. Sansei identifies Japanese-born (third-generation) immigrants, while Nisei identifies second-generation immigrants.

This has led observers to claim that we have entered into the era of what has been called global Christianity.[2] Clearly the nature of Christianity has changed irrevocably over the last generation, but this has sometimes led to exaggerated claims about Christianity: that its fundamental growth has invariably taken place without significant missionary presence or after missionaries have left; that the Western church is in decline and no longer plays a significant role in defining Christianity; and that now missions will no longer be from the West to the rest, but it will be a reverse mission such as we are seeing in Western Europe. In 2009 sociologist Robert Wuthnow responded to these claims by arguing that the American church is not in decline and in fact is internationalizing itself and increasing its presence and influence in many places of the world. For better or worse, Wuthnow argues, US churches still play a significant role in the increasingly diverse world church.[3]

In this book we want to avoid such polarized claims and simply acknowledge that the changing nature of Christianity, however it is understood, suggests that Christian reflection needs to be reconfigured in the form of a conversation between different parts of the body of Christ. Rather than seeing the flow of influences either as West to East (or South) or in the reverse, we want to argue that it needs to encompass multiple directions, including flows from South to South and within the Western churches.[4] Specifically we want to ask what this new situation of the church means for our corporate and continuing theological reflection.

Now one might think that these changes would have deep reverberations within Western theological education. But outside of missions and some pastoral theology courses, not much has changed in the theological curriculum—this despite the call of accrediting agencies for multicultural literacy. We will explore the many implications of this new reality throughout this book, but in this preface let us lay out the presenting problem: despite the dramatically changing character of the Christian church and global presence, the dominant theological paradigm studied in Western seminaries, and often carried by missionaries abroad, has been the received Western theological traditions. The tension between the changing circumstances of Christian

2. See Jenkins, *Next Christendom*. However, it is often unrecognized that Andrew Walls had been making a similar claim for more than a decade.

3. See Wuthnow, *Boundless Faith*. For its part, Wuthnow's critique has been challenged as being unfair to the world Christianity hypothesis, insisting wrongly that it saw no continuing role for the Western and specifically American churches. See Shaw, "Robert Wuthnow and World Christianity." A similar claim to Wuthnow's can be found in Noll, *New Shape of World Christianity*.

4. This was the argument of an earlier book by one of us. See Engel and Dyrness, *Changing the Mind of Missions*.

churches, along with the continuing focus on Western theology, constitutes what we might call the problem of global theology.

This book grows out of a set of observations about Christian theology today. First is the familiar claim that the Christian faith is changing: however one frames the changes, clearly the church has gone global. Not only is Christianity no longer predominantly a "Western religion," but also its most rapid growth today is outside the West, so that most Christians now come from places other than Europe and North America. But second, in spite of these changes, the teaching of theology in most Western settings has not changed. True, there are some new voices: Gustavo Gutiérrez, James Cone, and, if you're lucky, Kwok Pui-lan might appear on the syllabus of systematic theology, but the syllabus itself has not changed. Moreover, third, while theology is being done in many languages and settings, with ever-increasing variety and sophistication, these new theologians are frequently not in touch either with each other or, often, with much of what is discussed in Western theology classes. Perhaps this is a necessary result of the growing pluralism and multiculturalism of our settings. Or maybe it is simply a stage that we will pass through while a real global conversation emerges. In any case it is our assumption not only that this situation is changing but also that it needs to change in important ways.

This book will explore this state of affairs and do what it can to promote a more diverse conversation. We believe there are biblical grounds for such a project. In Ephesians 4, Paul lays out what he believes is God's own program for the maturity of the church, the body of Christ. There he is clear that the Spirit, as a sign of Christ's victory, has generously given a variety of gifts to the church (vv. 7–8). Further, these gifts are expressly given to equip Christians for the work of ministry, and the goal of this diverse endowment is that all might reach the "measure of the full stature of Christ" (v. 13). All of us, Paul insists, should reach maturity in Christ, "from whom the whole body, joined and knit together by every ligament with which it is equipped, as each part is working properly, promotes the body's growth in building itself up in love" (v. 16). Part of what this means, surely, is that the cultural, historical, and biblical reflections of the whole body—the products of its teachers, prophets, and evangelists—are necessary for us, together, to come to maturity. While the corporate and communal character of Paul's appeal may sound strange to Western ears, it resonates widely with much of the church today. We need each other, in theological reflection as much as in economic, political, and cultural affairs.

We the authors recognize that the work of developing global conversations is not the work of any single book, or even a single generation, but a long and slow process of learning to listen to unfamiliar voices. This book makes no claim to do anything more than introduce the problem and make some initial suggestions of what a global conversation in theology might look like. Beyond that, we hope to invite many others to join in this exciting project of watching the worldwide body of Christ grow into maturity in Christ.

We would like to recognize debts that we have accumulated in preparing this book. The book itself has grown out of attempts of a group of us to create a course at Fuller Seminary that would introduce students both to the discipline of theology as it has developed in theological education and to the growing global conversation about theology—a course we have titled "Doing Theology in a Global Context." So we want first to thank our colleagues Charles Van Engen and Veli-Matti Kärkkäinen, who along with Bill and Oscar have contributed to developing this course. Additionally Chuck and Veli-Matti, in the course of many conversations, have helped us envision what we mean by a theology in global contexts. Bill would like to thank conversation partners in Africa, Latin America, and Asia as well as the United States for many stimulating conversations that influenced what appears in this book: James Nkansah-Obrempong, Melba Padilla Maggay, Lorenzo Bautista, Juan Stam, Elsa Tamez, Jehu Hanciles, Kwok Pui-lan, Dwight Hopkins, and Bryant Myers. Oscar would like to express appreciation to his students from the Centro Latino at Fuller Seminary (especially his wife, Karla); from *Nuestra América* colleagues from the FUSBC, UBL, as well as Francisco Mena Oreamuno; from the US Latina diaspora, many theological partners like Catherine Barsotti, Juan Martínez, Tommy Givens, Elizabeth Conde-Fraizer, Miguel De La Torre, Eduardo Font, Amos Yong, Luis Rivera-Pagán, Santiago Slabodsky, Claudio Carvalhaes, Gregory Cuellar, Débora Junker, and Gabriela Viesca (research assistant). Beyond this we thank our Baker Academic editors: Bob Hosack, for encouraging us to pursue the book and for supporting it through the approval process, and Lisa Cockrel and Brian Bolger, who made it a better book.

September 2014
Pasadena and Manila

1

Transoccidentalism and the Making of Global Theology

Oscar García-Johnson

A Banana Republic Theologian

I was born in the Banana Republic, a name for Honduras coined at the end of the nineteenth century by the North Carolina novelist O. Henry in *Cabbages and Kings*. My early childhood was spent in the port of Tela, a coastal city very much like Coralio in the story by O. Henry. These two cities belong together in O. Henry's satirical narrative but also in the story of my own ancestral roots and upbringing. My great-grandmother took refuge in Trujillo when fleeing with her children from an uprising headed by Augusto César Sandino in the mines of San Albino, Nicaragua. Since my childhood, I have been told that the mines of San Albino were home to my British ancestors, the very scene of Sandino's founding insurrections against the Nicaraguan conservative forces in the first quarter of the twentieth century.

I got to meet my great-grandmother when she lived in the port of Tela, 150 miles west of her arriving point. We called her Mama Sara, and she died at the age of 108. A refined and articulate old woman, she tended to retreat in the precincts of San Albino. She enjoyed pomposity, abundance, and status in her lifetime as a member of the Europeans who came to the Americas to civilize the natives and improve their land. She certainly made sure that her family would appreciate its European pedigree, a distinctive heritage of a revered Western lineage distancing us from the local residents and Afro-Caribbeans. Memory and race were all she had left, for she lost her fortune and prestige when migrating to Honduras.

My mother, whose white father was from the southern United States and white mother was a British descendant, married a handsome *trigeño* (dark-skinned) man. My father was quite a Latin American representation of *mestizaje*, a blending of Amerindian, black, white, and Middle Eastern. Naturally, my grandmother never saw him as a fitting companion for a daughter with "pure" white blood. Nevertheless, my father managed to get hired by the prestigious United Fruit Company, a transnational Anglo-American banana industry company later to be known as Chiquita Banana. Being one of the two major companies that ruled the Honduran economy for several decades, by the 1920s the United Fruit Company had acquired over 650,000 acres of the most productive land along the Atlantic coast. *La compañia* (the company), as we used to call it, had control of railroads, ports, and key politicians, since bananas came to represent more than 80 percent of the nation's exports during the first half of the last century.

O. Henry's novel astutely anticipates the keen Anglo-American entrepreneurship and political maneuvering that had yet to be fully realized in the rich alluvial plains of Honduras's Atlantic coast. O. Henry's depiction is inviting.

> Taken and retaken by sea rovers, by adverse powers and by sudden uprising of rebellious factions, the historic 300 miles of adventurous coast has scarcely known for hundreds of years whom rightly to call its master. Pizarro, Balboa, Sir Francis Drake, and Bolivar did what they could to make it a part of Christendom. . . .
>
> The game goes on. The guns of rovers are silenced; but tintype man, the enlarged photograph brigand, the kodaking tourist and scouts of gentle brigade of fakirs have found it out, and carry on the work. The hucksters of Germany, France, and Sicily now bag its small chance across their counters. Gentleman adventurers throng the waiting rooms of its rulers with proposals for railroad and concessions. The little *opera-bouffe* nations play at government and intrigue until someday a big, silent gunboat glides into the offing and warns them not to break their toys.[1]

Due to my father's employment status, I spent a good portion of my childhood and early adolescence living in designated areas built for the privileged

---

1. Henry, *Cabbages and Kings*, 173, 184.

middle to upper management, which were located at the borders of the banana plantations. The local people referred to this area as *la zona Americana* (the American zone). The name was well earned, for it represented a life at the margins of the Honduran population—an elitist and privileged margin, I might add. *La zona Americana* was furnished with all the commodities that one would expect of an upper-middle-class lifestyle in the States transplanted into a "third world country."

La zona Americana was a geographical icon that inspired a sense of amazement and fueled the aspirations of many locals to somehow and someday belong to such a splendid society and culture: the Anglo-American culture. It goes without saying that life outside the borders of this American zone, in the banana plantations, was a very different scenario. Ironically, it so happened that my maternal grandmother (daughter of Mama Sara) lived in such a neighborhood, and I got to spend three months of every year in that unappealing place. No better words can depict the life in the plantations than those of Ramón Amaya-Amador, a banana *bracero* (manual laborer) himself who had a gift for words and angst for social change. His provocative novel *Prisión verde* (Green prison), published in 1950, partially captures the living conditions affecting workers in the banana plantation.

> Among that miscellaneous [scenarios] of *braceros* and bananas, sunshine and plagues, sweat and machines, creeks and malaria, the haughty cry of foremen was heard, [as well as] the whistle of moles, and the supreme power of the gringos gabbling with overconfident pride. So, all day, the grueling working of the *campeños* [field workers] was suspended until nightfall, when with tired shaky legs they would leave the green banana prison to embed themselves in the prison of soulless, empty barracks.[2]

As the political horizon changed and the land concessions granted to *la compañia* were challenged by a different generation of national leaders in Honduras, it began to move operations back home. Between the 1970s and 1990s, banana production in Honduras fluctuated significantly due to a number of hurricanes damaging the plantations and the spread of Black Sigatoka fungus. Consequently, most of the transnational operations of *la compañia* began to leave the country, leaving thousands of acres of land and thousands of *familias costeñas* (coast-based families) in ruins, jobless, and poorer than ever. *La compañia* left Honduras to go back home, but those who stayed home remained imprisoned in extreme poverty. Thus the life of many Hondurans on the northern Atlantic coast became intolerable to the point of exile or death.

2. Amador, *Prisión verde*, 66, my translation.

Many embarked on a deadly journey north. Some left by plane and many others by train, but whatever the means, the journey was a potentially deadly one for *los costeños* as they trekked toward the United States of America.

This case illustrates quite well the point made by Juan González in his book *Harvest of Empire: A History of Latinos in America*.[3] The harvest of Latin American immigrants González refers to is the result of the powerful Anglo-American companies' manipulation of the economic, geographical, and political resources of Latin American nations for their own interests. Many immigrants—a harvest of empire—are coming to the United States, suggests González, on the very tracks built by the Anglo-American politico-economic machinery. My parents were part of this harvest.

After coming to the States and going through the acculturation process, I have had to come to terms with a question that sooner or later haunts every theologian who comes from a former European colony. It is the question of where exactly my home is when doing theological reflection: Do I choose to do theological reflection out of the privileged "American zone" or the unappealing "green banana prison"? Throughout this book you will notice this struggle expressed in moments of self-questioning, self-affirmation, and reimagination. By the end of this chapter, I hope you realize that these two "universes" coexist along the continuum of a theological imagination that transcends the dichotomous categories of the West and finds a home in the transoccidental horizon of the global Triune God.

The Politics of Locality in Theological Studies

What is the point of beginning this book on global theology with a narrative that, although representing some trends among Latin American people, lacks the kind of universal representation we typically find in a theological manuscript? This is a pertinent question, since biographical theology has formidable objectors in the West. From their point of view, self-deception and self-fictionalization ("theology only of the self") might be reasons to dismiss this theological genre.[4] Interestingly, this suspicion vanishes when they approach documents such as Augustine's *Confessions* or Boethius's *De consolatione philosophiae*. Undeniably, the politics of location—where we do theology from and why—tends to inform the delivery and reception

3. See González, *Harvest of Empire*.
4. As pointed out by Derek Nelson, the list of objectors includes Martha Nussbaum and a prominent list of German theologians. See Nelson, introduction to *Theologians in Their Own Words*, 7–9.

of knowledge broadly speaking. In this regard, Willie Jennings, the African American Duke theologian, has much to say in his book *The Christian Imagination*. He thinks that "the story of race is the story of place. Geography matters for race as well as for identity, vision, and the hope of how one might live life."[5] Concurrently, stories of ethnicity and migrations may enrich theological elaboration with insights that could help the theological eye perceive what might otherwise be overlooked in the making of Christian theology, namely, imported ideas, histories, and epistemologies that construct Western typologies while communicating the message of the gospel in the majority world.

It is widely known that Western knowledge (its epistemology) has always been tied to particular Western geopolitics, which has been transmitted to the colonies and the world at large in the form of notions, practices, and utopias.[6] Latin America and Africa, for instance, have been experimental grounds for the historical projects pursued by the West. On the positive side, the rhetoric and practices of Western modernity have led to moments of emancipations, but the price that has been paid is great: ethnocultural neglect, discursive misrepresentation, and geopolitical dominance. Acknowledging the fact that predominant Western theologies have been operating out of an imperial-colonial core, influential theologians and missiologists in recent years have assumed the task of identifying theological paths bold enough to understand and meet the challenges presented by the epistemological captivity of the West in the theological process. Arguably, the so-called global theology enterprise is one of those paths. The goal is to carry out theological discourse while immersed in a post- or non-Western globalized context.[7] Not surprisingly, this global trend in theology faces resistance from both ends of the theological spectrum: both classical theologians (in fields such as history, systematics, ethics, biblical studies, and philosophy) and theologians from the margin (Liberationists, feminists, ethnicists, indigenists, etc.) tend to resist such projects. The former seek to retreat to the "golden age" of Western scholastics, while the latter are suspicious of this path as a new attempt to regulate (or recolonize) the theological diversity accomplished so far.

In an elementary yet constructive treatment of North American church involvement in global missions, Paul Borthwick acknowledges that pluralism,

5. Jennings, *Christian Imagination*, 289.

6. See, for instance, the category of "history of epistemology" as it appears in Edwards, *Encyclopedia of Philosophy*. It unfolds the history of the theory of knowledge as a Western evolution rooted in Greece, Rome, France, Great Britain, Germany, and ending in the United States.

7. Wheaton College, Fuller Seminary, Regent University, and others continually host events that seek to understand and engage global realities and global missions.

globalization, and territorialism are challenges Western Christianity faces.[8] In the words of a Zimbabwean brother, "What you in the West call 'globalization' we call 'Americanization.'"[9] But this resistance to occidentalization exceeds the boundaries of the mission field; it has been fermenting in the theological establishment of the West for a while. Hence, Western theologies are under the charge of occidentalism[10] and theological colonialism in respect to the way their classical and modern disciplines, methodologies, and conceptualizations represent God, the West, and the rest.[11] Implicit in this charge is the insubordinate attitude of the non-Western/ethnic "subaltern" that resists being reduced to an object or subject of study and adopts instead a protagonist role when attempting self-interpretation and self-representation. The tendency in modern Western disciplines has been to investigate members of the non-West as "ethnographic subjects," hoping that in the process they will speak for themselves, that is, become "subjects of study." As long as the West continues to use its own paradigms and methodologies when investigating the non-Western other, the effort of discursive representation of the other will suffer from inaccuracy. As Gayatri Spivak has pointed out, in this condition of representational asymmetry (investigated/non-Western—investigating/Western), the subaltern cannot speak as a subject but rather only as a fabrication of the West.[12]

This brings us to a central question: How appropriate is it for us to use the term "global theology" when talking constructively about discourses happening elsewhere? The representational asymmetry typical of Western discourse, I suggest, should prevent us from using the term "global theology" uncritically in a way that might give the impression that we are letting our subjects speak for themselves within our Western paradigms. This would make our theologies *globalizing*, not truly global. Correspondingly, we cannot properly be called *global* theologians if what we do is investigate and represent others in our

8. Borthwick, *Western Christians in Global Mission*, 69–76.

9. Ibid., 75.

10. This term is used critically by Enrique Dussel to indicate how "Western culture has positioned all other cultures as primitive, pre-modern, traditional, and underdeveloped." See Dussel, "Transmodernity and Interculturality," 15. Walter Mignolo further develops its epistemological implications in Mignolo, "Postcolonialismo." Obviously, "occidentalism" alludes to the groundbreaking work by Said, *Orientalism*, which underwrote the field of postcolonial studies. Yet occidentalism is not used in the same way Said uses "orientalism." The former centers on the Occident as a self-projected representation that portrays superiority and universality. The latter centers on a series of Asian misrepresentations and stereotypes serving also to enshrine the West as a superior culture.

11. See, for instance, Greenman, "Learning and Teaching Global Theologies"; Isasi-Díaz and Mendieta, "Decolonizing Epistemologies"; Jennings, *Christian Imagination*; Kwok, *Postcolonial Imagination and Feminist Theology*.

12. See Morris and Spivak, *Can the Subaltern Speak?*

scholarship while neglecting their self-representing paradigms. This would degenerate our theology into *egology* (speaking of the self). Let us make no mistake on this point—every theology carries within it a geopolitical, historical, and ideological prerogative and commitment that makes it contextual, whether this is acknowledged or not.

When the "Subaltern" Does Speak

The subaltern is speaking in the context of the wider world and is causing a disruption. The words by Homi Bhabha, a noted Indian-born postcolonial theorist, capture with precision the crucial moment of disruption in which Western theology finds itself at the present time. "Let us remember the terrible epiphany that overwhelmed Rahul Singh, the protagonist in V. S. Naipaul's novel *The Mimic Men*, when he came to the realization that the great stone walls of London posed neither a unique weight nor an unsurpassed resonance; those stones were the same stones one could find anywhere, everywhere; other stones were not a pale shadow of London ones."[13] I contend that any attempt at doing theology in today's globalized contexts, whether by Westerners or non-Westerners, must begin by taking into account Rahul Singh's epiphanic realization that the Western ways are no longer considered "unique, superior, or unsurpassed." In the same breath, a sense of astonishment (*Verwunderung*) and humility, to borrow from Karl Barth, might well be the proper attitude needed to discern where God is active, what divine movements point the way of God's revelation, and which competencies and commitments are required of us as we move forward to fulfill the theological task in today's globalized contexts.[14] If one is open to being astonished, strives for humbleness, and becomes attentive to God's manifestations around the world, an inevitable conclusion would be that the theological task as we have come to know it in the West is facing a transformation of its cartography and of its historical archives. The territory, texture, and phenomena of Christian practice are heading away from the West. The new cartographies of Christian practice, both in non-Western territories and also within the West in the form of "third spaces" or "back alleys of society," are shifting to include a theological self-representation coming out of decolonial theological categories that neither necessarily abandon nor depend on Western culture but instead seek autonomy of thought.[15]

13. Bhabha, *Nuevas minorías, nuevos derechos*, 91–92, my translation.
14. Barth, *Evangelical Theology*. See chapter 6, "Wonder."
15. The term "third spaces" refers to the marginalized communities living interstitially in the urban settings of developed countries (e.g., Africans in France, Southern Asians in the

This insurrection against the theological status quo has been resented in the theological establishment of the West, which usually refers to these decolonial efforts with names such as "local theologies," "ethnic theologies," "Liberation theologies," "Black theologies," "Asian theologies," *mujerista* theologies," "indigenous theologies," "theologies from the margin," "ecotheologies," and so forth.

Today, non-Western and ethnic theologies are still being represented as subaltern theologies within the reigning academic and theological establishment. Classical theologies, on the other hand, are referred to simply by totalizing nomenclatures: "biblical theology," "historical theology," "systematic theology," "Christian theology," or simply "theology." Nevertheless, the resurgence of multiple modes of theological reflection is a precondition for an autonomous epistemology. Therefore, the naming of different theological discourses is more than appropriate when such names express self-reflection and self-representation. We need the same thing to happen with Western discourse (e.g., "Anglo-European Christian history" and not merely "Christian history"; the same goes for "British-German systematic theology," "Western spirituality," etc.). Juan Martínez's observation in this regard is judicious: "One of the most important contributions contextual theologies can make to U.S. evangelical theology is to help it name itself as a contextual theology. Because of the outsized influence of U.S. evangelicalism, it will be particularly difficult for it to name its theologies as contextual. But until that happens all 'minority' theologies will be marginalized."[16]

Two Views for Doing Theology in Global Contexts

A seminal question that should be dealt with when doing theology in global contexts is, To what extent is it necessary to use Western theologies in the construction of global theologies if indeed Western theology has been part of the problem in non-Western contexts? In this book the reader will face two distinctive approaches to this question. In spite of the cynicism surrounding the possibility of building a theological discourse of this magnitude in such a time as ours, William Dyrness and I believe that the coconstruction of theological discourse in globalized contexts not only is necessary and possible but also constitutes a communal act of worshiping the God of the global church as we learn to deal with our self-idolatrous tendencies.

United States, and Nisei Latinos/as in Japan). For uses of this term, consult Castells, *Power of Identity*; Davey, *Urban Christianity and Global Order*.

16. Martínez, "Outside the Gate," 193.

William Dyrness—who speaks for a growing community of committed Western theologians wanting to move forward with a constructive theological approach in globalized settings—will answer this question by affirming that the Western legacy is still an inescapable reality for non-Western Christianity. In the next chapter, Bill will point out that the Western church, for better or worse, has decided which cultural influences to accept and reject ever since early Christian times. The Western church produced the creeds, hymns, treatises, liturgies, artistic representations, and religious traditions that still influence Christianity today. Indeed, the Western church makes the Western heritage an inescapable reality for newer expressions of the Christian faith. Since the Western theological heritage is still inescapable for the theological task today, it would be impossible, if not dangerous, for younger churches and theologies to disregard it entirely. In order to develop a theological discourse in a way that is global enough, both Western theologians and non-Western theologians should disarm themselves of unnecessary cynicism and recognize that Western culture is generative and nuanced (not monolithic) and hence useful for today's theologizing. In the same breath, Western theologians should acknowledge the fact that we are living in a "postimperial" world; thus, the typical Western-centric instinct so pervasive in Western theologizing must be acknowledged when doing theology in globalized contexts.

On the other hand, I will argue that what seems "inescapable" is not so much the historical products of Western Christianity but the fact that Western modernity/coloniality has occupied Western theologies and Christianity in a way that has projected an image of inferiority and codependency on the former colonies of Europe (occidentalism) in matters of doctrine, institutions, and social practices. Consequently, the elaboration of theology in a globalized context will be conceived of as a dynamic process of theological decolonization and glocal (global and local) dialogue by means of an interlocal and intercultural effort that does not assume the universal Western center but maintains its pluriversality and polycentricity. Naturally, I have reservations about the willingness and capacity of Western theologies alone to acknowledge and deal with issues of epistemology, colonialism, race, ethnicity, power, and privilege apart from the decolonizing process. Therefore, I argue, the task of elaborating theology collaboratively, interdisciplinarily, and interlocally entails an act of self-interpretation and self-representation in the form of a discourse that acknowledges its own context as it pursues a constructive dialogue with the contextual other. This goes for all of us, not just the majority world. This project of mutual interrogation undergirds all that we will discuss in the chapters that follow.

Let me develop the framework of this project a bit further. In making theology in globalized contexts, non-Western and Western theological efforts should undergo a dual methodological process that I am calling "transoccidentality." My advocacy of transoccidentality draws on aspects of Enrique Dussel's transmodern cultural theory to emphasize the deepening and broadening process in theological elaboration. The deepening aspect seeks self-interpretation and self-representation by effecting an epistemic delinking from totalizing Western typologies. The broadening aspect seeks to build intercultural and interlocal dialogue. As we articulate these movements in our transoccidental approach to theology in global contexts, I will address the issue of how inescapable Western culture and heritage may be for both Western and non-Western churches and theologians. Bill will make his response in the chapter that follows.

How Inescapable Is the West?

To what extent is Western heritage and culture inescapable for the majority global church and indigenous theologies of today? Perhaps the question should be extended to ask, *for whom* is it inescapable and why? To answer these questions I will examine two cases, one from Africa and another from Latin America.

David B. Barrett, a missionary and renowned British scholar of African Christianity, argues in his pioneering work *Schism and Renewal in Africa* that the eruption of the African-Initiated Churches (AICs) movement during the early twentieth century showed a "striking number of parallels" with the Protestant Reformation of the sixteenth century and with other renewals in the history of the West.[17] Acknowledging the fact that AICs constitute an indigenous effort to delink the African church from "over-Europeanized Christianity" as embodied by mainline churches in African contexts, Barrett supports the fact that such efforts constitute a "radical mission of renewal and reformation" but holds that these initiatives are, as Allan Anderson notes, "not restricted to AICs alone."[18] Anderson, reviewing Barrett, follows a similar pathway when assessing the Pentecostal character of the AICs and linking the movement with the North American Pentecostal movement ignited on Azusa Street in 1906. In this way Barrett (and Anderson) attempts to set African religious phenomena in line with a more "universal" account of church history, namely, a Western account.

17. See Barrett, *Schism and Renewal in Africa*, 161–86.
18. See Anderson, "Types and Butterflies," 107.

Let me open a different hermeneutical window on the same African phenomenon. Allan Effa, a Brazilian-raised son of a missionary, and professor of intercultural studies at Taylor Seminary, explores the contours of African contributions to global Christianity (particularly to the Muslim world, Europe, and North America) in his article "Releasing the Trigger: The Nigerian Factor in Global Christianity." Instead of viewing African Christianity under Western categories, Effa remarks on Africa's racial, cultural, and religious contribution to Europe and the Americas since early colonial times. In order to understand the significance of Effa's approach to the AICs, we need to acknowledge the fact that it would be impossible for us to recognize the American continent of today if it were not for the multiple African contributions to this continent through the centuries. The two great slave empires of the nineteenth century—the United States and Brazil—would not exist as we know them today were it not for Africa. Latin America is irrefutably a *mestizo* continent that has been deeply influenced by African race, cuisine, music, spiritualities, and so forth. In the United States, the civil rights movement, which changed the landscape of human rights in the world, was propelled and led by African Americans in clear acknowledgment of their African (and Christian) roots. "West Africa's global influence continues today," adds Effa in the same breath, "but with a marked difference. West African diaspora is accompanied by a missionary vision that challenges and reshapes expressions of Christianity around the world."[19] Effa's article, remarkably, compares Nigeria's shape in the world map with that of a revolver. Effa borrows this illustration from the Nigerian pastor Brown Oyitso from Nigeria's Redeemed Christian Church of God. Pastor Oyitso is known, explains Effa, for showing the similar shape of Nigeria and a revolver, pointing out that "Nigeria occupies the position of a trigger" in the map of world reevangelization of the West and the Middle East.[20]

Comparing these two hermeneutical windows sheds light on the question of how inescapable Western typologies are for Western and non-Western theological modes. It seems to me that Barrett finds Western culture and heritage to be inescapable when attempting to make sense of the AICs phenomena. The need for a universal archetype—a necessary rational category for analytical theology—to communicate this valued Christian happening to the Western world moves him to find in the archives of Western heritage the historical artifact that he needs to represent what is going on in Africa today in a way that resonates with the West's course of history, particularly

19. Effa, "Releasing the Trigger," 214.
20. Ibid.

the Protestant Reformation. As noble as his attempt may be in the interest of situating African Protestantism within a more universal history, Barrett links the indigenous effort of the AICs to an imported history, thus depriving the indigenous movement of the very reason for its emergence as a movement, namely, to disengage from an "over-Europeanized Christianity in Africa."[21] This is what Western theologians might consider "inescapable." In contrast, Pastor Oyitso from Nigeria offers a remarkable hermeneutical window for understanding the African phenomena, that of a revolver. As grotesque as the metaphor may be for a classical Western typologist, a revolver has much more grounding in Africa's violent history than the Protestant Reformation does. So while the British Dr. Barrett speaks to the West in Western categories by going back to the West's historical archive and fabricating a metaphor that situates Africa for the West, Pastor Oyitso from Nigeria speaks in compelling ways to the majority world. Being a Latin American, I find Oyitso's metaphor quite familiar; a revolver is the symbol of violence and the slave trade. It is not the past, however, that informs this metaphor but the future (the hope), which triggers the desire of evangelizing with words and wonders those whose ancestors met Africans in the past with chains and weapons. This is the African factor affecting global Christianity today. Consequently, it seems to me that Western culture and heritage is much more inescapable for Dr. Barrett than it may be for Pastor Oyitso.

A second case regarding how inescapable the West is for the majority world comes from Latin America. Let me preface it by noting that even those Western theologians who see themselves as progressive and sympathetic to self-representational theologies seem to take issue when "subaltern theologies" dare to challenge their most revered intellectual projects (i.e., Western history and epistemology). A case in point is Manuel Fraijó, a distinguished Spanish scholar of theology and philosophy who studied in Innsbruck, Münster, and Tübingen. Fraijó provides an outstanding review and critical assessment of Latin American Liberation theologies.

> Originally, Liberation theology came from European theology. Many of their most notable representatives were formed in European universities. The political theology of Metz and the theology of hope of Moltmann were their main sources of inspiration. . . . But too soon they [Liberation theologians] began to accuse their spiritual fathers of being excessively abstract and too tied to their capitalistic world-system when doing theology. In this way a distancing process, that I have never understood, began to take place between them. . . . Lastly, I think, there are two giants of European theology . . . without whose

21. Ogbu Kalu argues correspondingly in this regard. See Kalu, *African Pentecostalism*.

influence there would be no Liberation theology and any other progressive theology [K. Rahner and R. Bultmann].[22]

This critique, whatever its merits, fails to acknowledge several facts about the process of origination and self-representation in non-Western discourses. It also manifests the great uneasiness that Western theologians experience when confronted with the possibility of a subaltern insurrection. Fraijó, and many others with him, seems to ignore several possibilities. It is entirely possible for non-Western theologians to produce a full-blown theological discourse without having to subscribe to Anglo-European epistemologies, methodologies, and conceptualizations. To suggest that Liberation theology had its primary origin in Europe is a sign of arrogance. The so-called distancing process could easily be counterargued as an occidental misrepresentation based on the mythical presupposition of the superiority of "being formed in Europe," which makes one's own non-European communal grounding, situated theorization, and committed actions irrelevant when compared with Western culture and intellectuality. I believe Fraijó's assessment misunderstands what is truly happening here, because it is much more radical than "anti-European chauvinism," as Fraijó describes it.[23] The instinct of Liberation theologians moved toward a process of epistemic resistance to, if not disengagement from, dominant categorizations, a move that constitutes—according to Aníbal Quijáno and Walter Mignolo—the initial step for the decolonizing of knowledge and the very genesis of a liberating discourse.[24] In addition, let us remember Bhabha's account of Rahul Singh's realization: it is now quite possible to forge local theologies without reference to Europe. One can be diligently engaged in one's local histories and narratives, which, as Mr. Singh realized, need not be "pale shadows" of the European ones.

It also seems to me that Fraijó, just like his British colleague Barrett, finds it very difficult to escape Western culture and legacy when explaining Latin American Liberation theology. Conversely, the opposite seems to be the case for the Latin American Liberationists, who refuse to acknowledge any such influence. Still, the less prominent claim—pragmatic in nature—could be made that non-Western/ethnic theologies in Western institutions have not been able to disengage sufficiently from Western paradigms to show that they hold an autonomous status and equal academic stature when compared to Western disciplines. Indeed, non-Western/ethnic discourses have been interspersed with Western categories to the point of marginality. So the lack of autonomy in

22. Fraijó, *Fragmentos de esperanza*, 331, 332, 336, my translation.
23. Ibid., 334.
24. Mignolo, *Desobediencia epistémica*, 14.

representation could translate into a subaltern neglect of Western resources that never reaches a level of academic rigor and methodological style comparable to its Western counterpart.

Nevertheless, the subaltern theologian has found in that very unevenness a space for self-representation, one that has proved fertile for theological thinking and has provided an opportunity for epistemic delinking.[25] Thus, it flourishes like a rhizome of non-Western theological categories, such as marginality, *mestizaje*, violence, otherness, exclusion, poverty, displacement, hybridity, and so on. For the non-Western theologian, a situated-theorization in these destabilizing and uneven spaces opens up a liberating path in the midst of an oppressive universal system. Theological elaboration from the margins happens even when it means doing theology outside the gate of recognition and affirmation.[26] This in the end turns out to be a great asset that non-Western theologies bring to the project of doing theology in globalized contexts, for globalized contexts are nests of unevenness and all kinds of human disparities as well as unforeseen opportunities. The contexts of dislocation and socioeconomic disparities are familiar to subaltern theologians.

In conclusion, when representing the majority world, Western theologies and typologies have proved to be not only inadequate but also, in many instances, epistemically colonizing. Doing global theology, then, will require us to use different hermeneutical windows from those we have considered normative in the West. When we are faced with a particular Christian phenomena such as the AICs in the non-West, our relocation in the global hermeneutical horizon might require us to carefully challenge, modify, or even dismantle our Western presuppositions. For instance, we might argue that neither the American continents nor non-Western ethnicities (African, Amerindian, Middle Eastern) should be understood *mainly* on the basis of European history.[27] Furthermore, after rethinking Europe in light of the colonial projects of modernity in the Americas and Africa, we might dare to say that Europe would not be the influential seat of Western culture that it is today if it were not for the contributions of marginalized colonies: silver and gold at the service of new discoveries, forced labor by Indians and Africans, new comestibles like

25. Mignolo uses the concept of "delinking" (French *déconnexion*), first introduced by the Egyptian sociologist Samir Amia, along with the concept of "disengagement" (Spanish *desprendimiento*), developed by Quijano, to advance this concept of *delinking* in lieu of disengaging knowledge from different systems of colonial power that intersect and produce multiple levels of oppression; hence a multilayer matrix of colonial control is presented (economy, natural resources, authority, gender and sexuality, knowledge and subjectivity); see ibid., 12–16.

26. I show this in my forthcoming book, *Spirit outside the Gate: Mission Pneumatology from the Global South* (IVP Academic, 2017).

27. See Horne, *Deepest South*.

Mexican *chocolatl* and the Incan potato.[28] Finally, the pragmatic questions seem more urgent to me than the question of how inescapable the West is for the rest: How realistic is it to expect Western theologians and institutions to humbly and attentively participate in the coconstruction of theological elaboration with non-Western/ethnic thinkers on the basis of fairness and mutual respect? Will they expect a significant contribution from the pen of a former "subaltern" theologian and allow it to be made in a non-Western fashion?[29]

The Transoccidental Imagination

Theorizing beyond the West

Having argued that the West is much more inescapable for the Western theologian than for the rest in the world, we now move forward to elaborate a theory that might help us escape Western-centrism. I will attempt to articulate a theological conversation with disciplines I never encountered in my Western theological formation. Latin American literature, cultural studies, urbanology, critical theory, postcolonial studies, transatlantic studies, and decolonial theories were all nonexistent in my Western theological formation. That said, it would be a mistake to think that theologians in the West have never used such unorthodox disciplines when elaborating theological discourse. An outdated list suffices. J. B. Metz and Jürgen Moltmann in Germany have experimented with political theories; R. Marlé and J. Audinet in France and Canada have made use of cultural studies when dealing with epistemological assumptions; Casiano Floristán and J. J. Tamayo have used critical theory and literary criticism when discussing theological methodologies; David Tracy, Don Browning, Kathryn Tanner, Sallie McFague, and others have been multidisciplinary and open to post-Western tendencies in their theological discourses. Thus we can surely expect our own studies to welcome nonclassical disciplines as we imagine newer paradigms.

28. This has been well argued in the world-system hypothesis. See Dussel, "World-System and 'Trans-Modernity.'"

29. Since the 1970s (if not before) there have been theological efforts attempting to cross the historical-contextual ditch separating the South from the North. See, for instance, Branson et al., *Conflict and Context*; Torres and Fabella, *Emergent Gospel*. Lately, a promising approach that seeks to build dialogue among theologians and missiologists of the global South (South-to-South) is reemerging. See "Transgressive Theological Voices"; Keener and Carroll, *Global Voices*. In addition, we can find theologians from the margins in North America doing constructive work by discussing theologians that have been separated by context but are nevertheless close in theological agendas. This is the case with Goizueta's fine treatment of Bernard Lonergan's and Enrique Dussel's methodological projects; see Goizueta, *Liberation, Method, and Dialogue*.

As I described in my biography above, since childhood I have been reminded that I am a man of the Occident. But I hesitate when I attempt to define my occidentality apart from my non-occidentality. This sort of hesitation can move us to explore more carefully the contours of hybrid identities. *Mestizaje* is one among a handful of concepts that I have used to name this existential and cultural ambiguity. However, *mestizaje* denotes a random movement in the self that recapitulates an ambiguous identity. Instead, in this chapter I desire to trace a trajectory that points to the process of self-representation, a process that moves us beyond the script of the West as the locus of personal meaning and Christian mission. For this reason the concept of "transoccidentality," which implies an otherness from but not negation to our Western heritage, seems appropriate to me.

What Is "Transoccidentality"?

The term "transoccidental" emerges as I reflect on two theoretical concepts: "postoccidentality" and "transmodernity." The Cuban poet and literary critic Roberto Fernández Retamar coined the former in 1976 in reference to the Cuban revolution hero José Martí in his notable essay "Nuestra América y Occidente."[30] Fernádez Retamar uses the term "postoccidental" for an autonomous Latin American discourse that has transcended its occidental limitations and reached maturity. I think that transcending occidentality, however, does not necessarily translate into negating the occidental imprint that most of us Latin Americans carry within. Perhaps the fact that I describe myself as a hybrid-*mestizo*-borderline person helps me reconcile these ambiguities. José Martí acknowledges that such a project of total negation of our Western legacies is impossible when he writes, "All of our works, of our robust America, will inevitably carry within the imprint of a conquering civilization."[31] At the same time, every conscientious Latin American in the history of ideological, political, and religious freedom has attempted to transcend coloniality. So Martí continues, "But it will better [itself], it will transcend." This suggests to me that Martí, like me, conceives of the possibility of a life at the edge of our occidentality, a life that reaches beyond our colonialized self, a life that struggles to disengage from the totalizing colonial center tying our existence to somebody else's story and will. Ultimately, it is a life that dares to imagine both another horizon of existence and another center beyond the shell of oppression and asymmetry of the West's misrepresentation of its colonial subjects in its

30. See Fernández Retamar, "Nuestra América y occidente." I became aware of Fernández Retamar from Mignolo, "Postcolonialismo."
31. Martí, *Nuestra América*, 8, my translation.

universal history. This is precisely what Enrique Dussel has in mind when he speaks of "the exteriority of Modernity," the space "outside of the universal modern culture" that neglects the value and history of the colonized subject (i.e., indigeneity, *mestizaje*, Nepantla, Aztlan, etc.).[32] In the case of Latin America, such hybridity was experienced at the cultural, ideological, religious, and biological levels in the form of *mestizajes*, or "blendings," that continued to happen in the histories of the territories and peoples of the Americas.

A Decolonial Theory for Theologies in Global Contexts

Enrique Dussel's transmodern theory of culture captures many aspects of our view on transoccidentalism and provides a tempting programmatic proposal. His seminal thought can be summarized as follows:

> The strict concept of the "*trans*-modern" attempts to indicate the radical novelty of the irruption—as if from nothing—from the transformative exteriority of that which is always distinct, those universal cultures in the process of development which assume the challenges of Modernity, and even European/North American Post-modernity, but which respond *from another place, another location*. They respond from the perspective of their own cultural experiences, which are distinct from those of Europeans/North Americans, and therefore have the capacity to respond with solutions which would be absolutely impossible for an exclusively modern culture. A future *trans*-modern culture—which assumes the positive moments of Modernity (as evaluated through criteria distinct from the perspective of the other ancient cultures)—will have a rich pluriversity and would be the fruit of an authentic intercultural dialogue, that would need to bear clearly in mind existing asymmetries (to be an "imperial-core" or part of the semi-peripheral "central chorus"—like Europe today, and even more so since the 2003 Iraq War—is not the same as to be part of the postcolonial and peripheral world). . . . "*Trans*-modernity" points toward all of those aspects that are situated "beyond" (and also "prior to") the structures valorized by modern European/North American culture, and which are present in the great non-European universal cultures and have begun to move toward a pluriversal utopia.[33]

In this chapter I am not able to develop all the implications embedded in Dussel's transmodern theory with regard to the production of what I call transoccidental and glocal spaces (though we will return to these ideas in the chapters that follow). Dussel's transmodern theory embodies part of what I see

---

32. Dussel, "Transmodernity and Interculturality," 25.
33. Ibid., 18–19.

represented in Martí's seminal thought. Martí and Dussel would agree that a life beyond the "imperial-core" of coloniality/modernity could not represent a cultural existence entirely free from the "imprints" left and reenacted by imperial dominations past and present. Nor can it be a life absolutely beyond that edge that defines our historic-existential self. But by adding another horizon of existence, a new imaginary, and by transposing our colonized self to another plane, a new point of self-origination emerges. A new life for the "emancipated subaltern" can be imagined under a different set of coordinates on the occidental shell. This life on the exterior of Western modernity/coloniality, which is free to accept its complex cultural existence and seek dialogue under a new set of conditions, is what I imagine transoccidentalism to be.

As a theologian and student of cultural theories, I am left with an intriguing question: What might hold together the reimagined communal self and physical community in a way that makes mutual coexistence with other decolonial communities and theologies possible? What takes the place of the colonial core that previously infringed on and informed our colonized identities in a way that now allows for polycentricity, polyphony, and glocality and provides the ground for interlocal and intercultural dialogue under the logic of love, respect, equality, and justice? Leonardo Boff's analogical-theopolitical model of the Trinity resonates with me.

> There is a fundamental human yearning for sharing, equality, respect for differences, and communion of all and with God. The communion of the divine Three offers a source of inspiration for achieving these age-old yearnings of all peoples and all societies. Each divine Person shares fully in the other two: in life, love, and communion. Each is equal in eternity, majesty, and dignity; none is superior or inferior to the others. Although equal in sharing in life and love, each Person is distinct from the others. The Father is distinct from the Son and from the Spirit, and so is each Person. But this distinction allows for communion and mutual self-giving. The Persons are distinct so as to be able to give out of their wealth to the others and to form eternal communion and divine community. The Blessed Trinity is the most wonderful community. How to realize this ideal in our dominant social systems today, capitalism and socialism? . . . [In capitalism, d]ifference is valued at the expense of communion. In socialism it is the sharing of all that is valued . . . but personal differences are little valued. . . . The trinitarian mystery beckons us toward social forms in which all relations between persons and institutions are valued, in an egalitarian way, one of kinship and respect for differences. Only thus will oppression be overcome and life and freedom triumph.[34]

34. Boff, *Holy Trinity, Perfect Community*, 64.

We might critique Boff's view as a trinitarian anthropomorphism that seems to deny God's transcendental otherness. But Boff is taking an Eastern theological approach from a Liberationist perspective (an interesting combination) to advance his trinitarian understanding, which entails the coexistence of analogy and equivocity. Someone who uses a strictly analogical framework (classical Thomism) or a univocal logic (Western Protestantism) would have difficulty with this view.[35] As a theologian I do not accept the (postcolonial and postoccidental) assumption that Christianity as a whole has been irreversibly constituted by Western colonial modernity. Nor do I accept unconditionally Mignolo's claim that "decolonizing epistemology means, in the long run, liberating thinking from sacralized texts, whether religious or secular."[36] This would mean denying the complex, polygenetic, and polyphonic nature of Christianity, which indeed predates, postdates, and transverses Western modernity *and* coloniality. The fact that Western Europe has become secular and the majority world is becoming Christian should prove my case. The issue is not Christianity in general but Christianity in specific cases. From a theological perspective, the trinitarian core,[37] as I have articulated it, can offer a theopolitical alternative to the dominant left-or-right options of Western modernity.[38]

I have proposed that the elaboration of theology in a globalized context should be conceived of as a dynamic process of theological decolonization and glocal dialogue by means of an interlocal and intercultural effort that does not assume the universal Western center but maintains and celebrates its pluriversality and polycentricity. In addition, in an attempt to delink our theology from Western-centrism (occidentalism), I shall follow a decolonial and developmental process as suggested by Dussel. Transoccidentalism used as a theological process of decoloniality and glocal dialogue—that is, a process of delinking from a Western center and a broader engagement with conversation partners—might constitute an important contribution to the making of theology in global contexts.

35. One might also critique his apparently patriarchal references to God, but this would be unfair to his well-known gender sensitivity and his location in the Roman Catholic Church, which insists on use of the name of "Father–Son–Holy Spirit" as the only valid divine designation in the baptismal formula.

36. See Mignolo, "Decolonizing Western Epistemology," 25–26.

37. In the same vein, Colin Gunton claims that a sound trinitarian theology—one that emphasizes a Triune God who enters into a "free relation of creation and redemption with his world"—far from being a stepping stone for non-Christian communities, is the best interreligious contribution that Christianity can offer to the non-Christian world. For this to happen, however, the Trinity has to become the "centre of Christianity," which has too often not been the case in the West. See Gunton, *Promise of Trinitarian Theology*, chap. 1.

38. This sketch is based on Dussel's diagram of transmodernity. See Dussel, "Transmodernity and Interculturality," 19.

Conclusion

I began this chapter with a biographical and geopolitical description as a way to embark on a decolonial process of forging the basis for a theological "communal future."[39] The idea is to *build theology at the service of the global population rather than use the population at the service of theology*.[40]

Most of Africa, Latin America, parts of Asia, and the Middle East have been influenced by Western modernity and coloniality. Walter Mignolo rightly affirms, "In the last few decades no global-political, epistemic, and aesthetic phenomenon can be explained without the concept of coloniality."[41] We noticed that colonial subalterns around the world are beginning to speak loudly and fearlessly as they begin to think decolonially. "Decolonial thinking," Mignolo reminds us, "means engaging in knowledge making and transformation at the edge of the disciplines."[42] I have argued that any attempt to do theology in a global context must begin by taking into account the realization that the Western ways are no longer "unique, superior, or unsurpassed." In fact, I have acknowledged a long-standing argument in political and subaltern studies that reverses the victim role of the Americas and Africa in relation to Europe: "Without an *ego conquiro* there is no *ego cogito*" (Dussel). In other words, the Enlightenment is facilitated by the colonial projects; there would be no Enlightenment without colonialism.[43] The assumption that the West is inescapable for the majority world when doing church ministry and theological reflection is disrupted by non-Western-initiated churches and theologians, such as the AICs, Latin American Liberationists, and popular religionists. Are Western theological institutions and theologians prepared and willing to coconstruct theology with former subaltern theologians in a decolonial way?

In this introductory chapter, transoccidentalism has been proposed to reframe the epistemic codes of human identity (self-understanding, self-representation, and multiculturality) outside of Western modernity/coloniality. This orientation, enriched by border thinking (e.g., diaspora discourses), is ready to embrace complex cultural existences (e.g., hybridity, *mestizaje*, Nepantla) and seeks intercultural dialogue under a new set of social and theological conditions. The following categorizations and disciplines are key to reframing theological dialogue in global contexts.

39. Mignolo, "Decolonizing Western Epistemology," 29–30.
40. Ibid.
41. Ibid., 20.
42. Ibid., 42.
43. See Castro-Gómez and Mendieta, introduction to *Teorías sin disciplina*.

1. *Decolonial studies*, as articulated by Dussel, Mignolo, Mendieta, and other Latino/a scholars, represent indigenous critical theory from the majority world and offer a critical framework that can significantly benefit theological studies and in turn receive valuable contributions from a sound theological process.[44] Decolonial studies begin with a rereading of history and a revision of its epistemological codes. In transoccidentalism, decolonizing epistemology is a point of departure that seeks to disengage or delink Christian knowledge from the epistemic captivity of Western modernity and coloniality.

2. An *indigenous rationality of resistance* to Western colonial experiments in Latin American history has been evident at all levels since the colonial birth of our continent. For instance, in literature we find Guamán Poma de Ayala, Garcilaso de la Vega, Sor Juana Inés de la Cruz, Simón Bolívar, José Martí, the writers of the Boom, and so forth. Culturally speaking, popular religion in the Americas constitutes a witness of cultural resistance to colonization and occidentalization, both in the form of popular Catholicism and indigenous Pentecostalism (and *Pentecostalismo criollo*). Yet when we move to the field of theology, we face great limitations. Apart from the European defenders of the Amerindians, Montecinos, Las Casas, and a handful of others, theologians find themselves in no position to match the literary school of the Americas. Hence, decolonial studies build on this literary tradition and provide a wealth of postoccidental studies in critical dialogue with postcolonial studies.[45] Our critical apparatus situates itself in the larger intracontinental context of Latin American and US Latino thought (*Nuestra América*).

3. *Transnationality* as a continental condition and *glocality* as a strategic organization assert that the Americas cannot continue to be defined solely on the basis of former geopolitics and national narratives. In the new transnational reality of the Americas, most people live in urban settings reconfigured by various types of migrations. Migrants bring with them their local religiosity; thus Christianity in Western settings is becoming increasingly transoccidental. Glocality is strategically conceptualized in transoccidentalism.

4. *Social doctrine of the Trinity*. Transoccidentalism is used in correspondence with a theory of Christian experience in which the unifying agency of the Triune God is mediated by the Holy Spirit's intersubjective participation in the formation of Christian identity, Christian community, and transmission

44. For more information on decolonizing theories, see Mignolo, "Epistemic Disobedience and the Decolonial Option."

45. Similarly, transoccidentality as a methodology is to be distinguished from classical Liberation theology (Gutiérrez, Boff, and Sobrino), the decolonial Marxist studies in Latin America, and the poststructuralist (Lacan and Derrida) and postcolonial (Spivak, Said, Bhabha) discourses in the West, though it has learned from all of these.

of the Christian faith in today's globalized contexts. The transoccidental self discerns God as the incarnate Spirit who participates in fashioning the identity of the person in the Christian experience (*imago fidei*—the believing self), resocializing the person in community (*imago commune*—the communal self), and incorporating the person into the globalized city (*imago civilis*—the political self).[46] The trinitarian alterity (functionally speaking) informs the discipleship and undergirds the theological reflection of God's people everywhere.

If we are going to continue using the term "global theology," it must represent a dialogical and culturally developmental discipline. It should be glocal and intercultural. Theologies in a global context should take for granted a displacement from any metacultural core in favor of a pluralistic (functionally trinitarian) one that allows for multiculturality. Multiculturality represents the mature coexistence of communities that maintain their polycentric inner cores while remaining linked transversely and perichoretically to each other and to God as their trinitarian, gravitational center.

The challenge for all of us, however, is to dare to exercise our theological imaginations. The Cuban poet and intellectual José Martí gives us a thoughtful paragraph, partially quoted above, as he was imagining the contours of a new continent, "Our America." He writes, "All of our works, of our robust America, will inevitably carry within the imprint of a conquering civilization; but it will better [itself], it will transcend [*adelantará*] and astonish [*sorprenderá*] with the energy and the pulling force of a people who is distinct in essence, superior in noble ambitions, and if wounded, not dead. It's already risen!"[47]

We are at the dawn of a new global conversation. This is a different global theology, a theology between the "global South" and the "global South in the global North." It is a conversation that needs to happen with the Nigerians from Africa and the Nigerians from Europe and the United States, the Nisei from Peru and the Peruvian-Nisei from Japan. On this basis, we may retell the story of Christianity from the standpoint of "our glocal America" and listen to the story of Christianity from the standpoint of "your glocal Africa"—and "your glocal Asia" and "your glocal Europe" and "your glocal Anglo-America" and so on—until a culturally developed, multicultural, pluriversal, polyphonic, and trinitarian conversation emerges as a witness of the new creation in Jesus Christ. My prayer is that Western Christianity does not end like my British grandmother, who retained only her memory and race.

---

46. Discussion leading to this understanding can be found in García-Johnson, *Mestizo/a Community of the Spirit*, 62–69; García-Johnson, "Eucaristía de comunión."

47. Martí, *Nuestra América*, 8, my translation.

2

Doing Theology Out of a Western Heritage: Gains and Losses

WILLIAM A. DYRNESS

A Midwestern Local Theology

I (Bill) was a war baby, born in a suburban Chicago town into genteel but hard-won poverty—or so I believed at the time. My parents remembered well the lessons of the Depression and had learned to squeeze a nickel until the buffalo squeaked. They often reminded us that they had worked hard so that we kids could "have it nice"—my father was a professor in a Christian college, and my mother, who had not been to college, did her best to make a home for our family. My grandfather, who died before I was born, had emigrated from Norway late in the nineteenth century and pastored a thriving immigrant church in Chicago. Holidays were spent in their second-floor walk-up with my extended Norwegian family, enjoying the Scandinavian delicacies my grandmother, who lived to age ninety-five, spent weeks preparing. Chicago had been a rough place for these newly minted Americans—my grandfather was once violently mugged walking home from church. The children knew there was a funeral when the undertaker's carriage was waiting out in front of the house. (It was considered indecorous to take the dead to the cemetery in motorized vehicles.)

The theology and spirituality of my family was derived from the pietistic stream of Norwegian Lutheranism—the tradition that, in America, gave birth to the Evangelical Free Church. Ours was a serious and rigorous piety, with prayers before setting out on trips and when parting from friends, regular evening devotions, kneeling around the table to pray for (what seemed to me) an endless list of missionaries, and attendance at two services on Sunday and, often, Wednesday prayer meetings. Our faith was serious and deeply felt but nondemonstrative. We would have been appalled at the emotional outbursts that have become so common in third-wave Christianity. Missions had always been important for our family, with Grandpa cofounding the Scandinavian Alliance Mission (which later became the Evangelical Alliance Mission, or TEAM) and Dad serving most of his adult life on the board.

But apart from reports from returning missionaries, actual influences from other parts of the world were nonexistent. Growing up I did not know a Roman Catholic, let alone a Buddhist or Jew. I remember vividly my uncle complaining vigorously when their Scandinavian neighborhood in Chicago was invaded by "those Italian Catholics." The only Christianity I knew was a Midwestern pietism that came to be associated with Billy Graham and the rising evangelical movement. (I came to faith at a crusade of one of Graham's associates at the age of ten.)

Two discoveries would shape my understanding of theology. The first was an encounter with philosophy my last year in high school, which led to my becoming a philosophy major in college. I was interested in exploring the roots of thinking, which I took for granted, in the conversations of ancient Greece and the medieval philosophers. This philosophical heritage and the great Christian thinkers like Augustine and Calvin gave my pietism a framework that allowed me to think outside the narrow confines in which I had been raised. This was a faith that had a rich history and had attracted some of the best minds. I was determined to pursue some form of Reformed ministry and enrolled in seminary, where I was further exposed to what I saw as the rich Western heritage of Christianity.

Though I loved the preparation in history and biblical studies and pursued doctoral studies in Strasbourg and Amsterdam, nothing really prepared me for my second great discovery. After a brief parish ministry in the United States, I was called to become a teacher of theology in a new seminary in Manila, Philippines. In many ways, though I had already studied theology for six years, my real theological education began when we landed in Manila. For there the world outside my Midwestern and European experience was opened for me—or better, the world I had known was overturned.

When my wife, Grace, and I arrived in Manila with our two young daughters, the Philippines had been under martial law for two years—student unrest and military checkpoints were a regular feature of urban life. The first Christian student group to invite me to speak asked that I talk about poverty and Marxism. How should Christians respond to these challenges? I was stumped. No course or reading that I had done prepared me to address these issues. But not only had I woken up to a world where issues of justice and poverty were inescapable, I realized—to my shock—that overnight I had become representative of oppressive neocolonial power in the eyes of many. Despite what to our minds was a meager salary—barely a third of what we had been offered for a pastorate in the States—by the standards of our new setting, we were suddenly unimaginably wealthy. I was teaching pastors who lived on a fraction of what we received as expatriate missionaries; on a daily basis we were confronted with persons who survived on what they were able to salvage from the garbage cans on our street.

This new situation raised questions about wealth and poverty, just and unjust uses of power, and cultural difference I had no theological categories for. I realized that the theology I had learned, which had seemed so satisfying and even inevitable in my home setting, was inadequate to address issues faced by a developing country with its deep-seated corruption and grinding poverty. It did not matter that the library of that young seminary was noticeably smaller than my own because its theological resources were answering questions my students were not asking. So I began a crash course of theological reflection—learning from my students, listening to local pastors, and reflecting on cultural differences with my wife, who began a graduate program in anthropology at a local university. I still remember the day a book arrived at our seminary library with the title *Water Buffalo Theology*.[1] In the book, Kosuke Koyama, a Japanese missionary in Thailand, proposed that theology must be done for people who live in a world of objects, not ideas, who know "sticky rice," "rainy season," and "leaking roof" but do not understand "incarnation" or "atonement." How can the gospel be understood in this setting? This was a revelation to me. Subsequently, I have come to question this simplistic way of framing the alternatives, but this dramatic encounter forced me to think about theology in new ways. At about the same time, we came across the work of Gustavo Gutiérrez and José Míguez Bonino, which described a situation in Latin America that paralleled our own in the Philippines.[2] What if we thought

---

1. Koyama, *Water Buffalo Theology*.
2. See Gutiérrez, *Theology of Liberation*, and Bonino, *Doing Theology in a Revolutionary Situation*.

about the gospel as liberation as well as forgiveness? What if the evil addressed by the cross is social as well as personal? It was not the case that the gospel was suddenly less relevant; quite the contrary, the gospel took on fresh meaning. The problem was with us—we had not properly understood the gospel. We had missed critical dimensions of God's dramatic intervention in Christ.

I would not exchange those years of learning and growth for anything. I continue to learn from my colleagues, many of whom have become distinguished theologians in their own right. But the experience did pose a challenge to me that was similar to Oscar's: How will *I* do theology? Will I do it now out of this new setting or my old one? Of course my innocence was gone, and I could not return to the naive perspective I absorbed in seminary. But I also realized that I would never truly be a non-Western theologian. I would always speak out of and reflect the setting in which I was raised and had studied. Though I am indebted beyond measure to all I have learned from others, I know that my default is to speak out of my Western setting—even as Oscar's default is to reflect on the struggles he knows as a non-Western theologian working in the West. Recognizing these differences, it seems to me, is the first step in learning from each other. This process of conversation is what this book intends to encourage—and embody. In the remainder of this chapter, I will reflect on what it means for me to do theology from my (tempered) Western perspective today.

What I lacked during my theological education, and what many theology students still lack, is an articulate voice from non-Western settings that can challenge what we in the West take for granted. This is where Oscar's contribution becomes irreplaceable, and this is why we have decided to write this book together. I can no longer do my reflection, especially on non-Western theology, on my own; I must be willing to hear those increasingly sophisticated voices like Oscar's now talking back to Western theologians. What we hope to model in these chapters is a real conversation between two important and different points of view. While there is much on which we can agree, we want to hold on to the texture of our different settings, the actual places from which our reflections have emerged, so that real mutual learning can take place.

Is the West, Theologically Speaking, Really the Best?

So let me seek to respond to the important issues that Oscar raises in the previous chapter. I will begin with the "problem" of the assumed superiority of Western theology. I have admitted that the Christianity I knew was dominated by Western voices. This was not because I or anyone I studied with assumed they were superior but because that was all we knew. As far as I knew, for most of Christian history, theology had been centered and developed in the West, and there was no other way of doing theology. But my experiences outside the West soon alerted me to the fact that there was something missing in this traditional account of theology. And this changed not only my view of how we do theology today but also my view of how it might have been done from the beginning. Our new situation of a global church made me realize that there has always been more diversity in our history than we had previously noticed. So one implication of Oscar's challenge is that we probably need to start by rereading Christian history. When we do this carefully, we discover that the standard accounts have left out much of that history. For example, in the early church, Egyptian and Syriac voices were reflecting on the Christian faith and interpreting the Bible in ways that differed significantly from those of their Western colleagues.[3] During this time as well, Eastern voices like Irenaeus and, later, Gregory of Nyssa and John of Damascus interpreted Christianity in ways that diverged from the Latin style of reasoning that dominated the Western church. This eventually resulted in the definitive split between the Eastern and Western churches in 1054.

During the Middle Ages, Arabic philosophers and Germanic and Frankish cultures all had a major impact on the development of medieval theology and its culture. Later, during the Renaissance, the Eastern Orthodox influences were again strongly felt. And of course the modern missionary movement brought back theological artifacts that have, from time to time, influenced theological thinking.

The implications of this are hard to overemphasize. A truly global discussion of theology today, whatever else it does, will surely recognize the great diversity of contexts and resulting reflection on the gospel. One of the conclusions to be drawn from a rereading of Western traditions is that diversity is nothing new; though it has often been suspect and actively suppressed, it has been characteristic of the Christian story from the beginning. To understand the reality of the church in Japan that Oscar visited, for instance, it will not do to ignore the importance of, say, Brazilian or Japanese culture, as if these traditions will no longer matter in the future. Rather, we must ask what these believers are now making of these traditions and what this means for the future. And so we argue that we also need to ask what they will make of their received (and traditional) understandings of theology: Where did they come from, and how do they call out for adjustment or reform? What happened when these traditions traveled from place to place?

3. See on this Walls, "Rise of Global Theologies," in Greenman and Green, *Global Theology in Evangelical Perspective*.

Difference Is a Good Thing: All Theology Now Is Comparative

Porous borders represent an important and often overlooked dimension of
Western theology, and we will pay a lot of attention to these in this book.
But Oscar is claiming something more far reaching than this. He is arguing
that despite global diversity, up until recently the authoritative interpretation
and response to it has carried the label "Made in Europe," or later, "Made
in America." In general, it was the Western church, for better or worse, that
decided which of these influences to accept and which to reject, and it was
this church that produced the creeds and theological treatises that continue
to influence Christian theology. As we will note below, this situation has
drastically changed, and the future will be very different. Up to this point,
however, European intellectual and cultural traditions have been inescapable.

A personal illustration might help make this point. During 1989–90 my
family and I lived in Africa, and I was able to teach in a seminary in Nairobi,
Kenya. During that time I began working on a book that sought to listen
to and learn from the non-Western theologies I was reading.[4] While I was
working on the book, an older Western missionary approached me. "I am so
glad to hear you are writing a book on this non-Western theology," he said.
"There is much about it that needs correcting." It seemed natural to him
that the special role assigned to Western observers and theologians was to
"correct" what was coming from the younger churches. And this was not an
uncommon assumption.

But we should not make the opposite mistake and suggest that the Western
traditions of theology are inherently biased and therefore need to be simply
corrected (or even discarded) by newer perspectives. Here we must be careful
not to essentialize "Western theology" as though this were a single thing. We
need to recognize ways this heritage has taken the form of particular historical
traditions that have carried and embodied influential Christian thinking. We
might think about these traditions as long-term conversations representing
differing emphases. They have been shaped by particular historical and cultural
circumstances. The traditions I have in mind developed originally in Europe
and later in America but have been exported in various forms to the nations
of the earth. There is no way we can understand the Christian presence in
the world today apart from these historical traditions.

Significantly, these traditions represent not only theological ideas and biblical emphases but also institutional forms and liturgical practices that express
these emphases. Let me define these forms in this way: *Theological traditions*

---

4. See Dyrness, *Learning about Theology from the Third World*.

are long-term conversations, growing out of particular historical and cultural circumstances, about what things are central to the faith, especially as these are carried in images, rituals, and spiritual practices as well as verbal confessions and statements. That is to say they are both "theological," containing assumptions about God and God's presence in the world, and "practical and liturgical," embodying assumptions about how belief should be performed and lived out. These major traditions, in roughly chronological order, are Eastern (and Coptic) Orthodoxy; Roman Catholicism; the Reformed, Lutheran, and Anglican (evangelical and mainline) traditions of the Reformation; the Anabaptist tradition of the radical Reformation; and the more recent Pentecostal forms of church life and belief.[5] I do not mean to suggest that this list is exhaustive but merely that these are suggestive of the variety that has emerged in the history of the Christian church. (An extended description of these five traditions can be found in the appendix.)

Location Matters

But the existence of traditions like these raises the fundamental question that Oscar is asking: Now that theology can no longer be described as a Western enterprise, what are we to make of these traditions? Oscar's chapter has highlighted the complexity as well as the inescapability of this question, and here I want to try to respond to his concerns. As Oscar reminds us, when we ask how traditions such as these are important, we are hiding (or ignoring) some previous questions: Important for whom? Important where?

Of course, for Western theologians, who learn about these traditions in beginning theology and church history classes, these traditions are the starting point for doing theology—often one or another tradition is assumed to be normative from the outset, and others are introduced to show their inadequacy. The general assumption is that these traditions (or one tradition) are relevant for everyone, everywhere. But as my experience in the Philippines illustrates, when confronted with a wholly different cultural and historical situation, these prevailing conversations appear inadequate at best and positively harmful at worst.

Here we get at Oscar's central concern: these predominant Western theologies have "operated out of an imperial-colonial core." Western theologians

---

5. These of course are what sociologists might call ideal types. To be sure, communities on the ground may be influenced by more than one of these or indeed by others I don't mention. These are meant to be exemplary rather than definitive—to illustrate the continuing role of Western traditions in theology.

have not only been blind to the radical challenges offered by the situation of younger churches and the inadequacies of Western readings of Scripture, but they have not even noticed that these differences reflect serious economic and political imbalances. Here we come upon a typical misunderstanding on the part of those who teach out of these traditions: rather than being universally applicable versions of the Christian faith, they are in fact contextual theologies that have been formed in particular historical and cultural situations. This did not become evident to me until I spent some significant time in a very different cultural setting, and it eventually would involve what Oscar has described as a new "self-representation."

The first invitation to speak to a student group on Marxism and poverty in the Philippines was, in a sense, an invitation to reflect on these cultural differences and the resulting political imbalances and respond in a Christian way. I certainly would not say that nothing I had learned in theology was relevant to this challenge, but I at least had not been taught to make the necessary connections. Lest we be accused of harboring some radical agenda here, let me provide one simple illustration of this imbalance: the publishing of religious books. In 2006 (according to Bowker.com statistics) there were 292,000 books published in the United States, 18,000 of which were religious titles. Compare this to 300 published in Kenya, 76 of which were religious, and some 1,200 in Nigeria, 203 of which were religious.[6] And try ordering any of these books from Kenya or Nigeria—they are not available through Amazon! Clearly this flow of information from North to South does very little to promote any genuine exchange of ideas. And this imbalance reflects deeper cultural and economic issues that Oscar (and other postcolonial thinkers) has asked us to consider: What economic and political arrangements have led to this imbalance? How should Christians think about and respond to this?

Our attempt to promote global exchange is one attempt to correct this imbalance, but even our good-faith effort, as Oscar points out, is likely to be resisted at both ends of the spectrum of theologians—classical theologians on the one hand and feminist and LBGT theologians on the other. One suspects that we are veering dangerously in the direction of syncretism; the other suspects that we are still ignoring where the real injustices lie. But I would like to point out a further resistance that we need to recognize. Oscar is a very unusual non-Western theologian, one who is speaking out against the hegemony of Western voices. I have been teaching and lecturing overseas

6. These figures are from 1994 to 1995 and represent the most recent available data from UNESCO. The inadequacy of such data is a further illustration of the problem I am underlining. By 2006 these figures would be higher, but not much higher!

for more than thirty years, and too often I have encountered the opposite problem. Among theological students around the world, there is often too little awareness of the theological implications of their political and economic situations or of the imbalances that have resulted.

Once we became aware of these imbalances in the Philippines, I remember advocating to my students that more theology needed to be done in Tagalog (the Philippine national language), that they needed to begin doing their own vernacular theological reflection. I still remember my shock when they responded that since most of the books they wanted to read were in English, they should learn theology from Western teachers who were educated in Western universities, and they should read and write their theology in English. There were important exceptions of course, and their number is increasing all the time, but complacency about global inequalities and injustices are often as common in the majority world as in the West. All of this suggests that the work of raising consciousness, what Latin American theologians call "conscientization," must be part of our theological agenda.

Then consider Oscar's focus on the geography of theology. Perhaps the most important work that theologians like Oscar perform for us is very simply to remind us that place matters. Theological reflection looks different to a Manila squatter than to a university student in Chicago, and much of the difference reflects the look and feel of places and the situations of people who live in those places. In his important study of these issues, Willie Jennings points out the contrast between the place-making history and aesthetic of the Apache Indians and typical Western historiography. "This aesthetic looks at Anglo-American (Western) historiographic practice . . . as 'geographically adrift' because it is detached from local landscape with 'few spatial anchors,' with places often not identified, obsessed both with dating historical events and placing them in 'tightly ordered sequences' organized through some totalizing theory."[7] Notice the irony of Jennings's comparison: while Western thinkers seek a universal temporal structure, they are often blind to their own physical location and the influence of this on their imaginations; pretending to speak about all places and times, they speak from no place in particular.

One of the first implications of the importance of place is the painful difference between the places where theology is done in the world. As we will frequently note, non-Western theology often grows out of economic and existential challenges that Western theologians know nothing about. A

---

7. Jennings, *Christian Imagination*, 55. Jennings is discussing here Keith Basso's description of Apache history writing. He later states, "Traditioned intellection fails to enter into the spatial and landscape logic of these new people" (113).

Ugandan pastor often finds him- or herself living in a community ravaged by HIV/AIDS with minimal medical resources, for instance, and an evangelist in North India may face frequent persecution by radical Hindus while the police turn a blind eye. The typical Western pastor, by contrast, has learned her or his theology in academic and classroom settings, where debates about precise terminology and arguments are appropriate. Brothers and sisters from Uganda and India want us to understand that these places matter, and that theology done in the West is neither unique nor superior. Indeed, in these contested settings, it often appears quite inadequate.

Allow me to linger a bit more on the importance of context. Historically violent events represented, for instance, by the conquest of Latin America, European colonization, slavery, apartheid in South Africa, and Western-endorsed dictatorships inevitably inform non-Western theological reflection; these historical experiences constitute a living narrative and the context out of which non-Westerners do life, ministry, and theology. Oscar will press upon us the term *locus theologicus*, which refers literally to the place from which, or in terms of which, theology is formed. Thus, when non-Western pastors and teachers begin their theological reflection, violence, poverty, segregation, cultural marginalization, and so on often make up the loci of theology interpreted by Scripture—they are inevitably places that stimulate theological reflection. By contrast, when Western theologians do their historical and theological research, they consult their intellectual heritage—Augustine, Aquinas, Calvin, Kant, and so on—to construct theological discourse.

This is not to say majority-world theologians have no heritage of their own to consult. When non-Western theologians attempt to reflect on Scripture within their own context, they also find rich indigenous civilizations and aboriginal theologies whose cosmologies, political organizations, and ritualistic practices provide a rich storehouse for shaping theological reflection. We will explore this heritage in the next chapter. But here we face a problem: these sources are mostly deemed unacceptable and are usually disregarded by Western theologians; they are not "proper" theological sources. As a result, the study of these civilizations has not been part of the theological curriculum. When one looks carefully into the historical data, one finds notable figures such as Antonio de Montesinos and Bartolomé de Las Casas, who early on challenged the validity of the project of Western Christianization in the non-Western world. However, none of them are esteemed on the same level as Luther or Calvin.

In spite of all these obvious disparities and blind spots of the Western theological enterprise, autochthonous theologies in the form of Liberation theologies, indigenous theologies, popular religiosity, ethnic theologies, and postcolonial theologies have developed as a way to voice the narratives deemed crucial for non-Western theologians. These have become sophisticated expressions of the Christian faith and will henceforth make up part of the data of theology; they can no longer be ignored. In short, Oscar reminds us, Western theology simply cannot continue to do theology in the previous self-centered way.

Transoccidentalization

Of course Oscar is not proposing that non-Western theologians ignore the Western tradition of theology; that would be both impossible and unwise, as he admits. Here he wants to point out a different sort of problem. Part of the challenge faced by non-Western theologians has been the damage caused by colonial patterns, both political and economic, and the resulting dependency, both economic and epistemological. In certain parts of the world this residual harm has left people with a sense of inferiority that was reflected in my students' response to my call for contextualization. This often reflects a hidden assumption: only those with the wealth and education that characterize the West can do proper theological reflection.

People and groups in such settings are tethered to Western theology in a particularly poignant sense: not only do they not have a voice, but they often lack the sense that they ought to have one! This was well illustrated by the case of Manuel Fraijó, which Oscar cited. Fraijó's Eurocentric understanding of how theology originates convinced him that Liberation theology must have had its roots in European theology after all. A parallel situation is illustrated by competing accounts of the rise of Pentecostalism in Africa: surely it could not have indigenous roots; it must have had its origin in Western Pentecostalism.[8]

The answer of course is that these have multiple sources, but even these examples underline our central question: To what extent can we use Western theology in constructing global theology if Western theology itself has been part of the problem for non-Western theologians? Can it free itself of its colonial, imperial core? The answer that Oscar has proposed is suggested by what he calls a "transoccidental imagination." This involves recognition not only of other voices—understanding the world as a "pluriverse" rather than a "universe"—but also of other methods in the production of theological knowledge: critical theory, cultural and literary studies, and the social sciences.

Let me try to describe what I think is at stake here. Oscar's chapter makes use of methods that are widely discussed in Western universities—critical

8. See the debate in Kalu, *Pentecostalism in Africa*. Kalu disputes the consistent overemphasis of foreign influences.

theory and social-science methods, for example. But interestingly, these newer methods have only recently become part of *theological* conversation in the West. So in the same way that majority-world voices have called attention to overlooked perspectives in the history of Christianity, they are also pointing out Western resources for doing theology that Western theologians have overlooked. So, intriguingly, Oscar may be highlighting a new role that Western resources, and therefore Western voices, can play in the global conversation. With the new angles of vision provided by these newer methods, Western theologians can learn to speak with accents that contribute to the interlocal dialogue rather than impeding it. So we conclude that it is not so much a matter of escaping influences as proposing new horizons that are not bound by settled perspectives and inherited habits of thought. As Oscar puts it, transoccidentalism implies both a deepening and a broadening rather than a narrowing of the theological conversation.

Are There Perennial Theological Questions?

The conclusion of much theological discussion in the younger churches, as we have seen, has often been that Western traditions are irrelevant to the problems and challenges faced by churches elsewhere. This was also my impression when I first landed in the Philippines. Influenced as it is by various streams—Greco-Roman, medieval scholastic, and the modern Enlightenment, influences that may often go unacknowledged—Western theology is often accused of being fatally compromised, even syncretistic.[9] These influences not only are missing elsewhere but are often difficult to even explain in non-Western settings. But does this mean that theology has no relevance outside the context that shaped it? By no means, for this would deny not only the continuing validity of Scripture over time but even the value and role of history. So let me try to respond to this view. I think there is more to be said about the continuing role of Western theology in two respects. One is the continuing relevance of basic theological perspectives, and the other is the role of theology in biblical interpretation.

The first point rests on the assumption that the human experience raises perennial questions that theologians have attempted to answer through the ages. To illustrate this point, I refer again to Willie Jennings's complaint about

---

9. See the description of these criticisms in the excellent article "European Theology" by Hille, in Dyrness and Kärkkäinen, *Global Dictionary of Theology*, 285–94. Similarly Balcomb, in his article "African Evangelical Theology," argues that evangelical theology in Africa differs fundamentally from that in the West because the former did not experience the Enlightenment.

missionary and colonial theology. In one chapter he describes the work of the Jesuit missionary José de Acosta in Peru as transforming the New World into an ever-expanding classroom where the natives could be taught the way of Christ. In the resulting pedagogical framework, Jennings notes, "Acosta's quest to teach and thereby create orthodoxy even in those he designates the most ignorant flesh . . . produced a reductive theological vision in which the world's people become perpetual students, even where and when faith is formed."[10] The resulting pedagogical imperialism, he thinks, can be said to infect much of subsequent missionary history and is in turn reflected by the abstract and indexical notion of much of Christian theology. Jennings characterizes this as a discipleship within teaching rather than a teaching within discipleship.

For someone who has spent much of his life teaching in missionary situations, this charge struck a chord (or even a nerve!). But I think there is an appropriate response. True, missionaries often taught people how to read and translate the Bible and even how to think about God. But their pedagogies reflected certain convictions about God and the world that I'm not sure I want to give up. Take the case of Acosta, for example. His teaching the Indians about Christianity reflected, among other things, a conviction about God's creative work and the natural law that results from this—lessons he learned from his Catholic tradition. He believed that certain aspects of creation reflect God's continuing purposes over time. Other, Protestant missionaries also taught out of the conviction that God's purposes and instructions have a continuing validity for all times and places. In this case, their teaching often reflected what is called "the third use of the law"—the belief that the biblical instructions, both in the Old and New Testaments, not only convict of sin and keep society from destroying itself, as Luther (and many Anabaptists) taught, but they are to be applied to communal and family life both inside and outside the church. God wishes to see his purposes reflected in politics, economics, and social relations. And if one has this conviction, then a teaching ministry reflecting this is perfectly appropriate. In other words, the practice of missionary teaching (as well as institution building) reflects specific traditions of Western theology that respond to universal human needs and longings and specific core themes of Scripture. These specifics may well be challenged, but if they are given up, *some* formulation will have to be developed that will respond to the specific questions of human life: How do we live as a family? How is political and economic life to be ordered fairly and justly? And if these questions are to be answered, it is foolish to ignore the responses that God's people have developed through the centuries.

10. Jennings, *Christian Imagination*, 112. The reference to discipleship is on p. 106.

What are we to make of the common charge that Western theology has a penchant for turning theology into intellectual abstractions? This is a bigger and more important question than I can deal with here, but let me make some suggestions by way of introduction to the discussions that follow. It is perfectly true that Western thought bears all the marks of its unique history and therefore of the influence of Greek philosophy and its subsequent history, especially in the Enlightenment. Theology in the West has come to mean, for most students, the study of what the church has taught as this has come to be represented in creeds and statements of faith. But as our brief survey has shown, the varying *interpretations* of this faith—the *traditions* of theology—reflect a wide variety of cultural and historical circumstances. That has resulted in an important variety of expressions of Christianity. In other words, Western theology is not one thing—it developed in multiple directions, and these differences had consequences. So it is naive to think that the differences in interpretation of the Christian faith are either unimportant or merely a Western habit that younger churches need to discard. Ideas will always be guides to human behavior—they help people explain, understand, justify, and sometimes rationalize their behavior. As historians have pointed out, when colonized societies sought leverage to resist oppression, they often had recourse to Western—and frequently biblical—doctrines to formulate and promote their resistance.[11] At the very least, the Western traditions of reflection, if not normative, may be useful models that can help avoid the biblicistic proof texting or the reduction of theological reflection to moral inquiry all too common in many places today.

Theological Interpretation of Scripture

Perhaps an even more important way in which Western reflection has continued relevance is in biblical interpretation. One of the fruits of recent biblical scholarship is the recognition that no reading of Scripture is theologically or culturally neutral. So however intent non-Western theologians are to "read the Scripture for themselves," they will be doing so from particular perspectives. Even the assumption that inherited theology must be discarded because of its Western provenance can become a stumbling block for non-Western interpreters. The reason for this resistance is often unacknowledged: the faith younger churches espouse was introduced in terms of one of the traditions that we have pointed to (or by some combination of these). The original missionaries might have believed they were bringing the "simple gospel" to people, but

11. A classic expression of this process is Sanneh, *Translating the Message.*

they were in fact bearers of long-standing theological assumptions that call for recognition and, sometimes, critique.

This is partly a result of globalization. Given the reality of global cultural flows and modern communication technologies, the circulation of theological ideas is inescapable—think of the worldwide impact of the new apostolic movement, health-and-wealth preachers, or the various forms of Liberation theology. It is to be expected that no expression of the Christian faith will be entirely sui generis; it will inevitably bear the marks of its cultural, historical, and social context. But it will also bear the marks of previous formulations of the gospel message.

So the appeal to simply let people read the Scriptures for themselves turns out to be more complicated than one might expect. But let me try to put this in a more positive light: perhaps theological frameworks can enable interpretation rather than impede it. This is the view of a newer perspective on hermeneutics known as theological interpretation. Rather than interpreting Scripture simply in terms of its original cultural and historical setting, scholars are pointing out that truly formative readings are embedded in communal convictions about God and the work of the Spirit. Joel Green, one of the leaders of this movement, puts this practice of theological reading in perspective: "The horizons of interpretation of [biblical] texts include the particularity of the ecclesial community. This means that the measure of validity for Christian interpretation cannot be taken apart from the great creeds of the church, a concern with the rule of faith, and the history of Christian interpretation and its embodiment in Christian lives and communities."[12]

In other words, since all readings of Scripture employ theological assumptions about God and how we learn of his purposes, we should welcome the opportunity to explore and learn from theological options from other places and times. Since we all belong to a common body of Christ, we should welcome the opportunity to read Scripture with these other believers. This engaged and faithful reading of Scripture seems more attractive to non-Western Christians than the barren historical-critical method. It is a reading that both encourages spiritual formation and seeks to harvest the exegetical riches of the contemporary church and the church through the centuries.

Carriers and Institutional Forms of the Western Churches

But I also want to broaden the conversation and think about "theology" in a wider sense. In addition to specifically theological (and intellectual)

---

12. Green, *Practicing Theological Interpretation*, 127. This book provides an excellent introduction to theological interpretation.

developments, there are Western streams of spiritual and liturgical practice that provide a legacy that continues to nurture the church and have
important implications for theology. To take only two examples, consider
the traditions represented by the medieval mystics and by medieval and
Reformation liturgical practices. Nourished by the monastic movement,
and before that the desert fathers and mothers, medieval mystics developed
ways of thinking of the Christian's journey to God in terms of purification
and ascent. Treatises like Anselm's *Proslogion*, Bonaventure's *Soul's Journey
to God*, and Thomas à Kempis's *Imitation of Christ* provided insights that
stimulated the rise of Pietist movements in Europe and beyond. These are
central to the traditions of Catholic spirituality, but it is impossible to understand many kinds of Protestant Christianity, especially of the evangelical
variety, without taking into account this mystical and personal stream of
Christian spirituality.

Or consider the liturgical developments of the late Middle Ages and Reformation. Despite an environment that was deeply polemic and often an-
tagonistic, practices of personal and corporate worship—preaching, singing, prayers, confession, and sacraments—were developed from this joint
heritage that continues to influence Christians throughout the world. What
would Protestant worship be without the impact of the Geneva Psalter or the
hymns of the Great Awakenings? Recent movements of "worship renewal"
have suggested to theologians of many different traditions that this heritage
has a continuing validity and deserves fresh examination.

Considerations of spirituality remind us that the history of the Western
church is replete with vital figures whose lives and examples continue to influence not only what Christians believe but also how they pray and worship.
The church continues to be nurtured by the writings and testimonies of St.
Augustine, St. Francis, Teresa of Avila, Julian of Norwich, and so on, right
up to contemporary spiritual writers like Henry Nouwen and Mother Teresa.
What would the heritage of Christianity be like apart from Dante Alighieri's
description of the person's journey to God in *The Divine Comedy* or the
Christian pilgrimage to the heavenly city described in *Pilgrim's Progress* by
John Bunyan? Asian and African Christians, for whom elders and ancestors
play such a critical role, will acknowledge how important it is for this body
of witnesses to be acknowledged and appreciated, even as they begin to add
their own number to these voices. These are treasures and teachers not only
of the Western church but also of the church universal.

This argument might be summarized by the simple recognition that much
of the global church continues to be influenced by the history of the Western
church. The split between Eastern and Western versions of history is critical

for understanding, for example, events in Egypt and Ethiopia. Recently we have become aware of how events associated with the disastrous series of military crusades that Christian forces carried out in the eleventh and twelfth centuries continue to animate people's imaginations in many parts of the Middle East and Africa. Whatever the motives might have been, the results of these incursions continue to be influential (and often detrimental) for relations not only with Muslims but also with those between the Eastern and Western branches of Christianity.

We have referred already to the earthshaking events of the Reformation and Counter-Reformation of the sixteenth century. But consider the modern missionary movement that began in the eighteenth century and the Western colonial rule that often attended and facilitated this. Whatever the relationship between these developments, they continue to influence the shape of Christianity in many places in the world. Though we speak of our contemporary situation as "postcolonial," this certainly does not mean these chapters of Christian history no longer matter. In fact, much of the argument of postcolonial theologians is that they matter a great deal more than we let on. The heritage of these things, for better or worse, is inescapable.

A final aspect of the Western heritage that should be recognized is the continuing presence and impact of Western institutions. Indeed, these institutions determine in many ways the present shape of Christianity in the world and how it is represented. This includes of course what might be called the "denominational" shape of Christianity, which we have already described. But beyond this, let me call attention to the worldwide impact of other institutional forms that have resulted from the Western churches.

Western Christianity, for better or worse, has left an extensive heritage of missionary societies, educational facilities and practices, medical establishments, relief and development organizations and initiatives, publishers and literacy efforts, and many more. Think of the worldwide presence of World Vision, or ministries like Campus Crusade for Christ and the International Fellowship of Evangelical Students. What is perhaps even more significant, for most people in the world—especially those who are not part of the Christian church—these institutions constitute the face of Christianity. They represent what comes to mind when they think of Christianity. Moreover, one can argue that now more than at any time in Christian history, the continuing presence and influence of these institutions call for theological reflection and, sometimes, critique. What aspects of these institutions might constitute part of the multiple gifts that Paul refers to in 1 Corinthians 12? What part of this heritage might in fact inhibit the exercise not only of local initiative but also of various indigenous gifts?

Does the Majority World Need Western Theology?

But our opening narrative of the conference in Japan and Oscar's introductory chapter point out the sea change that is currently taking place in the makeup of Christian churches. Another change that is often unnoticed but will be important to our (especially Oscar's) reflection is the dissolution of Western empires and the global reach they facilitated. A century ago, a similar story might have gone as follows. A missionary couple from England and Germany plant a church in Nairobi that has members from several tribes in Kenya. Like the church in Japan, this church was, in a sense, a transnational and hybrid entity, but there was this clear difference: this effort represented the extension of a Western church and a political and economic system into Africa. It represented what has been called the "first globalization," that is, the expansion of the presence and impact of Western empires—British, German, American, and, in some cases, even Russian. The history of the twentieth century is largely the history of the dissolution of these empires, which, according to Donald Bloxham, collapsed in three progressive stages: World War I, the Great Depression, and World War II. The collapse of the empires that sponsored the first globalization has made possible a new, second globalization, whose character is polycentric and multicultural.[13] The implication of this for global theology is clear: though the Western church has had a decisive influence on the present character of the church, other influences have now come to play equally important roles. We are entering a new world of transoccidental theological reflection.

So this is my (Bill's) tentative conclusion. Even if we wanted to, we cannot escape this legacy. And for the most part, Christians from all parts of the world would want to both preserve this legacy and build on it while recognizing and counteracting its weaknesses where necessary. But whatever we think about all this, though Christianity is moving into a new world, it is burdened and blessed with a particular history. This history often, for better or worse, has its roots and characteristic interpretation in the West.

Of course, as a Western theologian, I will in fact do my theological reflection primarily out of the framework and in the light of the traditions that constitute my context. Oscar will continue to negotiate the in-between places he has described as his *mestizaje*, his hybridity. But for my part, now that I have heard from Oscar and seen the new accents that he brings to the conversation, I can no longer simply accept my own traditions uncritically; I will

13. This is the basic argument of Bloxham's book *Final Solution*. The polycentric character of the postimperial world was described along with its implication for mission in Engels and Dyrness, *Changing the Mind of Mission*.

acknowledge their limitations and even the damage they have done to others. But Oscar too has admitted that he needs to stay attuned to the diversity and complexity of Western theological reflections. Oscar's discussion of David Barrett's description of African Independent Churches and the response of Allan Effa provides an illuminating case study—one takes the Reformation as the dominant paradigm, the other the trigger of Nigerian Christianity. Oscar and I both agree that we cannot replace one with the other; rather, we need to allow them to illuminate each other. Clearly this cannot happen while one is considered superior or irreplaceable. Both are important in their different ways. Together they illustrate that the future of theology is comparative.

In a sense, I have lost my innocence as a Western theologian. My heritage as a Midwestern white evangelical has constructed the places (loci) with which I am most comfortable. But because of my experience as a missionary and my friendship with Oscar, I realize there are also other places, in the words of Augustine, we may be carried to—and others who may carry us—en route to our true homeland, which is in God.[14]

14. See Augustine, *On Christian Teaching* 1.

3

The Role of Indigenous Traditions
in Christian Theology

Our first two chapters described very different ways of approaching theology that reflect our different contexts. We used these differences to raise fundamental questions about the possibility of a global conversation in theology and the problematic (and contested) role of Western theology in this conversation. One of the major points we made is that *the place in which theology is formed matters*. Place matters because language, culture, and traditions are never neutral carriers of ideas; they always shape what they receive according to the values and inclinations of that place and its people. The implications of this may be stated in the form of a thesis that we want to develop in this chapter: theology develops in a particular place out of the interaction, not simply between the Scriptures and culture, but between some version of the Christian tradition and the indigenous traditions of that place—both cultural and religious.[1]

In order to explain and support this thesis we will turn our attention to the diverse, globalized world that provides such a wide variety of contexts for theological reflection. Christians often naively assume that there is some

1. This fact has led Oscar to insist that we must understand theological difference at the fundamental level of how we come to know about God, or theological epistemology. This is the subject of his forthcoming book.

simple form of the gospel that must just be translated into a local language, or that we must simply translate the Scriptures themselves into the various languages and let the people read them for themselves. While this is a necessary starting point—and we do want to insist on the priority of Scripture and the gospel—the theological reflection that results from simple translation is never as simple or straightforward as we imagine.

The word "Theology" (with a capital *T*) literally means "speaking about God" or "language about God." But all our speaking includes the assumptions and possibilities of our own particular cultural and historical situation. Even in Scripture it is clear that Abraham, though he heard and obeyed God's command to leave his home country, carried with him the cultural and even religious assumptions that he grew up with. So while theological reflection on Abraham in one sense begins with God's call in Genesis 12, in another sense it is formed by Abram's religious inheritance—his understanding of sacrifices, priests, family and hospitality, and so on. Though God was doing a new thing with Abraham—forming a nation that would bless the earth— God embodied this novelty in cultural and religious realities that Abraham already understood.

God's work of redemption always takes its start from the situations humans find themselves in. To further elaborate this, we want to pick up the discussion of chapters 1–2. Oscar described some of the problems the Western inheritance caused for younger churches and the differences they exhibit in the way they do theology. Bill noted the way Western churches inherited particular patterns of thought and practice that have decisively influenced the way they "do" theology. In some ways that whole discussion was acknowledging the main topic of this chapter: the inescapable influence and indeed the positive (and sometimes not so positive) contributions of indigenous traditions to the work of theological reflection and practice. God's Word must always be heard and obeyed from within some particular cultural setting and context—language, ways of thinking, and assumptions about the world and God (or gods or natural processes), together with the technology and artifacts that make up people's everyday lives. All of this will surely influence how people eventually understand who God is and how they are to respond to this. We cannot deal with all the aspects of human culture in this chapter, so we will focus on the presence and importance of the moral, religious, and even aesthetic values that animate a given culture—their indigenous traditions. All of these play a critical role in Christian theology.

But what role should these traditions play? While this question has caused a great deal of controversy throughout the history of the church, it has become especially contentious in the past generation. Our work in this chapter is to try to shed some light on these discussions. We will do this first by making some general comments on the problem as we have recently come to understand it and then discuss in some detail how this might be framed in two more specific settings: the Americas (Oscar) and Africa (Bill).

It became clear in our earlier chapters that this problem is not unique either to the Western traditions or to the newer churches; churches everywhere face and struggle with it. But the problem is complicated by the fact that not all churches have recognized their own cultural inheritance. Here I (Bill) have found it helpful to apply Jesus's teaching about judging others. In the Sermon on the Mount, Jesus tells his listeners not to judge others. He asks, "Why do you see the speck in your neighbor's eye, but do not notice the log in your own eye? . . . First take the log out of your own eye, and then you will see clearly to take the speck out of your neighbor's eye" (Matt. 7:3, 5). This is a helpful metaphor because Western theologians in particular tend not to notice how our cultural situation has influenced what we see and understand about God. The log in our eye is the twenty-first century, as Flannery O'Connor said of the twentieth century.[2] We could broaden that by saying, for Western theologians, the log in our eye is the Western tradition. And this tradition, with its special mix of influences—Greek philosophy, European paganism, medieval scholasticism, the Reformation, the Enlightenment—has shaped theology in specific ways. Let's pause briefly to reflect on this heritage.

The West: From Christendom to Contextualization

For most of Christian history, the Christian traditions have been closely bound up with a particular history and culture, which we usually designate as "Christendom." That is, in many places—Western Europe in the case of Catholic Christianity, and Eastern Europe and the Middle East in the case of Orthodox Christianity—a particular version of Christianity, along with special practices and a characteristic visual culture, was privileged. This meant not only that most people in these places followed these traditions but also that various kinds of influences were brought to bear to ensure that people conformed to this version of Christianity.

In the fourth century, once Constantine declared Christianity legal and then Theodosius declared it the official religion of the empire, they were able to apply considerable pressure, both military and economic, to support a particular form of the Christian movement. Their support, and that

2. See *Mystery and Manners*, 156–59.

of subsequent emperors, allowed the famous fourth- and fifth-century ecumenical councils, such as Nicaea in 325 and Chalcedon in 451, to meet and decide how Christians should think about Christ and the Trinity and what should be considered deviant. For the church fathers involved in these controversies, Scripture was of course the primary authority—in studying these early councils, one is impressed by how seriously these theologians took the actual words and phrases of Scripture.[3] But we should also recognize that they were working with cultural and social assumptions that influenced what they were able to see in the Scriptures. These factors included philosophical ideas that came from their Greek heritage. The language of the great councils—of substance and persons—was language that had been forged over centuries of philosophical debate. (The decisions and formulations of those councils also deeply affected how those very terms would subsequently be understood; the language of "persons" is a classic example.)[4] Similarly, attitudes toward law and justice inherited from their Roman forebears would have important influence on how theologians like Augustine, for example, would understand sin and forgiveness and also help us understand his later struggles with his Donatist adversaries. Peter Brown has argued recently that even beliefs about wealth and poverty reflected characteristic patterns of the declining Roman Empire.[5] In other words, though Western Christians have not always recognized it, as Oscar has forcefully reminded us, the traditions they have inherited are deeply marked by specific cultural and historical arrangements.

In the chapters that follow, we will have occasion to note how the emerging global conversations about theology have revisited various episodes of this history and brought new perspectives to bear on those important discussions. Some have asked, for example, whether these Greek categories are the only ones that might help us understand the mystery of the Trinity—especially for those unacquainted with Greek philosophy. Others wonder whether Augustine's reading of sin and its penalties, influenced as it is by Roman law, is the most accurate reading of the biblical material. This is a welcome development because the inherent problem with "Christendom" was its ability to impose a uniformity that ignored or suppressed alternative points of view—it was sometimes uncomfortable with diverse readings of Scripture for political rather than theological reasons. At the very least, it sometimes proposed theological formulations that were difficult to put into other cultural frameworks, where, for example, there had been no previous conversations about "persons" and "substance."

3. The classic study of these developments is Kelly, *Early Christian Creeds*.
4. See Zizioulas, *Being as Communion*.
5. See Brown, *Through the Eye of a Needle*.

This is seen, for example, in what happened when the Roman Empire disintegrated after the barbarian invasions in the fifth century. Voices on the periphery of the empire had always spoken with accents that the dominant players found hard to understand. Churches in Syria in the early centuries focused on the humanity of Christ and a more literal interpretation of Scripture; Christians in Egypt, by contrast, were more insistent on Christ's divinity and championed a more allegorical reading of Scripture. These differing impulses reflected the indigenous traditions in these places and gave their theologies a characteristic flavor that was, at various times, seen as problematic or even heretical. But they also flowered into uniquely Eastern and African traditions that would prove influential as they spread, respectively, into China and India and into Upper Egypt and Ethiopia. And to this day, though these traditions continue to flourish, they are seen as marginal to the more central Western tradition and its interpretation of theology.[6]

Recent scholarship has uncovered a wide variety of Christian movements that coexisted after the breakup of the Roman Empire in a changing and kaleidoscopic pattern of relationship with other faiths—from Mar Thoma churches in India and Nestorian Christianity in China to various forms of Arian and Gallic Christianity in the West.[7] Moreover, Christians during this time came to various levels of accommodation and even cooperation with Islam and Zoroastrianism, to name only the better-known examples. In early medieval Spain, Jews, Christians, and Muslims created a culture together that was to have great influence on medieval Christianity—from the translation and preservation of Greek literature to the building practices of Gothic architecture. By AD 800, Islamic Spain had reached a level of civilization that Western Europe would not reach for another four hundred years.[8]

The Renaissance and Reformation are known as a time of both the recovery of the texts and artifacts of classical civilization and, in the case of the Reformation, the suppression of many aspects of the medieval religious legacy. Both of these—recovery and suppression—would play large roles in the Protestant Reformation, but they also produced a decidedly ambivalent attitude toward tradition in general and have gone on to play an outsized role in the way Protestants think about theology. The call of Reformers to return to the sources—to read and interpret Scripture in the original Hebrew and Greek—was a direct result of Renaissance humanism. But this return to the sources also fueled a call to free Christianity from

6. A helpful description of these differences is found in the early chapters of Moffett, *History of Christianity in Asia*, vol. 1.
7. See Brown, "Recovering Submerged Worlds," 35–37, and the books reviewed there.
8. See Menocal, *Ornament of the World*.

what the Reformers saw as superstitious medieval practices. In England and other places, altar pieces, rood screens, images, elaborate candelabras, and chalices were swept away. Many believed (and of course Protestants mostly still insist) that this was all necessary to restore a pure version of Christianity in an effort to return to the ancient tradition—it was a restoration of tradition, not a departure from it. But for many people it involved unsettling social dislocation.[9]

John Calvin displays this ambivalence toward tradition. On the one hand he could insist that nothing he taught was really "new." As he says in his preface to the *Institutes*, "I could with no trouble at all prove that the greater part of what we are saying meets the approval" of the fathers of the church.[10] On the other hand, when he comes to discussion of worship, he sets out to free worship from all the medieval practices, "human devising," that supported only superstition and all vain ceremonies that have no support in Scripture. But in doing so he gave up the whole visual and imaginative world of the Middle Ages. Late sixteenth-century English theologian Thomas Bilson also betrays this ambiguity toward tradition. In a 1585 treatise he describes true Christian subjection to tradition. "What part of our faith is not ancient?" he asks. Removing images is simply restoring the original forms of worship that existed in the early church. Protestants are recovering tradition, not denying it. But at the same time, the developing medieval tradition had to be challenged and transformed. How are these views reconciled? Here Bilson has recourse to the Protestant principle: faith cannot be built on tradition alone. "You may not build any point of faith upon tradition, except the Scriptures confirm the same."[11]

But this reflects a peculiar attitude toward "tradition" that ignores the cultural and social patterns people inherit. Reformers were ready to appropriate the tradition of theological reflection but were suspicious of the images and practices that expressed this in the Middle Ages. And at the same time, it sets up unrealistic expectations about the (independent) role of Scripture in developing theology. This ambiguity, moreover, led to several generations of struggle, and frequently violence, over the nature of Christianity and the cultural forms it ought to take.[12] Most Protestants of course celebrate this purification of Christianity. Others have not been as sanguine about the loss of medieval practices and attitudes. This iconoclasm, Eamon Duffy has argued,

9. This is being increasingly recognized in the newer readings of Reformation history. See Wandel, *Reformation*.

10. Calvin, preface to *Institutes*. Calvin's reference to biblical worship is found in 4.10.23–26.

11. Bilson, *True Difference*, 581.

12. See my discussion of this period in Dyrness, *Reformed Theology and Visual Culture*.

was nothing less than the disruption of social and cultural structures, the loss of a whole way of life.[13]

We want to emphasize these different views of tradition because they have characterized the complex and diverse history of Christianity since that time, especially the patterns of missions that resulted. On one side, Catholic attitudes like those of Duffy could lead to deep respect for indigenous traditions. The Jesuit missionary Matteo Ricci (1552–1610), for example, sought to adapt the Christian message to Chinese culture and earned the hearing and respect of many Chinese intellectuals.[14] And in the mid-twentieth century, Catholic missionaries first spoke about enculturation in their attempts to communicate the gospel across cultures. But there is also a weakness with this respect for tradition: the frequent association of Catholic missionaries with political and economic power in Latin America led to very different attitudes toward indigenous traditions there, as Oscar has pointed out.

The Protestant focus on texts and Scripture led to very different attitudes toward indigenous traditions. Here of course there is also much to celebrate. The earliest missionaries to India, for example, took the time to collect and translate much of the region's literature so that these traditions could be used in the communication of the gospel. William Carey (1761–1834), the Baptist missionary to Bengal, translated the Bible into Sanskrit and Bengali and also helped collect and publish classical Indian literature.[15] Such was his contribution that he proved in many ways to be the father not only of modern missions but of Indian classical literature as well. Carey represented what was to become the hallmark of Protestant missions with its focus on Bible translation and Bible teaching as the primary means of promoting the faith and its dissemination. This focus on education has often proved beneficial in missions and has consistently stimulated economic development.[16]

This has had great positive influence on the preservation of culture in many places, but it has also had some less positive results. The emphasis on texts, literacy, and publication, while fostering many educational initiatives, has led to a dominant missiological model of "translation." This model assumes that communicating the gospel is a matter of translating

13. See Duffy, *Saints, Sacrilege and Sedition*, 101–2. These changes had the effect of "making invisible, and indeed of abolishing some of the social complexity of the parish" (101). Duffy provides a Roman Catholic perspective on the Reformation.

14. For reliable and helpful discussions of Ricci, see Joseph F. MacDonnell, SJ, "Matteo Ricci, S.J. (1552 to 1610) and His Contributions to Science in China," Home Page of Joseph F. MacDonnell, SJ, www.faculty.fairfield.edu/jmac/sj/scientists/ricci.htm.

15. On Carey, see Moffett, *History of Christianity in Asia*, 2:253–63.

16. For support of this point, see the important article by Woodberry, "Missionary Roots of Liberal Democracy," 244–74.

not only biblical texts but also Christian truth into the idiom of the people. The danger here is that indigenous practices and values, frequently carried in songs, legends, and rituals, can be overlooked or in some cases actively suppressed. This threat has recently been highlighted by the work of William Jennings.[17] Too often in the missionary movement, Jennings argues, as in colonialism more generally, there is an inverted sense of hospitality (8). Rather than embracing people in their living traditions, people have been displaced both from their cultural (and racial) roots and, in North America for example, literally from their own physical place. Moreover, the focus on texts and teaching led to an evaluative modality and a pedagogical mindset—to a discipleship inside teaching rather than, as in Scripture, a teaching within discipleship (106). The results of this have included a disembodied spirituality that loses its connection to the artifacts of the past and to the larger created order—piety replaced, Jennings writes, "a material display of Christian belonging" (202).

In the twentieth century there have been important theological movements that have sought to recover a more holistic understanding of culture, and even the ability to see culture not just as an ethical and moral universe but also as a place where God is present and working by the Spirit. Movements such as Liberation theology—or on the Protestant side, *misión integral*—have worked to recover a biblical holism.[18] These movements, and theological reflection more generally, have been helped enormously by advances in the social sciences. Early in the last century, American Franz Boas opposed the organic and evolutionary views that had developed in the nineteenth century and coalesced into the Nazi idea of *volk*. Boas stressed the historical and geographical factors that influence the rich variety of cultures over against the reigning philosophy of biological determinism. By mid-century, scholars were recognizing the cognitive and symbolic dimensions of culture that come to expression in language and practices. Clifford Geertz is the most famous of these in suggesting that religion is best understood as a system of symbols that structures and orders both people's understanding and their practices. This idea has been very influential and, for many theologians and missionaries, has become a kind of default view of culture. Geertz argued that culture is "an historically transmitted pattern of meaning embodied in symbols . . . by means of which people communicate, perpetuate, and develop their knowledge about and attitudes toward life."[19]

17. Jennings, *Christian Imagination*. Page numbers in the text refer to this work.
18. See Gutiérrez, *Theology of Liberation*, and Padilla, *Mission between the Times*.
19. Geertz, *Interpretation of Cultures*, 89.

Geertz's view has been challenged as "ideological" by Marxist and feminist thinkers, who stress the material and bodily nature of culture and the "constraints," or even oppression, that too often characterize culture. Their point can be illustrated by highlighting how, for Geertz, symbols express something deeper and more real—"knowledge and attitudes"—which he privileges. Geertz's symbolic view has also been critiqued by Muslim scholars, who point out the Christian (and even Protestant) bias that is embedded in this model. Culture and religion, Talal Asad argues, do not reside in ideas in people's minds but in concrete practices that are formed by communities over long periods of time—the focus on ideas, he thinks, is a deep-seated bias in Western formulations that reflects its Christian (and Protestant) orientation.[20]

From Contextualization to Mutual Learning

Though Catholic missiologists in the 1960s under the influence of Vatican II began to speak about enculturation, the 1970s represented the decade in which the most progress was made by Protestants and evangelicals in understanding cultural context. Influenced by the Lausanne Congress on World Evangelization in 1974, evangelicals began to make use of social-science categories and to recognize the need to communicate the gospel in the languages and categories people would understand. Fueling this was a growing awareness that all formulations, even Scripture itself, come from and express some particular cultural setting.[21]

While this represented a great advance in understanding mission, it did not always escape its Protestant heritage, especially in its focus on an unchanging message that needed to be translated into various languages and cultures. There was not yet an awareness of the positive contribution of these settings to the understanding—and more important, to an expanded vision of the corporate practices—of the Christian faith. In this respect Christians had not yet caught up with Paul's admonition to welcome all the multiple gifts of the body of Christ in order to promote our corporate growth into maturity in Christ (Eph. 4:11–15).

Here an important influence for many of us has been Hans-Georg Gadamer.[22] Gadamer insisted that a people's tradition represents the structure of their identity and constitutes the terms by which they understand their world and interpret texts. Following Gadamer, one might define tradition as

20. Asad, *Genealogies of Religion.*
21. See Stott and Coote, *Down to Earth.*
22. Gadamer, *Truth and Method.*

the cumulative history that has shaped people's lives. But this tradition must be constantly reframed and reenacted; it is not so much a creed as a script or musical score that must be performed in the light of changing circumstances. To put this negatively, apart from the cultural situation we find ourselves in, it would be impossible for us not only to communicate with another person but even to make sense of our experience at all.

But the positive contribution of this is that understanding, following Paul's insight in Ephesians 4, is potentially cumulative as Christians throughout history and from a variety of points of view live out the Christian faith. Robert Schreiter has helped many of us understand this process of mutual discovery in terms of what the church believes and teaches, on the one hand, and how various cultural traditions enable Christians to live out this faith in their various settings, on the other.[23] That is, religious identity is always expressed both by belief and by practice. The first we might equate with the traditional expression of the *lex credenda*, that is, the principle or law of belief; the second might be expressed by the *lex orandi*, or the law of prayer. Both are necessary, and both are influenced by the language and values of the setting that produces them. What we call orthodoxy, or what is to be believed, is expressed in various places and times through creeds or confessions (*lex credenda*); the performance (*lex orandi*) plays out in the specific vocabulary of, say, Shona culture or Han Chinese culture. The former seeks to embody the central import of Scripture as Christians read and interpret this over time. The latter, the performance, not only changes through history but will obviously look very different in Africa and China.

But what we have only recently come to see is that a conversation, an interaction, is taking place between these two "laws." Faithful performance can at times challenge or refine orthodoxy and move it forward—and often it has been the younger churches that remind us of this necessity. As Japanese theologian Anri Morimoto puts this, "When we move from one place to another, we do not move our head alone, or head first: our head moves along with the body. Likewise, the orthodoxy moves along with the body of faith expressions."[24] The danger is either that the tradition of belief is so strong that local performances are discouraged or that the local situation becomes so powerful that the law of belief is overwhelmed. A study of both the rich history of the church and the diverse experience of Christians today can help us avoid these dangers. Christians have not always been good at discerning

23. Schreiter, *New Catholicity*.
24. Morimoto, "Contextualized and Cumulative," 46. The suggestion of "breathing room" is from Morimoto's excellent discussion.

what is good. Here Oscar will describe briefly the engagement with indigenous traditions in Latin America, and Bill will look into the situation in Africa.

Theological Traditions in *las Américas*

The *"Indian" and the Western Scholar*

In the *Historia natural y moral de las Indias* published in 1590 by the Jesuit Spanish chronicler José de Acosta, we find a section titled "How there is some knowledge of God among the Indians." We can see a fair representation of its content in the following lines.

> In many ways the light of truth and reason works in them to some small degree; and so most of them acknowledge and confess a supreme Lord and Maker of all, whom the Peruvians called Virachocha, adding a very excellent name such as Pachacamac or Pachayachachic, which means the creator of heaven and earth, and Usapu, which means admirable, and other similar names. They worship him, and he was the chief god that they venerated, gazing heavenward. And the same belief exists, after their fashion, in the Mexicans. . . . All those who preach the Gospel to the Indians today have little difficulty in persuading them that there is a supreme God and Lord of all, and that he is the God of the Christians and the true God. Yet it has greatly astonished me that even though they do have the knowledge that I mention, *they have no word of their own with which to name God.* . . . So those who preach or write for the Indians use our Spanish *Dios*, adjusting its pronunciation and accent to the properties of the Indian languages, which are very diverse. *This shows what a weak and incomplete knowledge they have of God, for they do not even know how to name him except by using our word.*[25]

This historiographical pericope describing the assets and liabilities of the inhabitants of the "New World"[26] can serve to identify a pattern that has oriented the line of Western theological investigation and representation of the inhabitants of the Americas for centuries since the birth of Latin America as a colonial project. As commentators note, this chronicle and its portrayal of the originating cultures appeared in a convoluted time in Europe due to the classical revival of the Renaissance, the eruption of the Reformation and Counter-Reformation, and the discovery of a new territory and the "exotic Indians."

25. De Acosta, *Natural and Moral History of the Indies*, 256–57 (emphasis added).
26. The Incan Empire called their territory "Tawantinsuyu" (now Perú, Bolivia, and Ecuador), and the Aztec Empire called theirs "Anahuac" (now Mexico, Guatemala, Nicaragua). See ibid., xx.

"The greatness of Acosta's book lies," comments Walter Mignolo, "in its conceptualization of the 'Indies' within a larger philosophical picture. Its feebleness lies in its assumption that Amerindian knowledge did not count in the same way that the Greco-Latin tradition did."[27] Contrary to popular Western perception, pre-Columbian civilizations embodied a wealth of theological knowledge. In Acosta's categories, he acknowledges "the light of truth and reason," "a supreme God," and "the creator of heavens and earth" in Amerindian theology. When reviewing the texts, codices, architecture, and artifacts of the originating cultures, one can easily conclude that there is a pre-Columbian epistemology organically related to their cosmology, religion, politics, and city planning. The latter, for instance, is illustrated by the Aztec city of Tenochtitlán (now Mexico City), which astonished the Spanish conquistadors with its sophisticated urban planning. This can be seen in Bernal Díaz del Castillo's chronicle in *The True History of Conquest of New Spain* (ca. 1567), where he narrates the moment when, on November 8, 1519, the great Aztec leader Montezuma shows hospitality to the Spanish conquistador Hernán Cortés and receives him into the city of Tenochtitlán. The narrative is colored with phrases like "who could now count the multitude . . . it was indeed wonderful . . . all these palaces were [coated] with shining cement and swept and garlanded."[28]

In short, the Europeans did not encounter a blank page in the history of the Americas. Neither did they find a collection of uncivilized savages. In fact, they were initially shocked by the level of architectural sophistication, urban planning, astronomy, written documents, and so forth that they encountered in civilizations such as the Incas in South America and the Mayas and Aztecs in Mesoamerica. The magnitude of the impact caused by the "discovery" of America in Europe, including the encounter with the originating civilizations and their natural resources, was captured three centuries later by Adam Smith's charged statement, "The discovery of America and that of a passage to the East Indies . . . are the two greatest and most important events recorded in human history."[29] The amazement over the "New World" in Europe, however, did not impede the development of a colonial project and the subjugation of the pre-Columbian people—indeed, all of these resources served the purposes of an imperial Europe and contributed to its development. Moreover, if Amerindians were not as humanly valuable as the Europeans, then violent colonial processes such as deicide (killing of the gods), ethnocide (killing of

27. Mignolo, introduction to de Acosta, *Natural and Moral History of the Indies*, xviii.
28. Del Castillo, *True History of the Conquest of New Spain*, 2:41–44, 55–59.
29. See Smith, *Wealth of Nations*, 4.3.

their ethnic value), and genocide (massacres) could be properly justified. In fact, Enrique Dussel goes so far as to suggest that *"ego conquiro, ego cogito."* That is, without the conquest of the Americas and the logic of colonialism, there is no Enlightenment, no modernity, and indeed no Europe as we have come to know it.[30]

It is no longer possible to deny the fact that *las Américas* are a land forged by colonial and neocolonial projects. In the case of Acosta's account of the Americas, there is no question that he was one of the finest Christian scholars to set foot in the Americas at the beginning of the colonial era and that his scholarship was one of the finest and most theologically attuned to the rubric of Renaissance scholarship. Yet this great scholarship that brought together an appetite for "objective" truth, the classical disciplines of Greece and Rome, and the willingness to rigorously investigate the "New World" was plagued with Eurocentrism, historiographic neglect, and misrepresentation—he was unable to see the beam in his eye. And in many ways theological reflection on Latin America is still plagued with these prejudices. Five centuries later, can we confidently say that Western education and scholarship have overcome these deficiencies in the field of theological studies? Or do we continue to hold Acosta's basic conviction that the inhabitants of *las Américas* "have no word of their own with which to name God," which "shows what a weak and incomplete knowledge they have of God"?

Colonial Christianity

Speaking from within the Roman Catholic Church in Latin America, Lucio Gera presents us with three portrayals of the Catholic leader in the historical development of Roman Catholicism in Latin America. He argues that the leadership that predominated in the Catholic Church during the conquest and colonization period can be labeled as "traditionalist, rightist, conservative." This type of leadership, notes Gera, was nourished by the ideal of Christendom or colonial Christianity. In spite of the fact that the Iberian colonial powers over Latin America were overcome at their independence, Christendom leadership has not disappeared from the Latin American church; it has remained in the form of "aristocratic national Catholicism."[31] In his work *A History of the Church in Latin America*, Dussel adds an important element to Gera's view. Dussel categorizes the history of the colonial period into five stages using a complex and original historical and cultural method. One of

---

30. See Castro-Gómez and Mendieta, introduction to *Teorías sin disciplina*.
31. See Gera, "Apuntes para una interpretación," 59. Quoted in Bonino, *Doing Theology in a Revolutionary Situation*, 3–4.

his conclusions is that a significant portion of the native population of the Americas still "longs for complete evangelization," hence supplementing the official religion with folk Catholicism. This form of Catholicism has always been present and today is the majority in the Americas.[32]

In short, the combination of an imperial-political self-understanding of the church, an incomplete evangelistic mission, and a Christendom-type leadership conspired to propagate *conquest theology*. In turn, a layer of epistemic colonial codes, along with the experience of an imperial church, has written an imperial script into the sociopolitical imagination of the Americas. Through the centuries, that script has been used to legitimize a tragic list of dictatorships, regimes, power structures, and Christian superstructures that have perpetuated oppression, exploitation, and violence against the most vulnerable: the indigenous population, the poor, women, children, and rural immigrants.

Evangelicalism *in* las Américas

There is little question that the birth of Latin America and its church are tied to the imperial program of the proclamation of the cross of Jesus Christ.[33] But this paradigm would soon be challenged. The nineteenth century brought with it a series of conditions that would change the sociopolitical and religious horizon of Latin America forever. Two of the most significant ones were the political independence of the new nations of Latin America and the introduction of Protestantism. The former significantly weakened the influence and control of Iberian Catholicism over Latin American civic and political life, and the latter would help build the layers of knowledge and power that would yoke Latin America to a new superpower, the United States of America. Both conditions would contribute to forge new theological patterns in Latin America. One of these patterns resonates with triumphalism and health-and-wealth preaching. The other pattern counteracts it by seeking to represent theologically the vast impoverished and oppressed majority of Latin Americans through two distinctive discourses: Integral Mission theology (in the Protestant wing) and Liberation theology (mostly in the Roman Catholic wing). The latter pattern will be described in our next section.

---

32. Dussel combats the reductionistic concept of "mixed religions," or syncretism, by arguing that not all the layers of understanding of the indigenous people gave up to Christian knowledge as presented by the Christendom preaching of that epoch. See Dussel, *History of the Church in Latin America*, 62–71. Today we find fine Latino Catholic scholars, such as Orlando Espín, who argue that popular Catholicism has represented in Latin America and its diaspora the "least invaded cultural creation of our people and the locus for the most authentic self-disclosure." See Espín, *Grace and Humanness*, 148.

33. See Dussel, *History of the Church in Latin America*, 27.

Latin America was ready for a Christ that would provide an exit from historical tragedy, poverty, and spiritual emptiness. And for better or worse, this came with a new generation of Protestant missionaries after World War II and, in the next generation, a third wave of Pentecostalism. These brought a glorious theology with a triumphalist Christ—one we can find in selected biblical narratives, certain aspects of Western creedal formulations, and several Pentecostal hymns. This living Lord was passionately embraced and conceptualized as the living Christ of the *evangélicos* in diametrical opposition to the "other Christs" of the Americas, particularly the Spanish-Catholic crucified Christ. Finally! At long last we would sing the Protestant hymns; Christ has reached Latin America. The epistemological and ecclesiastical shift that characterized the Protestant Reformation in Europe three centuries earlier had now set foot in the Americas—along with the excesses accumulated by the post-Reformation thinkers: to be Protestant is to be anti-Catholic and fight against all forms of popular piety that attempt to give meaning to the Roman Catholic faith by means of "idolatrous" rituals. In the same vein, a popular saying came to capture the spirit of *la fe evangélica latinoamericana* (Latin American evangelical faith): *el Cristo de la Biblia es un Cristo vivo, no un Cristo muerto* (the Christ of the Bible is a living Christ, not a dead Christ). Along with a passionate proclamation of the glorious gospel of Jesus Christ, Western Protestantism and Pentecostalism introduced to Latin America an ethereal, truncated, and docetic Christology that had forgotten its way to the cross and suffered from the Anglo-Saxon fundamentalist-liberal divide.

Latin American Misión Integral *and Liberation Theology*

But there were other influences that soon would bear important fruit toward a holistic understanding of Christianity. John A. Mackay, a Presbyterian educator and evangelist, lived and worked in South America in the 1930s. His pioneering work on Christology paved the way for a contextual Christology in Latin America and offered a searing criticism of conquest theology. Mackay argued that the Christ that embarked to the Americas with the Spanish *conquistadores*, that is, the Christ known by the originating cultures and who gave birth to Christianity in the Americas, was quite simply a tragic and lifeless figure. Through Miguel de Unamuno's eyes, Mackay depicts quite poetically his critique against the docetic Christology he found embedded in South American Catholicism during his time. Mackay's depiction is worth citing in full.

> Christ too came to America. Journeying from Bethlehem and Calvary, He passed
> through Africa and Spain on His long westward journey to the pampas and

cordilleras. And yet, was it really he who came, or another religious figure with his name and some of his marks? [I think] that Christ, as he sojourned westward, went to prison in Spain, while another who took his name embarked with the Spanish crusaders for the New World, a Christ who was not born in Bethlehem but in North Africa. This Christ became naturalized in the Iberian colonies of America.[34]

If Mackay's perception is accurate, conquest theology seems to have conceived some infamous ideas in the embryonic subconscious of Latin America: (1) suffering is a God-given historical reality, and it is inevitable; (2) Christ illustrates tragedy and invites it; and (3) God blesses the other-in-power and allows him/her to use violence to accomplish his/her divine mandate.

Growing from this precedent, during the second half of the twentieth century, Latin America gave birth to twins, a theological pattern in two interrelated and yet distinct discourses that would shake the dominant paradigms of Western Christianity: Integral Mission on the evangelical side and Liberation theology on the Roman Catholic side. A fair description of both discourses in such a short space is beyond the scope of our presentation. Suffice it to say the *locus theologicus* shifted from the European categories of reason—*sola scriptura*, the church, individual subjectivism—to more indigenous categories. That said, Integral Mission was greatly overshadowed by the political and economic tone of Liberation theology. The time was right for such a tone; a historically situated discourse able to problematize the hegemony of neocolonial political and economic powers over Latin America was long due. Because of this fact, the diffusion of the Latin American Fellowship (FTL) and Integral Mission as a Latin American indigenous theology has remained partially in the shadows of theologizing in the West and the world.

If the "other Spanish Christ" of the Catholics brought death and fatalistic views, the *Cristo vivo de la Biblia* of the Anglo-American Protestant and Pentecostal missions did not bring enough life and seemed to have forgotten the way of the cross. It is on points like this precisely that Integral Mission constitutes an in-house criticism to transplanted epistemologies and imported histories by showing the irrelevancy of Western Protestant theology in the Americas. René Padilla, a founder of the FTL and an Integral Mission theologian, elaborates: "Despite its theoretical acknowledgment of Christ's full humanity, evangelical Christianity in Latin America, as in the rest of the world, is deeply affected by Docetism. It affirms Christ's transforming power in relation to the individual, but is totally unable to relate the gospel to social ethics and social life. In our case, Mackay's challenge remains unmet."[35]

34. Mackay, *Other Spanish Christ*, 95.
35. Branson and Padilla, *Conflict and Context*, 79.

These words represent not only a critique of Western theologizing in the Americas but also an attempt to bring about an evangelical indigenous theology, a discourse that by no means seeks to mimic Western theologizing but that struggles to be contextual, biblically faithful, and socially relevant.

In the case of the widely spread Latin American Liberation theology, one must recognize that a great part of its success is due to the keen epistemic relocation of its discourse. In short, the *locus theologicus* in classical theology underwent a relocation from abstract Western categories and sources to contextual, historical, and practical ones embedded in the daily political life of the people. Traditional theological categories from the West focused on reason, tradition, Scripture, and experience were replaced by a hermeneutics of communal suffering, poverty, and injustice in light of Jesus's way to the liberating cross. In this sense, Liberation theology represents a reversal of conquest theology and provides an alternative reinterpretation of the cross: the movement from a colonial legacy where Christ is assumed as victim of the historical tragedy to the option of Bartolomé de Las Casas and his solidarity with the poor, the invisibles, and victims of violence-producing powers. Interestingly, while Mackay looks at the "other Spanish Christ" through the lens of Unamuno and finds in it a Christ that is a child and a victim, Liberation theologians look at the *living and liberating* Christ through the praxis of Father Montesinos and Bartolomé de Las Casas. There they find a Christ that defends the civil rights of the indigenous population in a time of exploitation, genocide, and social injustice.

A series of external and internal factors (modern dialectics, the Cold War, the rise of Pentecostalism, and so forth) prevented Liberation theology from gaining the kind of public acceptance in Latin America that one would expect. Nevertheless, to disregard Liberation theology as something from the past would be naive since its ethos and method have been disseminated and integrated, for instance, in decolonial discourses in the global South and diaspora theologies in the global North.

Diaspora Latino/a Theologies

Immigration has had an effect on theology, at least across the Americas. The growth of Latino/a Christianity in the United States called for the training of religious leaders and contextual reflection. Latino/a theology, which developed almost side by side with Latin American Liberation theology and Integral Mission theology (FTL), concentrated on anthropological themes during its foundational and early developmental stages. A driving question at the early stages of Latino/a theology was, what does it mean to be Latino/a and to theologize out of our own contextual experience? Although Latino/a theology was heavily influenced by Liberation methodology, distinctive theological categories were identified to produce an autonomous discourse: periphery (Costas), *mestizaje* (Elizondo), *mujerista* theology (Isasi-Díaz), *mañana* eschatology (González), accompaniment (Goizueta), diaspora theology (Segovia), exile (García-Treto), popular Catholicism (Espín), Liberating Spirit (Villafañe), ethics from the margin (De La Torre), and so forth. For instance, when comparing how US Latinos/as do Christology in contrast to Latin Americans, one notices a distinctive difference. With regard to Christology, the concept of *mestizaje* and *mulatez* (as polemic as it is) has played an enormous role among Latino/a Protestants. The *mestizo-mulato* was considered for a long time, in Europe and Latin America, as a hybrid aberration, a product of the mixing of unequal races (Europeans with Amerindians and Africans). The Latino/a experience of *mestizaje-mulatez* offers a corresponding hermeneutical paradigm for understanding Jesus Christ as God among us.

In sum, in contrast to Latin American and Western theologies, diaspora Latino/a theology does not attempt to deny ambiguity for the sake of "clear" and "distinct" theologizing; instead, it tends to theologize ambiguity, subsuming in alterity corresponding historical memories, present struggles, and future utopias. Latinos/as in the global diaspora are aware of our borderline existential condition in ways that Latin Americans living to the south sometimes are not. Our subalternity is experienced at multiple levels with regard to the dominant Western and Latin American cultures. Our living constantly and subversively at the border has precipitated a way of dwelling and thinking on the border of knowledge and power. This way of life makes decoloniality a language of survival and subsistence for us. While many Latin Americans tend to experience the rhetoric of modernity and the impact of occidentalism from the outside, US Latinos/as experience it at the exteriority of modernity/coloniality (to use Dussel's terminology in his theory of transmodernity). This is to say that we are at the dawn of a new global conversation that needs to happen across the Americas. This is a different pattern of theologizing, with different agents and from different locations, a theology between the "global South" and the "South in the global North."

Africa: "The Determinative Nature of Founding Narratives"

Here I (Bill) will look to Africa and observe what that context might offer to the theological enterprise. The continent of Africa has witnessed the largest growth of the Christian church over the last century, and thus is often cited as the place where Christianity's future is being played out.[36] Yet interestingly Africa also boasts the longest continuous history with Christianity in the form of the Coptic Orthodox Church in Egypt and Ethiopia. So is Christianity a late arrival in Africa or part of its long-term heritage? Well, it is both. This ambiguity reflects a deeper tension over Christianity's relation to African traditional religions. Missionaries, and even African Christians today, have never been quite sure whether this indigenous spirituality must be replaced or simply purified by Christian beliefs and practices. Theology in Africa reflects a similar reticence: Should theology engage primarily with issues that arise in the African setting (a very common view among theologians in Africa today)? Or should it simply apply theological conversations (and traditions) that are prominent in the West? Or is it possible that some combination of these provides a way forward?

Taking these questions as our starting point, I will discuss two prominent and different views of Christianity's relationship to indigenous traditions, that of Ugandan Emmanuel Katongole and the late Ghanaian Kwame Bediako. Katongole, after studying theology at Makerere University in his native Uganda, earned a PhD at the Catholic University in Leuven, was a professor at Duke Divinity School, and recently was appointed to the faculty of theology of the University of Notre Dame. His recent book *The Sacrifice of Africa* presents a thoughtful and authoritative picture of the form theology might take in Africa.[37]

Katongole recognizes the importance of African indigenous traditions, but he understands them in a particular way. Africa today (much like the Latin America that Oscar described), Katongole thinks, is working from a particular political script that has deeply determined the shape of its life and witness and thus its theological reflection. The church has allowed itself to be formed by various projects of nation building and the alleviation of poverty, violence, and tribalism. Christians have become convinced that these are the fundamental issues that must be addressed, so they have shaped a Christian discourse that responds to these challenges, one that speaks the language of democracy and human rights. This discourse has taken various forms—spiritual, pastoral, and political—but all of these have taken on a prescriptive stance that seeks to affirm and encourage these human aspirations.

The basic problem with this, Katongole argues, is that it restricts Christianity to the religious sphere and does not question the underlying imagination, which has been defined for it by the secular nation state. Drawing on the work

---

36. This point is made, with accompanying statistics, in Jenkins, *Next Christendom*.
37. Katongole, *Sacrifice of Africa*.

of Basil Davidson, Katongole believes contemporary Africans have become "recaptives"; like slaves that were recaptured by naval blockades and set free, they have been alienated from Africa's social history. Whereas for the freed slaves their alienation was a matter of fact, for Africans today it was a *learned* sentiment; in fact it was the goal of education to "teach the story of Africa as a 'dark continent' and one 'with a history' that became unquestionably valid."[38]

What is needed, Katongole insists, are not programs of economic or political reform, nor even a recovery of traditional African values, but an alternative imagination that would replace this political script with another based on the Christian story, to offer people better stories than the ones they live by. Christianity is well suited for this because, at base, myths are the stuff of this faith. As he puts it, "The realities of the Christian tradition—the Scriptures, prayer, doctrine, worship, Baptism, the Eucharist . . . point to and re-enact a compelling story that should claim the whole of our lives."[39]

These historically embodied realities thus represent an alternative political imagination. Quoting William Cavanaugh, Katongole notes that this "imagination is the drama in which bodies are invested," and it challenges all other ways of organizing society. Katongole insists that this imagination is a social imagination through and through, concerned with feeding the hungry and bringing estranged bodies together in everyday life.

The bracing reminder that the resurrection of Christ has changed everything about human society is the core of Katongole's argument, and it is surely much needed in Africa. The obvious question is what this might look like on the ground—what Christians might do to embody this new imagination. And Katongole responds to this question in the third part of his book, providing three chapters that describe Christian initiatives in Africa: Paride Taban, who resigned his position as bishop of Sudan to set up a peace village; Angelina Atyam, who established the Concerned Parents Association in northern Uganda to model forgiveness and reconciliation in the face of the brutal Lord's Resistance Army; and Maggy Barankitse, whose Maison Shalom in Burundi provides a real-life example of Christ's feeding of the five thousand and a new vision of what it means to be the church.

The emphasis on a Christian imagination, along with these moving accounts of people who have struggled to realize such a vision, is a major contribution to reflection on theology in Africa. But there is a troubling undercurrent of radical critique, not only of African traditions, but also all contemporary efforts to orient Christian practice either to these traditions or to modernity.

38. Ibid., 70.
39. Ibid., 61–62.

Katongole ignores (or avoids) all the problems associated with the clash of these traditions with modern global culture. While he does not believe engagement with these issues is a bad thing, doing so does not, in his mind, address the central problem: the need for a new political imagination. But this raises a fundamental question: What then are we to do with poverty, tribalism, and the secular nation state? All indications are that these are facts on the ground that will not disappear any time soon. Katongole implies that if there is any "solution" to these issues (he shows a preference for this dismissive use of quotation marks), it will be when the church begins to live out its unique calling. All his examples are people who form alternative structures and communities rather than seeking to bring about any significant change within existing social structures. He believes such efforts represent the only way to influence the larger society.

For theological guidance, Katongole provides a valuable study of the Cameroonian priest Jean Marc Ela. Ela proposes what he calls a "shade tree theology," which, "far from the libraries and the offices, develops among brothers and sisters searching shoulder to shoulder with unlettered peasants for the sense of the word of God in situations in which the word touches them."[40] This begins, Ela writes in another place, "with the concrete practices and alternatives wherein the memory and resistance of our people have been articulated." With a method that recalls the Japanese theologian Kosuke Koyama, Ela here proposes a kind of pragmatic encounter between African traditions and the day-to-day living of the gospel. He too rejects the limitation of faith to a spiritual realm that never touches the social and political realities, but he seems also, like Koyama, to reject any grand theological schema. But here the argument of Katongole takes a surprising turn. Later in this same chapter he erects his own theoretical (i.e., theological) framework and turns to John Milbank and Stanley Hauerwas, a British and an American theologian, respectively.[41] Both of these argue for a Christianity firmly situated within concrete practices that define a radical Christian politics. While Katongole makes no general characterization of these thinkers, they represent a particular tradition of Western theology that reflects a decidedly negative attitude toward culture.[42] This tradition focuses on the church as an alternative society, one that lives out the reality of the gospel over against a secular world that operates with

40. Ela, *African Cry*, quoted in Katongole, *Sacrifice of Africa*, 103. The subsequent quotation is from 105–6.

41. See the discussion in Katongole, *Sacrifice of Africa*, 112–22.

42. While Hauerwas is a Methodist theologian and Milbank is Anglo-Catholic, their views of culture are in different ways closer to Anabaptist attitudes toward culture. See the description of this in appendix 1.

opposing assumptions. Because of this framework, any attempt to enter and engage the secular institutions will be doomed to failure or, worse, will end up compromising the concrete reality of the gospel—a reality only consistently lived out within community called the church of Jesus Christ.

A case might be made that this (Western) framework is particularly suited to the situation in Africa today and needs to be deployed alongside other important strategies, but Katongole makes no such case. Rather, his argument proceeds as though this "alternative imagination" were privileged. The problem is that most Christians in Africa today would agree with this imaginative vision; they simply have a variety of ways of seeking to embody this within their own traditions and practices. But alternative theological frameworks, for Katongole, are dismissed as mistaken strategies rather than addressed on their own (theological) terms.

This is seen most clearly in his discussion of Kwame Bediako, whom Katongole dismisses as an example of the (mostly evangelical) spiritual paradigm.[43] This paradigm, Katongole thinks, seeks to form in believers a "*spiritual* identity." Referring to Bediako's book *Christianity in Africa*,[44] Katongole notes that, for Bediako, recognizing God as the source of power and Christ as our supreme ancestor both ennobles politics and curbs the tendency toward dictatorship. The secret of this, Bediako argues, is to see the way the gospel "imbued local cultures with eternal significance and endowed African languages with a transcendent range." Oddly, Katongole sums up these observations by saying, "This is the fruit of having come to a new spiritual identity in Christ." But nothing could be further from Bediako's intention, either in this book or in any other of his writings.

Kwame Bediako (1945–2008) went to study for his doctorate in African literature in France, where he experienced a radical renewal of his Christian (Presbyterian) faith. This led him to study with missiologist Andrew Walls in Aberdeen for a second doctorate in theology. He dedicated his career to founding and leading a study center in Ghana that sought to reflect on Christianity within the context of African culture and spirituality.[45] His doctoral work was subsequently published as *Theology and Identity*.[46] The purpose of this work was to demonstrate that "the ethnocentrism of a large part of the missionary enterprise not only prevented sufficient understanding of African religious traditions, but also led to a theological misapprehension of the nature

---

43. See the discussion in Katongole, *Sacrifice of Africa*, 33–34.
44. See Bediako, *Christianity in Africa*, 12, quoted in Katongole, *Sacrifice of Africa*, 33.
45. The Akrofi-Christaller Institute of Theology, Mission and Culture; see www.acighana.org.
46. Bediako, "Identity and Integration." Page numbers in the text refer to this source. This was subsequently published as *Theology and Identity*.

of the Christian gospel itself" (iv). To argue this thesis, he compares the coming of missionaries to Africa with the attempt of early Jewish Christians to make gentile converts become Jewish as well as Christian. In his conclusion he notes that no Christian theology is simply repeated; it is always a synthesis adapted both from previous Christian traditions "in the service of new formulations of the problem of the life of the universe" and from humanity in relation to the will of the Creator (523). In the gospel both the early Hellenistic writers and modern Africans find an "overall integrating principle" because Christianity is, in part, a historically developing understanding of human life with the Creator.

Rather than focus on the resurrection of Jesus and his continuing life in the church as Katongole does, Bediako wants to place these theological realities in the larger framework of God's power and purposes in creation. These clearly include reflection on the indigenous spiritual traditions in Africa, which are so important to the African understanding of community and indeed to its identity in general. But Bediako is equally concerned with placing African cultural practices within the larger story of God's kingdom. It is *this* African life and *these* African contexts that Christ's resurrection and the pouring out of the Spirit have transformed. Because of Christ we cannot look either at these realities or our place in them in the same way. So Bediako has, like Katongole, a radical and transformative political vision, though one that connects directly with the material and spiritual heritage of Africa. Rather than seeing this Christian vision as supplanting Africa's indigenous imagination, as Katongole holds, Bediako believes it fulfills its deepest aspirations.

Bediako's preoccupation with the traditions that shaped him and his Akan people led him later to reflect on the history of Christianity in Africa, insisting on its ancient presence stretching back to Clement of Alexandria and Origen (whose very name, he reminds us, recalled the local deity Osiris).[47] He argues in an article that describes this heritage that any social analysis (and we might add any political one) that ignores religion, and particularly Christianity and its role in African life, "is bound to miss a great deal of what actually explains Africa now in the present, and by implication also, what the African future is likely to be." Citing his mentor Andrew Walls, he notes that the crucial activity is the exploration of Christian interaction with the ancient culture of Africa (and, he proposes, of Asia and Latin America). The quality of this interaction, Bediako believed, will depend on whether the churches grow toward maturity in Christ. So in response to Katongole, Bediako might say

---

47. See Bediako, "Africa and Christian Identity," 153–61. The quotation is from p. 160.

that it is surely true that Africa needs a Christian imagination, but it is equally true that Christianity needs an African imagination as well.

These two examples are instructive not only for the differing attitudes they express toward the Christian use of African values but also for the way they illustrate the role that Christian theological traditions invariably play in theological conversation. In the first case, Katongole applies a lively theological conversation in the West (represented by Milbank and Hauerwas) to the current situation in Africa; in the second, Bediako works from his Reformed heritage and seeks a more appreciative understanding of Christianity's relationship with African traditions. Together they provide a vivid display of the continuing debate over theology's use of indigenous values.

Conclusion

These brief examples illustrate our emphasis on seeing theology as a conversation among many voices contributing to the enlarging and developing understanding of Christianity—a transoccidental conversation. This is not an assertion of relativism, that all readings of Scripture and tradition are equally true. It is rather an insistence that the full meaning of Scripture will emerge only as Christians throughout history and around the world read and respond to it together and, as Paul says, "all of us come to the unity of the faith and of the knowledge of the Son of God, to maturity, to the measure of the full stature of Christ" (Eph. 4:13). This project of mutual listening will constitute our work in the remaining pages of this book. But before turning to some more specific theological issues and particular settings, let us try to summarize what we have learned about tradition and its relation to the understanding and practice of our faith. These assumptions will guide our discussions in the remainder of the book.

1. What Christians seek to make out and follow is the story of the trinitarian God, who created and redeemed the world and calls and empowers people from every tongue and nation, as that story is authoritatively laid out in Scripture. Theology is a matter of following God and obeying God's Word. It is first an active response, a matter of the obedience of faith, centrally involving practices of prayer, praise, and love of neighbor, and only then is it a reflection on these things in disciplined and systematic ways. This means that the church belongs to God and is nurtured and sustained by God. (This point will be filled out in our discussion in chap. 4.)

2. But the hearing and following of this story is always conditioned by the language and habits of some particular culture. And as we have recently

learned, culture is neither fixed nor finished but changing and dynamic, with multiple (internal and external) influences. Culture shapes people, but people are also agents who make and shape the culture their children will inhabit. Kathryn Tanner has helpfully emphasized the dynamism and porosity of cultural forms. They "cannot . . . be artificially frozen, separated off from changes they might undergo at the hand of social actors."[48] Yet culture also contains contradictions and power differentials that constrain or limit the ability of people to flourish. Thus a major dimension of theological method consists of careful and critical sociocultural analysis.

3. All of this implies that theological formulations on the local level not only are inevitable but also should be encouraged. Too often in the church's history, difference has been feared rather than appreciated. These fears have been associated with worries about "syncretism"—versions of the Christian story that are contaminated to one degree or another by cultural (or religious) elements seen to be incompatible with Scripture. But if cultural differences are a given and a reflection of the diversity of God's good creation, we should find ways to listen to new formulations—using syncretism, as Robert Schreiter says, not as a stick but a voice.[49] They are to be seen as part of the church's growth to maturity as it rereads its scriptural source and the traditions that have grown from it. Differences can then be seen more positively as potential assets, forcing us to rethink and reimagine the faith as God continually does new things, even if we may finally judge one or another view as inconsistent with Scripture.

4. Historical traditions of Christianity, and traditional formulations of the faith, which we discussed in the first two chapters, will continue to play an important role. For these represent long-term conversations about the faith that have learned both from each other and from the historical experience of Christians in many places. But these should now be seen in relation to the various settings of the younger churches, which will forge the theological agenda for the future together.

5. Finally, none of this means that evaluation of this or that expression of Christianity is impossible. Kathryn Tanner goes so far as to imply that any definitive expression of the faith is a kind of idolatry since all our human attempts are dogged by our sin and limited perspectives.[50] But this view is unwise and ultimately impossible. For to hold ourselves open to any possible expression of the faith would make coherent response and obedience

---

48. Tanner, *Theories of Culture*, 51.
49. Schreiter, *New Catholicity*, 82–83.
50. Tanner, *Theories of Culture*, 123–24.

impossible—we would always be waiting for some further instructions. But this is also unwise in the light of the guidance promised by Christ in sending the Holy Spirit, who moved the writers of Scripture and would lead believers into all truth (John 16:13). Further, we have the guidance of various Christian traditions in which we find our theological home and in terms of which we are able to discern what is right. Of course, there is a sense in which all judgments are provisional since we currently "see through a glass, darkly" (1 Cor. 13:12 KJV), but this humility does not exempt us from making provisional judgments by which we can, as Paul says in Philippians 4:9, keep on doing the things that we have learned.

4

God, Creation,
and the Human Community

"God is no stranger to African peoples, and in traditional life there are no atheists."[1] This is the way John Mbiti characterizes African spirituality, but it could apply equally well to almost all cultures of the world. Even in the West, with its growing population of "nones"—those without religious persuasion—belief in God still hovers around 90 percent.[2] Mbiti in fact claims that in the three hundred groups in Africa that he studied, without a single exception, people assume that God, the supreme being, exists as an all-powerful creator. This knowledge is carried in proverbs, traditional prayers, and stories rather than formal statements or creeds. This traditional Pygmy hymn even recalls the opening verses of the Gospel of John.

> In the beginning was God,
> Today is God,
> Tomorrow will be God.
> Who can make an image of God?
> He has no body.
> He is a word which comes out of your mouth.

1. Mbiti, *African Religions and Philosophy*, 29. The Pygmy hymn quoted below is from pp. 34–35.
2. See www.religion.pewforum.org/affiliations. Their most recent survey lists "unaffiliated" in the United States at 16.1 percent.

That word! It is no more,
It is past, and still it lives!
So is God.

In Nigeria, traditional Igbo morning prayers are offered by the head of the household, who, after a ritual washing, squats in the center of the compound and greets God as a way of sanctifying the new day.

Obasi (creator God) who dwells above
Glorious and powerful King
The incomprehensible and ineffable One.
Unfathomable waters
King of the Heavens
The King who dwells above and is above all
And yet whose garments reach the earth
The immanent one.
I submit entirely to you in homage
We are still here
The land and place you allotted to us
And in the condition you last met with us . . .
Give us life, worthwhile life. (Ezi Ndu)[3]

Even from these prayers it is clear that God's presence and purposes relate to the whole of life, to all times and places. Mbiti notes that many groups believe that God established not only the laws of nature but also the customs of peoples. The Ashanti, for example, believe "God created things in an orderly fashion."[4] The rising of the sun, agricultural practices, patterns of marriage, even the ability to give birth can all be attributed to God. Though God is the supreme being, in many African cultures he is thought to be a distant deity, or to have been offended in some way and withdrawn. So in order to manage their affairs properly, people often have recourse to a wide variety of spirits and ancestors (who are called the "living dead") to bless or heal. Despite the disruption caused by relocation from the rural areas to the city and by modern education, these impulses and beliefs continue to influence Africans. God and the powers are a central aspect of everyday life. Indeed, African traditional religions have experienced something of a revival in the last generation.

However these basic beliefs have been altered or challenged, it is safe to assume, as Mbiti argues, that belief in a transcendent, powerful God appears "natural" for most people—that is, they need not be conditioned to believe,

3. Okorocha, "Meaning of Salvation," 67–68.
4. Mbiti, *African Religions*, 40; he is quoting R. A. Lystad.

though they can be educated *not* to believe. As an Ashanti proverb has it, "No one shows a child the Supreme Being."[5] If this is so, the ordinary assumptions about God and God's working become important data in developing a people's theology. And they influence decisively what readers will find when they turn to Scripture.

A Pre-Columbian God

We have seen already that, in Africa, the Supreme Being is regarded as above all the giver and preserver of life. In Mesoamerica this God was called *Quetzalcóatl* (Feathered Serpent) in the Náhuatl language. Costa Rican theologian Elsa Tamez has reflected on how this indigenous faith can be understood in the light of God's revelation in Scripture.[6] Quetzalcóatl, she notes, was worshiped in all the stages of Mexican history and is the supreme source of all the other, lesser powers and spirits. Especially interesting is the consistent characterization of this God as acting always on behalf of humanity, creating the new human person, giving them corn to grow and wisdom to build homes, and helping them invent the calendar and make art. Most surprising is the way Quetzalcóatl is shown struggling against the lord of death, even injuring himself in order to give humanity life (37). According to this story, the blood from this injury is mixed with human bones and rescues them from the world of death. Those who have told this story across the generations confess their continued life is due to this self-sacrifice of Quetzalcóatl. (In one version of the story, other gods realize they have to model the self-sacrifice of Quetzalcóatl so that life in the universe can continue.) Tamez concludes that "these are the revelations of the God of life, the God who understands, a compassionate being who gives life to God's creatures" (39).

Though this God is remembered with affection, in the militarism of subsequent Aztec history this God was betrayed, and the Sun God (*Huitzilopochtli*), the warrior and conqueror of other people, was imposed (40). Though they continued to honor Quetzalcóatl, the military violence and associated human sacrifices constituted a betrayal of the pursuit of interior perfection and the need for self-sacrifice that Quetzalcóatl had represented (42). What resulted, Tamez argues, was a struggle between the gods (43).

5. Ibid., 29. This view has received support by contemporary Western psychologists who argue that belief in God is hardwired into the human psyche. See Barrett, *Cognitive Science, Religion, and Theology*.

6. See Tamez, "Reliving Our Histories," in Batstone, *New Visions for the Americas*, 33–56. Page numbers in the text refer to this source.

It is not hard to see that something similar has happened, Tamez argues, in the history of Christianity. Indeed, her account recalls the words of the Lord through the prophet Isaiah:

> These people draw near with their mouths
> and honor me with their lips,
> while their hearts are far from me. (29:13)

Specifically, when the Spaniards arrived in Latin America, the God they claimed betrayed the biblical God of life. The God of life of the Bible, who freed the slaves from Egypt and gave life through the self-sacrifice of the Son of God, was betrayed by violence and massacres like that of Pedro de Alvarado in the high temple during the feast of Tóxcatl—a betrayal that exactly mirrored the violence of the Sun God acting in the name of Quetzalcóatl. Small wonder that Mayans witnessing the slaughter visited on them by the Spaniards saw this God as a betrayer. As the Mayan prophet Chilam-Balam expressed it, "Only due to crazy times, to crazy priests, was that sadness visited upon us with the arrival of Christianity. Because those who were very Christian arrive here with the true God, and that was the beginning of our misery and our charity" (46).

But just as there had been many who rejected the abominable practices of the Sun God and its human sacrifices, so there were those among the Spaniards who spoke out against their brutalities. In a famous sermon, Father Antonio de Montesinos, on the day before Christmas, boldly denounced his people. "I have risen up here to be the voice of Christ in the desert. . . . That voice says that you are in mortal sin, and therein will you live and die, for the cruelty and tyranny that you have used against these innocent people. Are they not human beings? Do they not have a rational soul?" (49–50). For his pains, at the instruction of King Ferdinand, Montesinos was recalled to Spain. But his cause was taken up by others, Father Bartolomé de Las Casas among them. Tamez demonstrates that it is not simply a case of confronting the Christian God with the pagan gods that were present before the conquest. In fact, for many, the missionaries did not bring the "good news" at all, even though the continent was Christianized; what they brought resembled more often the Sun God the natives knew all too well. As for Quetzalcóatl, Tamez implies, the missionaries missed the opportunity to show, from these indigenous traditions, the goal of justice and life that Christ came to make possible.

This account is reminiscent of Paul's sermon in Acts 17, where Paul reminds his listeners what they already believed about the gods. Missing in Mesoamerica on the part of missionaries was the sensitivity to see that God had been present and speaking for centuries before the arrival of the Span-iards, and that now a new opportunity was being given in this place to pursue life through the death and resurrection—the self-sacrifice of Christ. Rather, these missionaries insisted the people leave all that they knew about God and how he worked. But this was to ask them to lose their identity—to stop being who they knew they were. The plaintive tone of an indigenous priest makes clear what was at stake. In a 1524 "Dialogue of the Twelve," the priest makes his defense: "You have spoken to us a new word, and we are disturbed by it. . . . Shall we destroy the ancient rule of life? Because in our heart we understand to whom we owe our lives, to whom we owe our birth, to whom we owe our growth, to whom we owe our development. For that reason the Gods are invoked" (52).

These had been the terms by which they understood the cosmos, and the world the Spaniards brought—from the mass baptisms to the *encomiendas* (forced resettlements)—was not a world that made sense to them (we do not "take it as truth," this priest went on to say). Tamez thinks it was only with the coming of the Virgin of Guadalupe that both Gods were brought together into a single image, making possible an integration of Christianity with the indigenous vision of the cosmos (55).[7] In this image native people were able to retrieve the meaning of their ancient worship in terms of Mary. For Juan Diego, the Náhuatl who reported the vision, heard a word from this God addressed to them by Mary in their own language. This made it possible for the Náhuatl people not only to accept the Christian God but also to make it a part of their own vision of the cosmos. They were finally able to accept this Christian God of life because it made sense in terms of their cosmology; at the same time they were able to recover their own religious tradition in the new circumstances of colonialism. But we Christians, Tamez observes, have not had an equivalent humility to recognize the Giver of Life in other cultures. "However," she pleads, "*that is our God* who is revealed to us in Scriptures, who has revealed Self in the past and will always reveal Self in the history of every culture" (56, her emphasis).

Tamez's discussion is a powerful reminder that God's revelation in Scripture does not come to people as though they were a blank slate. It is construed, in the first instance, within the assumptions by which they have lived their lives. They need, first, to fit this disturbing news into their views of the world and the way it works. Moreover, this account of pre-Columbian beliefs reminds us

---

7. See a fuller description of this integration of faiths in the Virgin in Burkhart, "Cult of the Virgin of Guadalupe in Mexico," in Gossen, *South and Meso-American Native Spiritual-ity*, 198–208.

that God has not left himself without a witness among any nation or people but has been present, calling and urging them toward justice and life.

Initially, this is how God's reality will be discerned when missionaries bring the Scriptures, but that is not the whole story. And Tamez does not tell us this other part of the story in this article, though she knows it well. When the Scriptures are finally read and reread in a people's own language, the truth of God's renewing work in Israel and Christ gives new accents to ancient assumptions, even "news" that those beliefs did not, indeed could not, comprehend. In the case of Africa, the Scriptures claim that the distant, powerful God has become a part of this world in Jesus Christ, that the gulf between God and humans, which all the spirits and powers seek vainly to manage, has been closed once and for all. John V. Taylor, the great missionary-theologian, has put this in striking terms: "This discovery that the vague and distant creator is the center and focus of every moment of all being is so catastrophic that it may overshadow for a time everything else in the gospel."[8] As we saw in the last chapter, for Kwame Bediako, Christ helped Africans not only to make deeper sense of their ancestral and spiritual heritage but also to go beyond it.

In Latin America, recent reflection on Scripture has led theologians to react against a view of God "from above," one that reminds them of the oppressive power of the colonial regime and ignores the plight of the poor and marginalized. Rather, in Christ people have found a God who walks along with them and shares their sufferings on the cross and yet at the same time is the one who creates and sustains the world.[9]

Western Views of God

For the people whose views of God we have reviewed, there is no doubt that God plays an active role in the world. Whatever their exact beliefs about God, we have seen a deep commitment to divine rule. In terms that theologians commonly use, we might say that most people in the world, whatever their professed beliefs, are functional theists. That is, they live their lives from day to day in the faith that an all-powerful God in some way controls their affairs.

By contrast, most educated people in the West and the elites of the majority world are what might be called functional deists. That is, whatever their professed beliefs about God, they live their daily lives as if they alone were

8. Taylor, *Primal Vision*, 122. His discussion of Christ "closing the gulf" is found on pp. 86–108.

9. See the classical expression of this in Sobrino, *Christology at the Crossroads*, and a more recent expression addressed to the Latino/a diaspora in Goizueta, *Caminemos con Jesús*.

responsible for managing things. (Deism is the view that God created the world but plays no role in its continued functioning.) God is for many only a distant, even mythical figure who leaves people to their own devices. Though there are exceptions, in the American tradition at least, an ethos of individual self-sufficiency has deep roots in its own past and in Anglo-Saxon culture.[10] From Benjamin Franklin's program of self-improvement to the Horatio Alger myth, Americans have believed that through their own efforts they can lift themselves to a better place. In short, many Americans from the dominant culture believe that God helps those who help themselves. (Those from minority cultures, Oscar would remind us, have very different views of God's presence and activity.)

Recently Charles Taylor has given careful attention to what he calls the "buffered self," a self isolated from any direct influence of God or even other people, in contrast to the "porous self," which sees itself as open to other powers and spirits. As he describes this, "Living in a disenchanted world, the buffered self is no longer open, vulnerable to a world of spirits and forces. . . . The fears, anxieties, even terrors that belong to the porous self are behind it. This sense of self-possession, of a secure inner realm, is all the stronger, if . . . we have taken the anthropocentric turn, and no longer even draw on the power of God."[11] Taylor's argument is that this view has become the default view in post-Romantic Western culture—people may not consciously know or understand this, but it is assumed much in the same way that the activities of God and spirits are assumed to be operative in Africa.

This is where the term "functional deism" becomes relevant. This view, which has received confirmation in recent research, holds that Americans largely live their lives as if God were not an active participant.[12] They may even be Christian and profess a belief in God's presence in the world, but they live their lives *as though* God were distant or even absent—calling on him only in times of special need. God is considered a support of the projects and efforts that make up human life; the primary responsibility for these, however, rests with the individual.

This assumption may help explain the rise of those who profess no faith in God. On these grounds, if I can become a stronger, better educated, and more successful person on my own, I can do without God—I do not need the support God offers, even if it may be necessary for others who are less well

---

10. See the description of this ethos and resulting theology in Dyrness, *How Does America Hear the Gospel?*

11. Taylor, *Secular Age*, 300–301.

12. See Smith and Denton, *Soul Searching*, who have defined this default spirituality as a "moralistic therapeutic deism."

off. This recalls Christ's observation of the difficulty wealthy persons face when seeking to enter the kingdom of heaven—it is more difficult than for a camel to go through a needle's eye (Matt. 19:24).

If Western readers of Scripture bring these assumptions with them to their reading and interpretation, how might Scripture "talk back"? How might the biblical material challenge, enrich, and transform these default notions? We propose two ways. One is the emphasis Scripture places on God's active and continuous presence in the created order—the clear teaching of Scripture that God has a stake in the world. The second is that God is revealed in Scripture as Trinity: as a Father who creates and sustains all things, as a Son who enters fully into human and earthly reality to transform all things, and as Spirit who was poured out on "all flesh" at Pentecost to be the power of God for the salvation of humans and the renewal of creation.

Lutheran theologian Robert Jenson picks up on both these emphases in a striking expression. The Trinity, Jenson writes, "asserts that God in himself is in fact no other than he is in his history among us and with us."[13] In a word, Jenson is saying that there is no way of getting at God's person apart from the presence and activity of God in creation, indeed, in the events of our lives. This assertion profoundly addresses both of the ways that Scripture "talks back" to the default views of God found in American culture. God cannot be separated from the projects of creation and culture, and the divine engagement with the world is defined by God's nature as Father, Son, and Holy Spirit. This is not simply a statement about God's revelation in Scripture, though it is grounded there; it is also a claim about God's involvement with all human cultures and each human person in those cultures.

God in the Old Testament

Creator of All Things

God is the subject of the first sentence in the Old Testament and the primary protagonist of all that takes place from Genesis to Revelation. "In the beginning God created the heaven and the earth" (Gen. 1:1 KJV). The first chapters of Genesis make it clear not only that God is the sole cause of all things but also that *God irrevocably identifies with creation and especially with the human creation.* Genesis 1 can be read as a kind of progressive project of God coming to a climax on the sixth day when God's "image and likeness" appear in the form of the man and the woman. All this comes

13. Jenson, *Systematic Theology*, 1:19.

about by the simple word of God; all things—the sun, stars, animals, and sea creatures, which are worshiped in many cultures—are created by God's Word and completely subordinate to the divine will. And this teeming world is all "good"—a theme that will be repeated frequently throughout Scripture. As Paul says to Timothy, "For everything created by God is good, and nothing is to be rejected, provided it is received with thanksgiving; for it is sanctified by God's word and by prayer" (1 Tim. 4:4–5).

But beyond the general concern and oversight, a special tenderness and care are attached to God's relation to the human creation. First, there is a special consultation before this creation, and afterward God gives Adam and Eve a special blessing, charging them to fill and care for the earth. All this is "very good" (Gen. 1:31). This special creation and blessing is followed up by God's concern for Adam's home in the garden (2:8), his work (2:19), and his relationships with both created things (2:16–17) and other humans (2:18). A profound theology of divine hospitality emerges in these verses, one that is to be modeled by God's "image and likeness." Even after Adam and Eve have disobeyed God's instructions, God comes to them in the garden "at the time of the evening breeze" (3:8) and calls to them, "Where are you?" And so God does with everyone and with all the communities and cultures that would follow.

This is the story of God's great love for all that God made and the persistence of that concern even in the face of Adam and Eve's inconceivable lapse. Their mistake was serious; a moral order had been breached, and their disobedience became, with God's judgment, a disorder at the center of things. But the account is at pains to underline the hope and persistence of God's mercy that is evident even in judgment: though enmity with the serpent will continue, his head will be bruised by the seed of the woman; childbearing and caring for the earth—those original blessings—continue but are now doleful projects laced with sweat and pain. And when these predictions were over, God, as the merciful Father, made garments and clothed them.

What continues to astound is the deliberate concern of God for every aspect of human life: its intimacies, its work, even what is worn and eaten—all of which recalls Jesus's great Sermon on the Mount, where he concludes, "Therefore I tell you, do not worry about your life, what you will eat or what you will drink, or about your body, what you will wear. Is not life more than food, and the body more than clothing? Look at the birds of the air; they neither sow nor reap nor gather into barns, and yet your heavenly Father feeds them. Are you not of more value than they?" (Matt. 6:25–26). This all confounds the functional deism of American culture that feels no need either to depend on God's mercy or, worse, thank God for all the gifts God daily bestows.

God Suffers with Creation

This identification of God with birds, lilies, and especially human creation will be constant throughout Scripture despite the recalcitrance of this creation and its refusal to praise or even acknowledge this loving presence at the heart of things. A characteristic of God's commitment to creation follows from this: *God suffers with creation*. After the drumbeat of violence and alienation of the early chapters of Genesis, the writer records God's response in 6:5–6: "The LORD saw that the wickedness was great in the earth and that every inclination of the thoughts of their hearts was only evil continually. And the LORD was sorry that he had made humankind on the earth, and it grieved him to his heart." It is hard to overemphasize the importance of this response. The Hebrew words here express the deepest possible feelings of sorrow and suffering that God felt for (and with) the creation. If Adam and Eve are made to suffer for the disorder their disobedience caused, God will share this with them. This is a God the Náhuatl people would recognize, a God who suffers to bring life. God in these verses even determines to fulfill his original promise that eating of the forbidden fruit would issue in death and blot out all that was made. But God cannot do this, for Noah—and later Abram—find favor in the sight of the Lord.

God's sensitivity to the suffering of the people, and indeed suffering with and for this people, will be a continual theme through Scripture. God hears the cry of the slave people in Egypt (Exod. 2:24) and suffers with them in exile. In a famous passage in Hosea 11, God notes that while their exile is a fruit of their sin ("you plowed wickedness, / you have reaped injustice"; 10:13), still God cannot abandon them.

> When Israel was a child, I loved him,
>   and out of Egypt I called my son" (11:1)

But the more God called, the more they went away.

> Yet it was I who taught Ephraim to walk,
>   I took them up in my arms;
>   but they did not know that I healed them. (v. 3)

Though the people are "bent on turning away" (v. 7), God cannot abandon them.

> How can I give you up, Ephraim? . . .
> My heart recoils within me;
>   my compassion grows warm and tender.

> I will not execute my fierce anger;
>   I will not again destroy Ephraim;
> for I am God and no mortal,
>   the Holy One in your midst. (vv. 8–9)

This heart of God becomes the key to understanding the ministry of Jesus, who is especially tuned to the cry of widows and children, and who cries out to Jerusalem in his Olivet discourse, "Jerusalem, Jerusalem . . . ! How often have I desired to gather your children together as a hen gathers her brood under her wings, and you were not willing!" (Matt. 23:37). But as Jerusalem had killed and crucified prophets and wise men in the past (v. 34), so they would do again with Christ.

The suffering of God with creation has not been a prominent theme in Western theology. Indeed, it deeply challenges its "indigenous" notions of God. But as we have seen, it has ancient credentials in the Mesoamerican tradition and Liberation theology, and it makes a critical appearance in Asian theology in a book by Kazoh Kitamori titled *A Theology of the Pain of God*.[14] Kitamori takes his departure from passages in the Prophets like that in Hosea or Jeremiah 31:20:

> Is Ephraim my dear son? . . .
> Therefore I am deeply moved for him;
>   I will surely have mercy on him,
>   says the LORD.

Kitamori's personal struggle with tuberculosis and the anguish of his native Japan in the war led him to meditate on these passages. Kitamori thinks the suffering of God is a concept of God's relation, not part of God's essence; it is reflective of his love, specifically his determination to love the objects of his wrath (16, 21). But significantly, Jesus's suffering, Kitamori believes, becomes an act within God so that the essence of God can be comprehended only by "the word of the cross" (47). Kitamori thinks this gives new significance to human suffering, recalling as it does our estrangement from God (60–61) while at the same time becoming a potential vehicle of our service to God (81).

Here is a profoundly biblical reflection that picks up on the Buddhist theme of healing through suffering and on the Japanese sense of painful empathy for and with others—in Japanese drama, *tsurasa* is a deep personal agony suffered for others. For the Japanese, the deepest tragedy is one of broken personal relationship (135), and so Japanese playgoers weep shamelessly at the cries of agony of players. In this way, Kitamori believes, they are able to

---

14. Kitamori, *Theology of the Pain of God*. Page numbers in the text refer to this source.

experience something of the deep pain of God who suffers for a fallen but beloved world. Kitamori is also careful to point out that Scripture does not simply confirm these Japanese sensitivities but also challenges them by asserting that God's pain is seen most clearly in loving the unlovely and estranged person—something that is foreign to Japanese culture (138).

If God's suffering with and for those who are marginal and excluded is strange to Japanese culture, it has not been a dominant theme in Western theology either—especially in the Reformed tradition, with its emphasis on God's sovereignty. But this has changed since the Second World War, and the experience of Japan (and Kitamori himself) may have played some role in this change. The most famous treatment of the theme in the West is that of Jürgen Moltmann in his book *The Crucified God*.[15] Moltmann wants to explore a true Christian identity as a "crucified Christian," which, he believes, "can be demonstrated only by a witnessing non-identification with the demands and interests of society" (17). Early in the book, Moltmann describes a movement of Japanese students, along with the student protests in the West in the 1960s, who risked their lives in a series of symbolic actions to protest injustice "by taking the cross upon themselves" (15). Later he cites Bonhoeffer's famous reference to the God who let himself "be pushed out of the world and on to the cross." At this critical point, Moltmann references Kitamori's *Theology of the Pain of God*. Moltmann believes that this notion that in the suffering of Christ, God himself suffers—relevant to the suffering of the Japanese, to the poor in Latin America, and to the American slaves who saw an image of their own suffering in Christ's suffering—must be taken further (47–48).

Moltmann insists, echoing Kitamori, that the event of the cross is an event between Jesus and God the Father—it is, in other words, an event within the Godhead. The Trinity must be understood as a short version of the passion narrative of Christ; all human history is taken up into this "history of God" and integrated into the eschatological history of God (146). So rather than setting the death of Christ over against Christ's resurrection, the death of Christ can be seen as the immanent form of the resurrection. "The coming kingdom, the certainty of which the disciples found in the Easter appearances of Christ, has then, as a result of this Christ, taken the form of a cross in the alienated world" (185). Following Christ, on this view, takes on a new dimension. Moltmann concludes, "We participate in the Trinitarian process of God's history. Just as we participate actively and passively in the suffering of God, so too we will participate in the joy of God wherever we love and pray and hope" (255).

15. Moltmann, *Crucified God*. The phrase "crucified God" is from Luther (7). Page numbers in the text refer to this source.

Moltmann's movement into these areas has not been without criticism. Some suggest that he has bound God too closely to historical events or that he implies a historical process within the Godhead, but his work nonetheless has opened new ways of thinking about God that mine some of the most difficult and moving passages of Scripture. And his work has been accompanied by—perhaps even prodded by—what was in some ways the first real interaction with non-Western theology by a prominent Western theologian.[16]

God Calls Out a People

To emphasize God's suffering with creation, important as this is, risks leaving the impression that God is at the mercy of creation—a critique that has been leveled at Moltmann. And so this theme needs to be balanced with the initiative that God continues to take with the created order. His creative word continues to be manifest throughout the earth in a general sense (Ps. 19), but God's call also takes on a more personal focus in the calling of individuals and eventually of a people. Already in the garden, as we have seen, God calls out to Adam and Eve in their confusion, "Where are you?" (Gen. 3:9). After Abel is murdered, God asks Cain, "Where is your brother Abel?" (4:9). Finally, this merciful calling of God is directed toward Abram in Haran, where God says to Abram, "Go from your country and your kindred . . . to the land that I will show you. I will make of you a great nation, and I will bless you, and make your name great, so that you will be a blessing . . . and in you all the families of the earth shall be blessed" (12:1–3). Significantly, this promise includes specific geography, people, and a covenant "to be God to you and to your offspring after you" (17:7). Notice that God intends to bless all the nations through this one people, but to accomplish this, God calls a single man with no physical heir to be the "father" of this nation. This is consistent with God's practice throughout history: though he loves and cares for everyone equally, he selects individuals—first Moses and then David to lead the people—to fulfill the promises he made to Abraham, Isaac, and Jacob. Later he will call prophets such as Jeremiah and Isaiah to speak on his behalf. Just as God creates the world at the beginning, so he creates a people and its leaders; "it was I who taught Ephraim to walk," he reminds them in Hosea 11:3. And even when they are bent on running away, God will not forget them.

So God's unbreakable connection with creation leads to this bond with this specific people through a covenant that constitutes them as a people. They

16. In addition to the references to Kitamori and the Japanese students, Moltmann notes that the argument in the final chapter of *Crucified God* takes its start from the whole development of Liberation theology.

had been threatened with extermination as slaves in Egypt, and God called them out. God heard the cry of the suffering of these slaves and remembered the promises to Abraham. As in the garden, God's concern extends to careful instructions for their life together, their work, and their worship, which he delivers to Moses on the mountain—instructions that order their relationships with each other, with the earth and its care, with the animals, and most particularly with God: "I am the LORD you God, who brought you out of the land of Egypt, out of the house of slavery; you shall have no other gods before me" (Exod. 20:2–3). These instructions (*torah*) are the ones Jesus will interpret in his terms in the later Sermon on the Mount.

So God has created a particular people, has given them instructions on how they are to live, and now will lead them into a specific piece of land, an event that is described in the book of Deuteronomy. The author refers to the "good land" more than three hundred times, and it becomes an image of the "good creation" that God had made but that became broken and marred with violence. Now God seeks to restore that creation with a people who will listen to God's call and follow the instructions God gives. The land of Canaan, which Israel is to occupy, is meant to be a kind of down payment on the renewal of all creation that God envisions. God never allows Israel to lose sight of this promise to renew the earth. Even during the darkest hours of the exile, God gives Isaiah a vision of the peaceable kingdom God has in mind.

> For I am about to create new heavens
>   and a new earth;
> the former things shall not be remembered
>   or come to mind.
> Be glad and rejoice forever
>   in what I am creating;
> for I am about to create Jerusalem as a joy,
>   and its people as a delight. (Isa. 65:17–18)

This vision is repeated and filled out in the final chapters of Revelation, when John sees a new heaven and new earth and hears a loud voice from the throne saying,

> See, the home of God is among mortals.
> He will dwell with them;
> they will be his peoples,
> and God himself will be with them;
> he will wipe every tear from their eyes. (Rev. 21:3–4)

Significantly, this event will not be for God's people only but will involve all nations and every person. The promise is consistent throughout Scripture. As the psalmist says,

> There is none like you among the gods, O Lord,
>   nor are there any works like yours.
> All the nations you have made shall come
>   and bow down before you, O Lord,
>   and shall glorify your name. (Ps. 86:8–9)

Israel often found these promises hard to square with the sufferings they were forced to endure, especially during the exile. The book of Job, and wisdom literature generally, tried to make sense of these promises in the face of the disorder they were living through. But like Jeremiah in the book of Lamentations, Job insists on God's faithfulness and on a future vindication.

> I know that my Redeemer lives,
>   and that at the last he will stand upon the earth. (Job 19:25)

The skepticism Job demonstrates about the "goodness of creation" often finds resonance in non-Western theology. This too "talks back" to Western self-confidence and its expectation of progress.

God and the Ministry of Jesus

Job's reference to a "Redeemer" who will stand on the earth, along with the Servant Songs in Isaiah, Christians believe, anticipate the coming of one who is sent from God, Jesus the Christ. In this sense, Christians have always insisted that the Old Testament, the Hebrew Scriptures, is also a Christian book. Indeed, the perspective we have taken argues that God's essential nature and vocation in and with creation is clearly laid out already, even supremely, in the Old Testament. There we gain a perspective on God's presence and purposes that will be assumed in the New Testament writings, which simply fill out the Old Testament vision.

Other theological emphases in the West would not use this starting point. While they take seriously the Old Testament material that we have highlighted, many Christian theologians prefer to take their starting point and find their center in the incarnation of God in Jesus Christ. Karl Barth, who is perhaps the most important theologian to argue for this christological starting point, has put matters in these terms: "By being Father, the Son, and the Holy Ghost in his work in Jesus Christ, God is in the highest."[17] This is to say that it is only in knowing the self-disclosure of God in Jesus Christ that anything can be known about God or about God's relationship with the world. To know anything properly about the latter, then, we must begin not with the Old Testament material but with the New Testament witness to Jesus Christ. Only when one has heard the word that God has delivered in Jesus Christ can one turn to the Old Testament and properly understand it. As Barth describes this in his *Church Dogmatics*, "Faith in Jesus Christ contains within itself the knowledge of the secret of creation, the Creator and the creature."[18] That is all we need to know about creation and its nature, about the Creator as present yet separate from creation, and about the creature as responsible to God, who is discovered and known in Jesus Christ.

It is important to recognize that there is biblical support for Barth's emphasis. Especially in the Gospel of Matthew, Christ is shown to be fulfilling and elaborating the promise God made to Israel. Christ's birth recalls Isaiah's prophecy about the coming of Emmanuel, "God with us" (Isa. 7:14 in Matt. 1:23); at Christ's baptism in the Jordan a voice from heaven says, "This is my Son, the Beloved, with whom I am well pleased" (Matt. 3:17); at the transfiguration a similar voice comes from the cloud: "This is my Son, my Chosen; listen to him!" (Luke 9:35).

In Jesus the Creator Is Present

Like God in the creation account, Jesus shows his mastery over the creation by calming the storm, healing the sick and blind, and even raising the dead simply by speaking the word. And as in that early account, he calls out to those who will follow him, instructs them, and, as we have noted, expresses his intimate concern for all the aspects of their lives, even what they eat and wear. Above all, Jesus shares God's commitment to the created order to the extent of suffering with and for it on the cross. In the timeless words of John, "And the Word became flesh and lived among us, and we have seen his glory, the glory as of a father's only son, full of grace and truth" (John 1:14).[19]

God and the Sending of the Spirit

For Karl Barth, God's presence in Jesus Christ is the key to understanding God as Trinity. First, this is because Christ has truly expressed what God is

17. Barth, *Dogmatics in Outline*, 40.
18. Barth, *Church Dogmatics* III/1, 31 (hereafter *CD*).
19. As is well known, for John, God's glory is seen most clearly in the cross (John 17:1).

from eternity. "It is not without His Son but as the Father of Jesus Christ that God bears the name of Father in Scripture and the creed" (*CD* III/1, 49). But the proposition that God is Father and Creator can only be defended when "we mean by 'Father' the 'Father with the Son and the Holy Spirit'" (ibid.). But second, this Trinity of persons is revealed in the history of God's creation with the creature, and this is primarily seen in the appearance of Christ and in the sending of the Holy Spirit in Acts 2. As Barth describes this, "God wills and God creates the creature for the sake of His Son or Word and therefore in harmony with Himself; and for His own supreme glory and therefore in the Holy Spirit" (*CD* III/1, 59). This is an execution of the covenant of grace, Barth says, which God established with creation at the beginning. The meaning of history, then, is the realization of this covenant in a people.

The added meaning of the Pentecost experience is the birth of church—what Paul will call "the body of Christ," called to be God's agent of transformation in the world by the power of the Spirit. As Robert Jenson says, "As the Spirit shows his face, the Church appears."[20] And through the church, God is signaling and inaugurating the renewal of all things. As Paul claims, "So if anyone is in Christ, there is a new creation: everything old has passed away; see, everything has become new!" (2 Cor. 5:17). Paul consistently expresses this new creation in trinitarian terms (one cannot even confess "Jesus is Lord," Paul thinks, except by the Spirit) as well with terms heavy with Old Testament resonances in Galatians 4: "God sent his Son, born of a woman, born under the law, so that we might receive adoption as children. And because you are children, God has sent the Spirit of his Son into our hearts, crying, 'Abba! Father!'" (4:4–6).

His prayer for believers is trinitarian—for them to "be strengthened in [their] inner being with power through his Spirit, and that Christ may dwell in [their] hearts through faith" (Eph. 3:16–17). Even their worship expresses being filled with the Spirit, making melody to the Lord, "giving thanks to God the Father at all times and for everything in the name of our Lord Jesus Christ" (Eph. 5:19–20).

When the early church considered the nature of God, they began their reflection from their practice of meeting together to pray to God in the name of Christ. As believers who honored the Hebrew Scriptures, they assumed that God was one—they famously rejected the polytheism of the Greco-Roman world and suffered the consequences. But they had experienced the power of God in Christ as well as the renewing work of the Holy Spirit. The christological and trinitarian debates of the third and fourth centuries all

---

20. Jenson, *Systematic Theology*, 1:89.

centered on a single question: How are we to worship and reflect on God's manifestation in Christ and God's presence in the Holy Spirit in relation to the biblical commitment to one eternal Creator?

The Trinity and Creation in Contemporary Western Theology

In Western theology, this same question has received renewed attention in the twentieth century. As we have noted, Karl Barth has promoted a trinitarian theology that centers on God's revelation in Jesus Christ. In the process, he has produced what some have called the greatest treatment of the Trinity since the Reformation. And Jürgen Moltmann has argued that God can only be fully known in the history of his being in the suffering of Christ. As is evident in both Moltmann and Barth, this reflection has accompanied a fresh reading of Scripture and new attempts to come to terms with its emphases. And both have been concerned to understand God in historical terms rather than expressing God's being in philosophical categories alien to Scripture.

This discussion is important for our purposes because it has come to focus on the question of God's relationship to and activity within creation. Traditional Western discussions of the Trinity have argued that the one God is eternally three persons: the Father, who eternally "begets" the Son, and the Spirit who "proceeds" from the Father and the Son. This approach to the Godhead, understood in terms of these internal dynamics, is spoken of as the "immanent" Trinity. Only after this has been understood, in the traditional view, can one reflect on God's activity in creating the world. (God's external relation to the world as Father, Son, and Holy Spirit has come to be called the "economic" Trinity.)[21] The great achievement of modern discussions of the Trinity can be traced to Barth and especially the Catholic theologian Karl Rahner. Rahner argued that the economic Trinity is identical to the immanent Trinity.[22] This view, which is referred to as Rahner's Rule, insists that in order for our understanding of God to be truly biblical, we must always speak about God in terms of God's self-revelation in Christ and in the Spirit poured out at Pentecost. The economic and the immanent are merely two aspects of this single self-communication of God.

One can see the influence of Barth's emphasis on a christological starting point, but the historical thrust of Moltmann's work is also consistent with Rahner's insight. The most important interpreter of Rahner's work is

---

21. This term comes from the Greek word *oikonomia*, which refers to the management of the household, and from which our modern understanding of "economics" derives.

22. This is developed in Rahner's book *The Trinity*.

theologian Catherine Mowry LaCugna, especially in her book *God for Us*.[23] Picking up Rahner's focus, LaCugna believes the tendency to argue from the immanent to the economic Trinity—that is, from within the Godhead outward to creation—is problematic. Rather, she thinks, one must begin with and hold on to the economy of salvation as the key to understanding the Trinity. That is, God's person is revealed in the clearest light in the salvation of the world, which God promised to Israel and revealed in Christ and in the Spirit. She summarizes this by saying, "Who and what God is, is fully expressed and bestowed in creation and history, particularly in the person of Jesus and the activity of the Spirit" (221). This emphasis, she thinks, returns the focus to the actions of God in saving the world and, equally important, is more congenial to developing priorities of corporate worship and personal spirituality. In worshiping God through Christ by the power of the Spirit in prayer and praise, the believer is joined to the eternal being of God.

Rahner and those following him have been criticized for effacing the distinction between the inner life of God and God's presence and activity in creation. Critics question whether the emphasis on God's being "fully expressed and bestowed" in creation doesn't do away with an important distinction between God's person and work—a distinction which, on this view, need not imply a separation. But along with Barth and Moltmann, these theologians have done much to restore trinitarian teaching to the center of theological reflection.

A more Reformed expression of these developments has been offered by Colin Gunton, late professor of theology at King's College, University of London. The traditional overemphasis on the immanent Trinity, Gunton thinks, results from the continuing influence of Greek categories. Rather than understanding God in terms of "being," Gunton wants to use the more biblical categories of "God's actions." The problem he sees is not the tendency to move from within the Godhead outward to the world, as Rahner saw it, but the habit of moving from the abstract to the concrete.[24] Gunton sees the continuing influence of Platonic and Neoplatonic categories especially in Augustine and subsequently in the history of the church, which he traces in some detail in *The Triune Creator*. Rather than a hierarchical dependence of creation on God—and the risk of residual pantheism, Gunton thinks—we should envision a creation with its own time and space "which are given by God but not continuous with his reality" (142). This is why Barth's focus on Christ as a mediator of creation can be helpful. Christ can be seen as the

---

23. See LaCugna, *God for Us*. Page numbers in the text refer to this source.

24. This is the basic argument of Gunton's last book, *Act and Being*. See also his more substantial discussion of the Trinity in *Triune Creator*, 147. Page numbers in the text refer to this latter source.

"mediation of the one who is the way of God out into that which is not himself" (143). But this cannot be adequately conceived, Gunton thinks, without the Holy Spirit, "the one by whose mediation the Son became incarnate and is made the means of the relating of the creation to God the Father" (143).

This trinitarian mediation of creation by the presence and actions of Christ and the Spirit avoids both a demeaning of its materiality and a tendency toward pantheism (or panentheism—that all creation has its being only within God, a view that Moltmann has recently made popular). One sees here the influence of Barth, but Gunton is also critical of Barth. Barth continued, Gunton believes, if in an "improved" form, the tendency of the whole Western tradition "so to subordinate creation to redemption that the status of the material world as a whole is endangered" (165). Instead, a focus on Christ and the Spirit as the "two hands of God" (Irenaeus) helps us understand creation and redemption as parts of the same divine project, which is to return "the creation to its proper direction, its orientation to its eschatological destiny, which is to be perfected in due course of time by God's enabling it to be that which it was created to be" (56). If God's work in Christ and the Spirit provides a key to understanding creation, it must be in the whole of that creation, human and nonhuman, that God seeks to be glorified. And if creation is the place where those acts are manifest—as the theater for God's glory, to use Calvin's terms—then the work of Christ and the Spirit there gives us the fullness of God.

These developments need to be seen against the backdrop of the Western development and the West's subsequent preoccupation with science and technology. They provide a way of responding to these cultural projects in a biblical manner by giving them a theological and creational context. But they can be equally useful in non-Western contexts where a mélange of spirits and powers risk clouding over the biblical celebration of the material and the bodily. I remember hearing of an old African man who, when he was asked whether Christianity helped him understand the concept of soul, answered, "No, we knew about that. What Christianity gave us was the body." It could be that a more robust view of the Trinity in terms of God's creative and redemptive work in Christ and the Spirit will provide resources for traditional cultures facing the challenges of modernization.

God's Relation to Creation: A Cross-Cultural Conversation

We have spent a good bit of time exploring Western views of the relation between God and creation, especially those of Moltmann and Barth. But now we need to ask how this might contribute to theological reflection elsewhere.

Fortunately we have an important study by Peter Fulljames, which relates Barth's views on this (along with those of Wolfhart Pannenberg) to three major African theologians: Ghanaians Kwesi Dickson and John Pobee, and Tanzanian Charles Nyamiti.[25] A review of this can provide a possible model for theological conversation sensitive to its global context.[26]

Fulljames begins with an exposition of Barth's view of God's relation to creation, including Barth's focus on Christ as the key to understanding this relation. But Fulljames makes a further reference to the role of the covenant in creation. Barth characteristically relates the covenant fundamentally to Christ, arguing that it is primarily in Christ that we understand God's covenantal intentions in creation. In fact, in Barth's well-known terms, "The covenant is the internal basis of creation and creation is the external basis of the covenant." The reason God created the world is to be one with the creature in Jesus Christ (20; *CD* III/1, 43–44). Similarly, Christ helps us grasp God's relationship with creation more generally. This leads Barth to a second emphasis, which Fulljames describes: the analogy of relations (which Barth prefers to the scholastic "analogy of being"). That is, by analogy of the relation between God and Christ and the self-giving love it demonstrates, we can see how God is related to the created order (21). In short, all the traditional questions raised in the early chapters of Genesis—why God creates, what the image of God means, how God can be transcendent and immanent, the goodness of the material world—are answered in the appearance of Christ. Fulljames concludes, "Despite the ambiguity that results from the presence of evil in the world the essential goodness of the world is affirmed. Reconciliation is made possible by the free self-giving love of God in Jesus Christ" (31).

Kwesi Dickson and John Pobee, both Ghanaians, the one Methodist, the other Anglican, belong to what might be called the first generation of African academic theologians, and the first to attract notice by Western theology. Dickson's *Theology in Africa* is an impressive statement of theology from an African perspective.[27] Every Christian theologizes, Dickson insists, and Africans do so from a unique context—in his case, from within an Akan cultural situation. He notes the pervasive religious character of this culture and its frequent continuity with biblical culture. Fulljames notes that Dickson's

25. Fulljames, *God and Creation in Intercultural Perspective*. Page numbers in the text refer to this source. We will focus on the interaction of these African theologians with Barth rather than Pannenberg in what follows.
26. Fulljames is careful to say this conversation is asymmetrical. He is seeking to show what he as a Western theologian can gain from these other perspectives; he does not claim to say what they might learn from Barth and Pannenberg (ibid., 3).
27. Dickson, *Theology in Africa* (hereafter *TA*).

method, while not stated explicitly, is to put African culture directly in dialogue with biblical texts (45). Among the themes Dickson develops are community ("in our traditional African society we were individuals within a community"; *TA*, 177); unity with nature, the strong sense of connection that Africans feel with the natural environment ("he loves the environment, he fears it, and he senses something mysterious about it"; *TA*, 49); and the importance of spirit possession, which Dickson likens to (and contrasts with) the prophets being possessed of the Spirit in the Old Testament (53–54). Especially important for Fulljames is Dickson's stress on the importance of death as a means to life in Akan culture, which makes the death of Christ of major significance (55–56).

John Pobee's *Toward an African Theology* is a similarly important treatment of theology from an African perspective.[28] But Pobee is more concerned to have a contextual theology that counters what he calls the North Atlantic captivity of African Christianity. Pobee also writes substantially on creation, as one might expect of an African. His Akan heritage gives him a keen sense of God's presence in the whole of life, but his Christian faith gives him a sense of God's greatness. "God, though his presence and power may be felt in the world around men, is yet apart from nature, independent of the world and men, and is the source of their life. The Christian God is not part of the world like nature deified; God is the eternal initiating Subject yet intimately present to us" (*TAT*, 76).

Like Dickson, Pobee probes his cultural context but also wants to insist on the political context of theology—since God is sovereign, involvement in politics for the Christian is nonnegotiable (66). Wanting theology to be a practical discipline, he addresses the political situation in Ghana directly by proposing an ethics of power. Here Pobee goes further than Dickson in highlighting values of Akan culture that positively correlate with specific scriptural passages, and he justifies this through a theology of incarnation (70). This leads Pobee to focus on Christ in his humanity, his sinlessness, his healing power, and fundamentally his communication of life in its fullness to and through the community called the church, as well as his path to glory through martyrdom. Jesus is key. "To say Jesus is 'Nana' (i.e., Lord) is to let his standards reign supreme in personal orientation, in the structures of society, in the economic processes, and in political forces. It means in practical terms personal and social justice and re-creation" (*TAT*, 98).

This practical and holistic orientation leads Pobee to stress that humans are cocreators with God. Before the passage just cited, Pobee references the way an Akan chief carries out his mandate. If he says he can do something, then "he does it with his followers." In a similar way, humans, made in God's

---

28. Pobee, *Toward an African Theology* (hereafter *TAT*).

image, are called to carry out the mission of Christ to renew the earth. They are to stand against the economic exploitation, the excesses of technology, and the ravishing of the environment, involving themselves in projects that will transform the human community (85).

The reflections of Dickson and Pobee are grounded in their own Akan context and give their thinking immediate relevance. It is difficult to think of Barth's theology as "contextual"—much of his emphasis disconnects God's presence and actions from our human way of thinking. Barth famously wants to restore God's Word to its rightful supremacy in theology. But even to understand this insistence, one must know something about Barth's context—the anthropocentrism of theology after Schleiermacher, the liberalism of Harnack, and so on. The context of Barth, then, is primarily a theological one. Other dimensions—social and political—are important for him personally, but they do not directly impinge on his thinking about God and the church. For Dickson and Pobee, the cultural and even political context cannot be ignored, and their theology seeks to engage with issues the context raises.

Fulljames points out a number of ways in which these thinkers throw light on Barth's theology. While there would be deep and fundamental agreement on many points, not least on Barth's focus on Christ and the incarnation, both Dickson and Pobee would want to see God's relation to creation in more comprehensive and immediate terms. God's covenant may be seen to include all created things, and God's actions in the world may be discerned much more broadly than Barth allows—if you want to send a message to God, Pobee says, "send it to the wind" (TAT, 76). Even human activities, Pobee would insist, can be seen as God's activities when consistent with the revelation of Christ. Moreover, God is particularly interested in human relationships in community. Here Pobee goes beyond Dickson in his stress on community, in that the community forms the individuals within it, both for good and for ill (87). God is interested in the way communities can deform people (sin thus has a deeply social component) but is also invested in the way communities promote life—indeed, God's primary role for Akans is as the giver of life (88). Still, people can work with God to create life-giving communities. And here Fulljames sees an important contribution that Pobee might make to Barth. Barth's emphasis on God's sovereignty can at times seem to overwhelm the creature (Barth can even say that "creaturely events take place as God himself acts"; CD III/1, 133). But Pobee's notion of cocreativity implies that God acts through humans, and his focus on community ensures that humans act freely as they interact both with other people and with created things (93).

Charles Nyamiti, a Tanzanian who has taught for years at the Catholic Higher Institute in Nairobi, presents a wholly different way of thinking about both theology and culture as a Roman Catholic. A contemporary of Dickson and Pobee, his major work, *African Tradition and the Christian God*, appeared in 1976.[29] Both the phrasing of the title and the fact that it was published in Africa give a clue to Nyamiti's priorities. He wants to start with the African tradition and then confront that with the Catholic tradition of theology; unlike Dickson and Pobee, he does not promote a direct dialogue between African culture and Scripture. This method is evident in *ATCG*, where he begins with an elaboration of themes present in African culture, and Gikuyu culture in particular. Then he turns to the theological tradition developed in the church and seeks to put this in dialogue with the conceptual implications of the cultural values (101). Nyamiti is attempting a systematic theology in much the same way as it has been developed in the West but in serious dialogue with contextual values. He explores, for example, the similarities and differences of native understandings of God with the Christian God. While God is distant—a God of the Mountains—he is also present at all times. Thunder and lightning manifest his power; God gives life and health to people and animals. Nyamiti seeks to employ the symbolic power in African religion in explaining theology (106). This method is evident most clearly in his innovative study of ancestors as a theological theme, for which he is best known. Nyamiti uses the concept of ancestor in many ways, but his primary use of it, following the Gikuyu tradition, is as a parent-ancestor. He defines this as "the personal parent of another person, of whom he is archetype of both nature and behavior, and with whom he is entitled to have a regular sacred relationship through communication of some sort" (*ATCG*, 48). Note that the symbolic weight Nyamiti intends to capture is the personal relationship through which a person is meant to reflect the character of the parent. This helps us understand the relationship we are to have with Christ, who is both ancestor and exemplar (115). Kinship, of course, is important in many cultures, but to the Gikuyu there is also a sacred status and the right to communication, in addition to ancestors being exemplars of behavior.

In his discussion of the Trinity, Nyamiti thinks "ancestor" is a better term than "Son," because ancestor not only generates the descendant but is also a prototype of the latter. It provides, as Fulljames puts it, "a model that is to be reflected in the character of the descendant" (116). And in Christian theology the Spirit provides the means of communication. Nyamiti says, "Since in God, the sacred communication can only be made through the Holy Spirit, divine ancestorship and descendency demand by their very nature the

29. *African Tradition and the Christian God* (hereafter *ATCG*). His later work *Christ as Our Ancestor* has been even more influential.

presence of the Holy Spirit" (*ATCG*, 49). In this way, ancestorship provides a model for understanding the Trinity in a way that does not diminish—as Barth tends to do—the role of the Holy Spirit. Christ is acknowledged, especially in Nyamiti's book *Christ as Our Ancestor*, as our brother/sister ancestor, who shares a common parent with us and with whom we are entitled to have regular communication. In his role as healer and redeemer, Christ mediates the power that God deploys. Recalling the language of J. V. Taylor, Nyamiti understands redemption as a closing of the gap between the greatness of God and the human situation (118). Christ's death, then, is understood in terms of a life-giving ritual: "The crucifixion of the Son is the sacred communication and ritual self-giving of the Descendent to his divine Ancestor, whereas the glorification of the Son by the Father through the Spirit is the divine ancestral answer" (*Christ as Our Ancestor*, 46).

It would be unthinkable for Africans to construct a living theology in a way that excludes the role of ancestors, for in traditional thinking the ancestors are the guardians of the well-being of the community. Many rites of initiation and sacrifice are played out against this understanding. Nyamiti's argument is an important attempt to harness the emotional weight of these events in the service of a deepened understanding of the Christian tradition. There is no reason that these cultural values should not be pressed into service as a way to understand the communion of saints, in the same way as our Western tradition of individual heroes and role models has been used to understand the heritage of saints for Westerners. In fact, the symbolic power of rituals and expectations regarding ancestors offers energy that Western conceptions, most of which are symbolically impoverished, mostly lack.

Of course it would be impossible for a Western person to use ancestors in this way, since they carry no traditional meaning for Westerners. But Western theology can still learn from these emphases. Specifically, Fulljames suggests, Barth's attempt to understand covenant solely in terms of Christ's fulfilling the covenant relationship between God and Israel risks undermining any substantial role for the Spirit (125). Barth of course gives a formal role to the Spirit along with Christ, but unlike Nyamiti he does not provide any *necessity* for the Spirit's role. And this in turn tends to minimize the intimacy of God's relationship with the creation, which African theologians want to celebrate.

How can we evaluate this model of theological conversation? In general, we can appreciate the attempt of Fulljames to put these important thinkers in dialogue with one another; doing so allows us to see how these very different traditions can speak to one another and might learn together. But the conversation remains on the most general level. Discussion relies mostly on abstract formulations and comparisons at a fairly high level of generality—perhaps this is the besetting sin of the Western theological tradition that produced this comparative exercise. It could also be that this reflects the first generation of theologians in Africa, who were staking out a very large territory and could only map it by pointing out the major landmarks. But somehow theology has to be brought down closer to where people live—indeed, the discussion of Mbiti with which we began and the traditional prayers that we cited did precisely that. Perhaps it is up to the next generation of theologians in Africa to turn attention to the more immediate concerns of people. This may account for the fact that a brief survey of contemporary work in Africa finds a consistent focus on particular moral and social issues—one is tempted to describe this writing as being more about ethics than theology.[30] Perhaps this is what is most needed at the moment.

Violence and Poverty as Theological Issues

In an effort to move theology toward concern with more immediate issues, we close this chapter with brief comments on two major issues for emerging churches: violence and poverty. In the West, such concerns are relegated to courses on development or ethics—if they are raised at all. But in many parts of the world these are daily issues that call for theological response. How can God be present—holding all things together in Christ, as Colossians 1:17 has it—when that creation is riven with violence? In his commentary on the book of Job, Gustavo Gutiérrez moves the category of *violence and suffering* from the periphery of the Western discourse into the center of Christian theology by posing a fundamental question on how to speak about God in the Americas.

> Because in this continent (Latin America) we continue living, daily, the violation of human rights, the assassination, the torture that we rejected with the Jewish Holocaust forty years ago. Therefore, for us it is a question of finding a language about God in the midst of the hunger of millions, the humiliation of races considered inferior, the discrimination against women especially of the poor classes, the systematic social injustice, the persistent and high infant mortality, the *desaparecidos* (the "disappeared ones"), those that are unjustly jailed and deprived of liberty, the suffering of the people that struggle for their right to a life, the exiled and the refugees, the terrorism of diverse stripes, the common burial grounds full of dead bodies from Ayacucho . . . how to talk about the God of life when the innocent are killed massively and cruelly? How to proclaim the resurrection of the Lord where death rules, particularly over

30. See Diane Stinton, ed., *African Theology on the Way: Current Conversations* (London: SPCK, 2010).

children, women, the poor, and the native populations, the "insignificant" of
our society? . . . Job signals a path through his vehement protest, his discovery
of concrete commitment to the poor and to all of those who suffer unjustly,
through his encounter with God, and through his recognition of the gratuity
of God's project over human history.[31]

Gutiérrez and other majority-world theologians help us realize that in the
same way that Augustine and other patristic theologians struggled to find a
language to speak about God in their own pagan philosophical milieu, so we
must struggle to find our language in our own global world—a language to
speak about God in a violent, unjust, and impoverished world. Hence, violence,
poverty, injustice, and the like, although not classical theological items, are
not to be considered peripheral or optional categories for Christian theology
but central and substantial matters of reflection and practice. They are *loci
theologicus* (places in which theology is done).

The growth of refugee camps in Kenya and Jordan is testimony to the
fact that people seek security and relief from violence even before they seek
other amenities. In October 2008, on the occasion of the launch of the *Global
Dictionary of Theology*,[32] the distinguished African theologian Ogbu Kalu
presented a paper on the future of global theology.[33] Kalu noted that the reality
of actual violence in Nigeria (his home country) and Congo, to say nothing of
long-simmering conflicts elsewhere, is often fueled by religion—an observation
that remains relevant. This implies that violence is necessarily a theological
issue. He might have noted that it was, after all, a religious difference that
accounts for the first appearance of violence in Scripture, when Cain became
angry that God did not accept his offering. But Kalu cites other contributing
factors that must be considered: violence is often exacerbated by poverty
and exported through the processes of globalization. In other words, Kalu
argues, any theological response must consider the total situation—religious,
social, political, and economic—giving rise to violence. It is interesting that
a Nigerian theologian (formed in a Reformed theological perspective) should
underline the multiple factors that contribute to violence, implying that God's
purposes are to be pursued in the each of these domains.

Kalu proceeds to review the various discourses that have tried to capture
issues of violence: that it results from a cosmic battle of powers, class manipulation, religious fundamentalism, or a lack of good government. While
all of these are helpful, none, Kalu implies, adequately captures the scope of

31. Gutiérrez, *Hablar de Dios*, 184. Quoted in Feliciano, "Suffering," 47.
32. See Dyrness and Kärkkäinen, *Global Dictionary of Theology*.
33. Kalu, "Future of Global Theology."

the problem. We might add that the themes of this chapter suggest a broader canvas on which images of violence might be laid out: that God both creates a good and ordered creation and continues to uphold it by the grace of Christ and by the power of the Spirit, and that though human disobedience has brought with it the disorder that issues in violence, this has been confronted in the life and ministry of Christ in his death and resurrection and his gift of the Holy Spirit. Apart from this bigger picture, there would not be any explanation for why violence happens, nor any grounds for hope that violence can be overcome. But it has been overcome in Christ.

With this bigger picture in mind, Kalu proposes that the church can do the following things. (1) It can reimagine the world in which it lives—especially its public and social spaces and the role and function of government. Notice in contrast to Katongole, Kalu insists that this includes not just the role of the church but the places and institutions of society, for biblical teaching on creation would argue that God has an interest there as well. (2) The church needs to find ways to bring healing to these public spaces, specifically through mechanisms like that of the Truth and Reconciliation Commissions in South Africa and Burundi, seeking an active application of the reality that God was in Christ reconciling a hostile world to himself and has committed to God's people the ministry of reconciliation (2 Cor. 5:18–19). (3) The church must center its religious space by "promoting a culture of interfaith education through creating dialogue contexts that mine the interior theological bases of various faith traditions" and promoting an ethic that ensures peaceful coexistence on the continent.[34] Sadly, Kalu died shortly after presenting this paper and was unable to further elaborate his prophetic vision. But surely the most appropriate response to violence implies an engagement at all the levels he describes. As he says, the church "can theologize while engaging the public space in a mode of '*in actione contemplativus*'—a spirituality that worships Christ and celebrates his reign by fully engaging the forces that dehumanize and incite violence."

While violence may be more fundamental, poverty is the frequent and all-too-common by-product. Indeed, in Scripture the contrast is not typically between the rich and the poor but between the oppressor and the exploited, because, as Elsa Tamez has shown, "for the Bible oppression is the basic cause of poverty."[35] Since this is so, poverty, like violence, must be understood within a broader social and even political context. With a focus on oppression, which after all is a form of violence, Scripture helpfully reminds us that this

34. Ibid., 16–17.
35. Tamez, *Bible of the Oppressed*, 3. In this book she lays out the biblical vocabulary for poverty and oppression.

problem is an ever-present, disempowering issue. Conrad Boerma, in what is still one of the best books on poverty, highlights the multiple roots of the problem Scripture describes: traders who exploit the people (Hos. 12:7–8), corrupt judges (Amos 5:7), and the seizure of wages and property (Jer. 22:13). The poor have nowhere to turn and often resort to despair.[36]

Recent discussions of poverty have moved beyond simple economic explanations to recognizing the multiple dimensions of poverty. Bryant Myers, for example, makes use of the work of Robert Chambers, especially his picture of the "poverty trap," to show the entanglement that poverty involves. Chambers adds physical weakness, isolation (from services), vulnerability, and powerlessness. But Myers adds to these "spiritual poverty," bondage to spirits or powers, and the inability to believe that change is possible—that is, the absence of hope. In short, Myers highlights disordered relationships, which lead to a marred identity. Myers concludes, "So deeply embedded is this kind of poverty that the good news is no longer believable."[37]

How might such a situation be engaged theologically? Here the weakness of the Western tradition becomes painfully evident. For the default response to such a question is to attempt to understand or explain poverty, and it moves at once to the question of theodicy: Why did God allow such a situation to come about? But any exposure to reflection outside the West would find such a response irrelevant. The wake-up call has been provided to Western theology by Liberation theology in Latin America. In a word, Liberation theologians remind us that, given that the biblical category of oppression is fundamental to understanding poverty, the theological response to this was God's deliverance of Israel from Egypt. If oppression is the problem, liberation is the answer. Moreover, as they often point out, liberation in the first place was not an abstract theological category but a realization on the part of the church that the situation of poverty as it existed was intolerable.[38] It was not as though Christians in Latin America had some program of poverty alleviation in mind; rather, they knew that poverty needed to be actively opposed in every way possible and began doing so. Only then did they begin to reflect on God's possible presence and reread Scripture. Theology, as they like to remind us, is a second-order discipline—it is reflection on practice.

---

36. Boerma, *Rich, the Poor, and the Bible*. I am grateful for Ringma's "Liberation Theologians Speak to Evangelicals," in Wanak, *Church and Poverty in Asia*, 16–17, for reminding me of Boerma's work.

37. Myers, *Walking with the Poor*, 66–76; quotation is from p. 76. Chambers's discussion of the "poverty trap" is from *Rural Development*, 103–9.

38. Two indispensable sources for understanding Liberation theology are Gutiérrez, *Theology of Liberation*, and, especially for Protestants, Bonino, *Doing Theology in a Revolutionary Situation*.

If the primary response to God's Word is not reflection but obedience, then the most appropriate response to poverty is not explanation but practical ministry. Here the best teachers are those who have been involved as Christians in obeying God in the places where oppression is at its worst. Filipina Ruth S. Callanta, for example, was a professor at the prestigious Asian Institute of Management in Manila when she felt God's call to work among the oppressed. In the midst of her work, however, some theologians reminded her of biblical themes that gave meaning to her work and that empowered her and those she worked with. Once, when hearing someone describe the dynamics of the biblical Jubilee Year, she was so excited about its potential for ministry that she drove off the road into a rice paddy.[39] When she was asked to describe her strategy, she at once had recourse to the biblical themes that we have highlighted in this chapter. In her description of her work published in 2008, she began by saying, "The theme 'He has filled the hungry with Good Things' lays down the Church's most solid foundations for its preferential option for the poor. To us Christians, this passage from Luke [1:53], echoing Psalm 107:9, telescopes God's promises since the beginning of time until their fulfillment in our Lord Jesus Christ."[40] If oppression and the resulting hopelessness and helplessness are the problem, then the answer is the realization that God's intention, from creation to the present, has been to lift up the lowly and fill the hungry with good things.

From this starting point Callanta has developed an indigenous network of ministries that stretches throughout the Philippines and, as of 2008, had distributed $24 million in small loans, started schools, and created feeding and job-training programs. The strategy that Callanta derived from her biblical orientation, which is embodied in the Center for Community Transformation, starts with evangelism and then moves to the implications of this new perspective—the values and priorities it implies and the services that can meet their physical needs: microfinance, education, housing, health care, insurance, and relationship building. The final goal is community empowerment.[41] The retort to this might well be that this is all very good, but how is it a theological response to poverty? It is a theological response because God's intention to "fill the hungry with good things" is becoming visible in these programs. These programs do not pretend to explain poverty—Job's friends demonstrated the folly of all such pretensions—but they do exhibit a down payment on the future world that God has promised and made visible in Jesus Christ. They are theological artifacts.

---

39. I owe this account to Malcomb Bradshaw, who was riding with her at the time and sharing this biblical insight.

40. Callanta, "Transformational Strategy," in Wanak, *Church and Poverty in Asia*, 147.

41. Ibid., 153.

5

Jesus Christ and the
Good News for the World

In this chapter we come to the center of the Christian faith, the appearance of God in human form—the life and work of Christ, his death on the cross, and his subsequent resurrection. This appearance includes and continues in the pouring out of the Holy Spirit, whom Christ had introduced as another Comforter. In the chapter on the role of indigenous culture in theological reflection, we pointed out that God has not been without a witness in any of these places: God was present and working in the values and practices of the culture and even, we have claimed, in aspects of the religions that developed there. But in this chapter we make a claim that lies at the core of God's revelation in Christ, through the Spirit, and in Scripture: that if God was at work in all the cultures of the world, this revelation was incomplete.[1] In the first place, although God was present and people often had an awareness of and some relationship with this God, through the indigenous religious traditions they inherited, this relationship was defective in various ways. God was not known as a human person, and there was no knowledge of what God had done or could do to deliver them from bondage to the spirits or bring salvation.

1. Oscar would remind us that this does not mean that a (Western) rationality is needed to overcome a (non-Western) incomprehension. This incompleteness is a characteristic of all indigenous traditions, East and West.

Though God was known, what is called "the gospel" in the New Testament was unknown—the good news that God was in Christ reconciling the world to himself. The astounding claim of the New Testament is that the eternal God, the creator of all things, has appeared in human form both to fully reveal God and to bring salvation. As John 1:14 says, "And the Word became flesh and lived among us, and we have seen his glory, the glory as of the father's only son." This "news" about God and salvation, the New Testament asserts, is not indigenous; it must be introduced to all humanity from outside. (In Luther's famous phrase, it came to us *extra nos*.)

In the evangelical tradition we take for granted that Scripture is the privileged, premier, and authoritative carrier of the good news. This means in effect that the gospel comes through the tradition, teaching, and interpreting of Scripture. But our argument in this book has shown that the hermeneutics present in much evangelism and missions has not been innocent. The "traditioning," teaching, and interpreting have too often influenced the presentation of the gospel message in ways that were detrimental to target communities and cultures. In this chapter we will show how the *traditioning* of the gospel message—centered on the reality of Jesus Christ—though indispensable for Christian existence, is at the same time subject to human manipulation and misinterpretation and is constantly in need of the historically situated discernment of the Christian community and the guidance and correction of the Holy Spirit.

The Indispensable Gospel of Jesus Christ

Jesus of Nazareth was a Jewish teacher who lived in first-century Palestine and was crucified by the Roman authorities. In the Gospels he is called the Christ, the anointed one (i.e., the Messiah promised in the Old Testament). By his teaching, primarily his parables, and through the many "signs" (miracles) he performed, Jesus announced the appearance of what he called the kingdom (or reign) of God in the world. Through his death, resurrection, and the giving of the Spirit, this reign became visible in history. At the same time, the church was born and became the special locus of this reign and its primary witness. Even this brief, incomplete summary makes clear the staggering variety of issues that are at stake in the Christian claim that God was present and acting in Jesus the Christ. First, there is the claim that the distant Creator has come into human history, that God can be *seen* in Christ. Then, as the appearance of the Creator, Christ clarifies and transforms God's relation to the created order. Further, the New Testament claims that the whole reality of Christ's incarnation, life, work, death, resurrection, and continuing presence in the world represents a salvific cluster of events: Christ's life and death bring about reconciliation, renewal, and forgiveness, among other things. But finally, as the events of Christ's life unfold and as they are later interpreted in the New Testament, it becomes clear that Christ is inaugurating something that will grow and will one day issue in a renewal of all things. We could go on. It is not hard to see that the implications of all this are not only religious but also historical, social, cultural, political, even metaphysical (that is, having to do with the nature of reality).

As with other areas of Christian teaching, the way Christ is understood and presented has varied widely throughout Christian history and in the many cultures of the world. This is not surprising since God's appearance in human history was rooted in a particular Palestinian situation, and it has to be comprehended in terms of some particular language and culture. But we take this diversity to be an asset and not a problem. That is, today understanding Christ must involve learning from the variety of ways his life, teaching, and deeds have been understood and appropriated. To illustrate this point we will offer in what follows a selection of different approaches, which show how Christ speaks in different ways, in different settings, and in different times.

Christ in the West

To begin with a dominant Western understanding, consider New Testament scholar N. T. Wright, of St. Andrews University in Scotland, who has written a series of scholarly books on Christian origins. In the second volume of this series, titled *Jesus and the Victory of God*,[2] he seeks to explore how the pieces of the puzzle—all the angles by which Christ may be understood, like those that we listed in the previous paragraph—might fit together. What kind of portrait or silhouette can we draw of Jesus? For Wright, the urgency of this question is raised not only by the many directions that one might explore but also by the many studies, both Jewish and Christian, ancient and modern, of Christ's life. Wright summarizes the New Testament claim as he sees it: "Jesus' public persona within first-century Judaism was that of a prophet," and "the content of his prophetic proclamation was the 'kingdom' of Israel's god" (11). As he goes on to note, this implies that we need a history of the Jewish Jesus, however difficult this may prove to construct. Note that in laying out this starting point, Wright has referenced biblical studies from both Old and

---

2. Wright, *Jesus and the Victory of God*. Page numbers in the text refer to this work.

New Testaments, conversations with Jewish and Christian scholars, and the questions that have arisen in this conversation over a long period of history. But interestingly, he makes no reference to the life of the ordinary Christian or the impact on the contemporary situation—in fact, he specifically postpones the question of relevance to a final chapter. And neither has he admitted that this approach is tethered closely to Western understandings both of history and scholarship. In this Wright is not unusual, nor is he intentionally ignoring other parts of the world. Indeed, Wright is someone who is particularly committed to a more inclusive (and cross-cultural) scholarship. But he does exhibit a common assumption of Western scholarship: that exploration of the life of Christ must rest on the highest standards of scholarly method as these are generally understood, and that scholarly studies need not, in the first instance, address common believers or questions of relevance. Theology in the West tends to move from questions of theory (how things are to be understood and explained) to questions of practice (what is to be done). Let us move now to different, non-Western patterns of understanding, which tend to begin with questions of common experience and its challenges and which provide an instructive contrast to the classical understanding of history and theology in the West.

Christ across the Americas

Theologians situated in the context of the Americas have learned to resist viewing the reality of Jesus Christ—his incarnation, life, death, resurrection, and continuing presence in the continent—as compartments of truth that must make sense separately, as though they made sense in the abstract world of *un*situated ideas. In his thick volume on Christology (*La humanidad nueva*), José Ignacio González Faus, the distinguished Spanish theologian and professor of Jon Sobrino, undertakes an ambitious project in dialogue with his former student and other Liberation theologians of Latin America in the hope of remedying the tragic christological bifurcation between Christology and soteriology (the person of Christ and his redemptive work) that has maintained since medieval times in Europe. González Faus asks the following question in search of a christological synthesis:

> How can we attempt to confess the Absolute within the confinements of a concrete individual in history and, as such, contingent . . . ? How can we have knowledge of the unknowable; of what is Wholly-Other . . . [this is] the apparent contradiction of the two statements made by the evangelist: "Nobody can see God," but "whoever sees me, sees the Father." How to confess the

arrival of the absolute future into a history that is not about to come, but that is already in the past?[3]

González Faus proposes the following synthesis: "The problem of Christianity not being self-identified as a doctrine or ideology—but as the following of a person (except that from the beginning, that person is abstractly called *Logos*)—is that it turns it into a concrete-universal."[4]

It is therefore in the most concrete and particular act of following Jesus of Nazareth, according to González Faus, that one finds the most absolute and universal truth. Hence González Faus, and with him most Liberation and contextual theologians in the Americas, would come to adopt a theological attitude that would create a distance from the modern European views on Christology and soteriology. This attitude is keyed to the following pronouncement: *Christians are called to follow the historical Jesus while believing in the resurrected Christ.* Both theological efforts should be understood not as autonomous methodological options but as complementary paths that originate from faith and evolve as a means of maturing the critical thinking of the believer in the praxis of everyday life.

In a similar way, the Latino historian Justo González reminds us that dogma and history in Western Christianity have not been constructed and communicated innocently across time, geography, and theological schools; hence sociopolitical implications have had adverse consequences for non-Western communities.[5] In the Americas, as in many other contexts, the separation of the incarnation and the life of Christ from his redemptive work has generated a bipolar understanding of the Christian faith. In the context of the Americas, Christology and evangelization were used to fund violent imperial projects, which is why doctrines such as Christology and soteriology are not matters subject simply to speculation and theoretical debate among Latino/a theologians as in the West; they are matters of intense cultural and historical consequence.

As we have shown in previous chapters, since the time of the European conquest, evangelizing the "New World" has been an ongoing and unfinished project of Western Christianity that is often subsumed into the practice of a civilizing mission. The birth of Latin America as a colonial project is tied to the imperial program of the proclamation of the cross and death of Jesus Christ. The cross, in its material and symbolic form, was originally used as God's legitimizing seal for the Iberian campaign of invasion, cultural devastation,

---

3. González Faus, *Humanidad nueva*, 47. All translations by Oscar unless otherwise noted.
4. Ibid.
5. See González, *Mañana*, esp. chap. 5.

appropriation of the land, colonization, massacring, and evangelization of the Americas during and after the European conquest. Three centuries after the conquest, Western Protestantism would use the symbolic power of the cross to contrast and inspire a new Christian imagination (anti-Catholic and triumphalist) pointing to a new history in the religious makeup of the Americas. The new sense of continental history would suggest to the Americas the removal of the idea of "Iberoamerica" as an imposition of the imperial church of Spain and the adoption of "Latin America" connoting a group of countries on their way to becoming "nation states"—although still culturally and religiously tied to a southern, Catholic hemisphere. Meanwhile, North America as a British Protestant hemisphere above Latin America began to build and acquire power, just as had happened in Europe.

These political and religious realities affecting the makeup of the Americas inescapably shape any reflection on the good news of Jesus Christ in the continent and among its people, and these lead it in a different direction than the christological theories, debates, and motifs that have occupied Western theology across the centuries. This is not to deny the influence that Western doctrine and debates have had on the course of evangelicalism and Roman Catholicism in the Americas. Nor is it to deny that similarities exist among these very different contexts—much of what was affirmed by González Faus above resonates with forms of Augustinianism and Western Anabaptist teachings. But it is precisely the hegemony of Western philosophical and theological thought and its disavowal of historical realities that has resulted in a deficit of independent thought in the popular religious imagination of the Americas and its resulting bipolar religious personality. Theologians across the Americas have understood that this bipolar personality in the Christian imagination of the Americas is due to an inherited theological language imprisoned in a Western colonial/modern logic based on two accounts of history—Western history and its theory over against the real-life, imperial history of Latin America. This dual account of history in Western theological language constitutes a Western crisis for understanding God, creation, and the Christian self. In 1970, Rubem Alves, a Protestant Liberation theologian, articulated the Western theological crisis with the following words.

> Traditional theological language is in crisis. This new [Latin American] situation has created a radically new concern that is in foundational opposition to the [traditional] languages previously mentioned. . . . The ultimate concern of traditional ecclesiastical language lies in the understanding of eternity, God, and the salvation of the soul. The relationship between these notions and the world, life, and history (even when it is not negative) is purely tangential. . . .

Thus, within this arrangement the concern for life, land, justice, and future is never the ultimate concern, but the penultimate concern, which derives from the previous notions (God, soul, eternity, salvation, etc.). Within this logic, we love life because we love God; we make our lives dependable upon a metaphysical *a priori*. This is the language that is in crisis.[6]

Samuel Silva Gotay, a Puerto Rican historian, echoes Alves's critique and adds that "Latin America will have to be deployed into a radically new theology," a theology where only "one history" is affirmed.[7] Here lies the great difference between Latin American and Western theologies, affirms Silva Gotay, in that the "two worlds" notion of the West (transcendence-immanence) ought to be conceived as one real history—the history known to our land here in the Americas—one that is recognized in the Bible.[8] In sum, it is impossible to understand Jesus Christ in the particular context of the Americas without understanding the history of the Americas. Likewise, the Americas cannot be understood without the introduction of the gospel of Christ and the cross. As in no other context, both the Americas and the gospel are inseparably fused in a spiral of tragedy and hope. Let me (Oscar) reflect further on this spiral.

Coloniality and the Cross as Salvation History

At the beginning of the Americas there were two crosses:[9] the historical event of the conquest and the theological meaning of that event in light of the biblical Jesus. This incipient conundrum shapes the theological imagination of many of us Latin American and Latino/a theologians when trying to make sense of the good news of Jesus Christ in the Americas. Leonardo Boff, in a clever article originally published in 1984 under the title "Como pregar a cruz hoje numa sociedade de crucificados" ("How to preach the cross today in a society of crucified ones"), captures this understanding fairly well: "We all carry on our shoulders . . . or in our hearts some cross. And every cross, as little as it may look, is onerous, but can be lived as a tribulation or a liberation."[10]

No matter where one stands in the wide spectrum of Latin American Christianity and its global diaspora, be it in the Protestant faction (liberals,

6. Alves, *Apuntes para un programa*. Quoted in Gotay, *Pensamiento Cristiano Revolucionario*, 95–96.
7. Gotay, *Pensamiento Cristiano Revolucionario*, 96.
8. Ibid., 96
9. A reworking of Moltmann's famous quotation: "At the beginning of Christianity there are two crosses." See Moltmann, "Cross as Military Symbol," in Trelstad, *Cross Examinations*.
10. Boff, *Cruz nuestra de cada día*.

evangélicos, Pentecostals, ethnic)[11] or in the Roman Catholic faction (official religion, popular religion, Liberationist movements), Christology faces two crosses. One will take us right to the conquest and back to deal with the historical consequences in our time. The other will take us to the reality of Jesus Christ, our source of life, hope, healing, liberation, and salvation. The cross and the sword arrived in the "New World" as inseparable pieces of a shock-and-awe Spanish campaign pretending to appropriate the natural resources of the "newly discovered" land in order to fund the continuation of the Crusades in the Holy Land. It goes without saying that Christopher Columbus's acquisition practices when arriving at the "West Indies" centered on marking the land by inserting a cross. In a letter to the Spanish royalty, Columbus writes, "And in every land where your Highness' ships arrive, and in every cape, I send out the order to place a high cross."[12] With this distinctive practice, comments Luis Rivera Pagán, "Columbus placed crosses in strategic spaces as a symbol of [his] taking of possession."[13] Violence, invasion, and Christian faith are united under the symbol of the cross, marking the Americas as a territory under the possession of the Church and the Spanish kings. "Behind the evangelizing cross," concludes Rivera-Pagán, "hides the not-so-veiled conquering sword."[14]

As we have shown in chapter 3 (in discussing theological traditions in *las Américas*), fatalism and historical determinism came to condition the self-understanding of what it means to be and live as a Latin American during the colonial period. Fatalism as a script informing the Latin American religious imagination is well articulated by Georges Casalis in his lucid essay "Jesús: ni vencido ni monarca celestial": "Everyone seems to find a reason to submit to fatalism and chance (*suerte*) and to accept their destiny as defeated and dejected people."[15]

Furthermore, the legacy of colonial Catholicism communicated a Christ that exemplified tragedy in daily life and invited contemplation. Casalis, again, offers a compelling interpretation.

> This discouraged Jesus is nothing but the representation of the defeated Indian; the representation of the poorest in those villages where, ever since Cortes, nothing has changed. This Jesus represents the miserable one that inhabits the

11. See the four descriptions, or faces, according to Bonino, *Faces of Latin American Protestantism*.
12. Columbus, *Cuatro viajes*, 245.
13. Rivera-Pagán, *Evangelización y violencia*, 15.
14. Ibid.
15. Casalis, "Jesús," in Bonino, *Jesús*, 120.

immense slums of the great cities, where the subhuman state surpasses words and understanding. But this is the very same Jesus who, seen from the distance, appears as the port of salvation for those who are exploited and hungry in the field.[16]

It is not difficult to see why some of the most important intellectuals and national leaders responsible for the political independence of the Latin American nations in the nineteenth century would consider delinking from the Roman Catholic Church to be a necessary tactic for national autonomy. The issue for the Americas, however, was beyond the church as an institution. The colonialist mentality had already permeated the DNA of *Latinamericanism*, hence facilitating the emergence of dictatorships, regimes, power structures, and Christian superstructures that have perpetuated oppression and legitimized violence—particularly against the most vulnerable members of society: the indigenous population, the poor, women, immigrants, and children.

As we have shown in previous chapters, although the beginnings of the Protestant missions in Latin America showed promising levels of relevance and biblical faithfulness, as Protestantism advanced, a new wave of missionaries reshaped the landscape of Latin American Protestantism. Many of them were victims of the fundamentalist/liberal struggle and spoke in a dispensationalist twang. In addition, many missionaries were attracted to the mission field not just by the gospel calling but by a sense of Manifest Destiny, which at the time was openly embraced by many in North America.[17] In the words of Josiah Strong, in reference to the "great missionary race,"[18]

> It is to the British and North American people that the evangelization of the world has been entrusted . . . so that every man may be elevated to the higher light of Christian civilization. If we add to these considerations our steadfast and growing development in modern times, we will have a very clear confirmation that God is not only expecting our Anglo Saxon civilization to be the stamping seal for the people of the earth, but that He is also preparing, along with that seal, all the necessary power to make that impression.[19]

16. Ibid., 122.
17. The concept "Manifest Destiny" derives from an intertwining of religion and politics associated with the idea that providence has assigned the United States dominion over other countries. This ideology "represents one of the central nuclei around which North Americans have integrated a cultural and religious point of view of their own nation in a specific point in history," which triggered a cultural imperialism that has accompanied, in most cases, the North American missionary organizations in their evangelistic efforts around the world, especially Latin America. See Lores, "Destino manifiesto y la empresa misionera."
18. Strong, *Our Country*, 209.
19. Ibid., quoted in Lores, "El destino manifiesto y la empresa misionera."

In short, along with a faithful proclamation of the glorious Christ, Western Protestantism/Pentecostalism introduced to Latin America a new sense of historical beginning encrypted in the doctrine of salvation by means of a dualistic historical account. On the one hand, salvation here and now was promoted via Panamericanism and the doctrine of development. On the other hand, salvation yet to come was communicated to the Latin American public as a dispensationalist gospel rooted on an ethereal, truncated, and docetic Christ that had forgotten his way to the cross and was about to come at any moment to take up his suffering servants. In any case, salvation history in the Americas became intertwined with US nationalism and evangelicalism.

El Cristo de Nuestra América: In Search of the Jesus of Our History

It is against this spiral of hope and violence expressed in colonial history (European conquest) and occidentalism (North American expansionist assimilationism) that indigenous Latin American christological expressions would emerge as a way to articulate the incarnated and resurrected Jesus for the Americas. On the Roman Catholic side, Liberationist theologians such as Leonardo Boff and Jon Sobrino, for instance, would center on the Jesus of history and the relevance of this for Latin American history. In 1971, hoping to bypass the repressive military agencies in Brazil, Boff began to publish monthly articles under the title "Jesus Christ the Liberator" in a religious magazine named *Sponsa Christi* ("Spouse of Christ"). In March 1972, Boff collected his articles and published his controversial title, *Jesus Christ Liberator*. The singularity of the book at the time consisted in presenting Jesus as a religious and political liberator—the founder of a cosmic and sociopolitical revolution capable of awakening the conscience of the community in their struggle against all forms of oppressions. It was, Boff claimed, Jesus's public defiance of the religious and political order that took him to the cross. The resurrection of Jesus of Nazareth constituted, for Boff, the great liberation and the great insurrection against all structures of evil. The one resurrected, according to Boff, was not Caesar or the high priest but a crucified person, a victim of institutional evil. And with the crucified victim now resurrected as the Christ, a new hope arises for those Latin Americans who, like their Lord, are also unjustly persecuted and tortured. Hence, there is hope that the executioner will not triumph over his victim. The climax of Boff's book is captured in the way Jesus's disciples would come to remember Jesus of Nazareth as the Son of God: "Only God can be so human."[20] In spite of Boff's lasting impact, it was Jon Sobrino who further developed Liberationist Christology in the Americas by pointing to suffering as the hermeneutics connecting the historical Christ and the Latin American people. Jesus of Nazareth certainly understood suffering and even the abandonment of his Father at the cross. The poor and oppressed of Latin America, argued Sobrino, can identify with such a Christ: the crucified Jesus, the kidnapped leader, the tortured and assassinated defender of the poor and oppressed, the abandoned-by-the-Father spiritual figure who died for the sake of justice. All these portraits of the historical Jesus appear sympathetic to Latin American eyes. And all of them stand in stark contrast to a lifeless Christ on the cross or a helpless baby, the two dominant images of traditional Latin American Catholicism. For Sobrino as for Boff, Jesus's resurrection is his vindication, that is, the validation of the historical process Jesus went through in order to fight injustice and attain liberation.

René Padilla, and later Samuel Escobar,[21] voiced Latin American concerns from an evangelical perspective. In an essay titled "Toward a Contextual Christology in Latin America," Padilla directly addresses who Christ is in Latin America and his role in human history. After elaborating the way traditional Western views on Christology are incorporated within a caricature of personal piety and civil religion, Padilla proceeds to show that these portraits are not only sociopolitically irrelevant to the Latin American continent but also unfaithful to the witness of the New Testament. In Padilla's own words, "The portraits of Christ in Latin America continue to be mainly, almost exclusively, . . . the Christ of dogma, the political Christ, and mainly *el Cristo de mi tierra* [Christ of my land], the dead Jesus."[22] For Padilla, two conditions are required when elaborating a contextual Christology: a biblically faithful account of Jesus Christ is (1) historically relevant and (2) based on the incarnational character of Christology. Padilla pictures a Jesus Christ who discloses prophetic authority and intimacy with the Father—someone who is a social leader, a miracle worker, an example of social ethics, and a political-transformational influence. Padilla's portrait of Christ suggests that the role of this contextual Christ is multifaceted and biblically based, and it clearly manifests an evangelical tendency. Some have argued that such a reconciliation of the Jesus of history and the Christ of faith, as presented by Padilla, is simplistic and uncritical. For Padilla, however, a contextual Christology helps us see a historical Jesus (the Latin American historical

---

20. Boff, *Jesus Christ Liberator*, 179.
21. See Escobar, *En busca de Cristo*.
22. Padilla, "Toward a Contextual Christology," in Branson and Padilla, *Conflict and Context*, 103.

Jesus) who is still the Lord and savior of history and still the agent of social transformation.

In short, salvation history and the understanding of Jesus Christ in the Americas portray a strange and unceasing dance of death with life, of vicarious sacrifice with utopic liberation, of historical tragedy with victorious vindication. The melancholic Christ of colonial Catholicism will encounter the triumphalist Christ of evangelicalism. Both are inadequate representations of the continuing presence of the biblical Christ in the Americas and have worked to this day against indigenous efforts to bring *el Cristo de nuestra América* (the Christ of our America) into the religious imagination of the Americas, particularly into the daily practice of faith. *El Cristo de nuestra América*, however, is *ni vencido, ni monarca celestial* (not a defeated victim nor a celestial monarch). *El Cristo de nuestra América* is a Lord and savior of history, a liberator, a healer of humanity, a cultural emancipator, and a political-transformational influence. In this new scenario, the spiral of suffering and hope is no longer avoided but embraced and transcended. In the words of the US Latino theologian Luis Pedraja, "The cross liberates us by affirming that we are not abandoned or rejected by God when we too encounter our own crosses. Nor does our suffering and death occur in vain, for at the cross, God vests our own crosses with meaning and the hope of life in spite of death."[23]

Benigno Beltran's Filipino Christology of the Inarticulate

Let us consider now the christological articulation of Father Benigno Beltran, a Catholic professor in the Philippines who for many years served as a priest to the scavengers who worked in the garbage dumps of Manila. In 1987 he published his study of Christ, titled *The Christology of the Inarticulate*.[24] There he sought to portray what he called the Filipino face of Christ, which "symbolizes the particular elements the Filipino experience adds to, or emphasizes in, the universal understanding of Christ" (1). In doing so he wants to take into account the language and symbols of the people in terms of which they are drawn to Christ and to discover the ways in which they show this devotion.

Beltran's method is to take the results of a survey of people in his parish and put them in conversation with some of the classical teaching on Christ. He notes, for example, that the Council of Chalcedon (AD 451) sought to reconcile the idea of person with nature. They were asking, *who* is Jesus and *what* is his nature (82)? But these notions have long histories in the philosophical

---

23. Pedraja, *Teologia*, 156.
24. Beltran, *Christology of the Inarticulate*. Page numbers in the text refer to this work.

traditions of that time and appear strange to Filipinos. As Beltran points out, "There is no such articulated philosophy in the Philippines" (216). Since the Filipino imagination is oriented to the concrete and experiential, abstract formulations like this will not suffice (146). Rather, Beltran argues, one must start with the concrete experiences of Filipinos in their processions and feast days, ceremonies in which Christ is portrayed as Santo Niño or the crucified Christ. These practices and the images associated with them, Beltran thinks, serve less as "cognitive landmarks than as evocative objects to arouse religious sentiments, shape values and guide behavior" (127). By engaging in these communal practices, whether it is following the crucifix or praying before the image of the Santo Niño, Filipino believers not only witness God's presence but also participate in the life of God among them (128).

Beltran recognizes that these folk practices carry danger. The focus on the sufferings of Christ can lose sight of the final victory guaranteed by the resurrection; in a matriarchal society, a focus on Mary's influence on Jesus can be an instance where cultural values overshadow theological ones; and the overemphasis on Jesus's divinity can lead to a docetic view in which he did not share our real humanity. In calling attention to these risks, Beltran is clearly applying the authority of Scripture to illuminate and critique local practices. But the discovery of the local, or vernacular, theology of the people is nevertheless an essential starting point both for instruction and for pastoral care (135–39). Nor does this imply that the classical tradition of Christianity and its creeds should play no role, as Beltran's study makes clear. But it does imply that a theology that takes on the flesh and blood of a people must speak in the language and images of that people.

Cyril Okorocha and the African Meaning of Salvation

A final illustration is now drawn from the African context. Nothing could be more mistaken than the presumption that Western missionaries encountered in African cultures a tabula rasa. In fact, Cyril Okorocha's study among the Igbo people of Nigeria shows that "it is a people's inherited ideas about salvation as the goal of humanity's religiousness that determines their response to a new religious system."[25] To understand the Christian notion of salvation among the Igbo people, one must begin by understanding their primal notion of salvation, since this inheritance constitutes a central theme of African religiosity (60).

25. Okorocha, "Meaning of Salvation," in Dyrness, *Emerging Voices*, 59. Page numbers in the text refer to this work.

Many Africans think of salvation in terms of *Ezi Ndu*, a "viable life" or a "life of total wholeness." Such a vital life is materially abundant (financial and economic progress, etc.), but it must also include justice and morality. This salvation is mainly achieved through a spiritual battle between good and evil forces. Okorocha argues that conversion in Africa is understood as an encounter of powers from several systems of salvation, resulting in a movement in the direction of power—what they call *ihe*. Thus "power . . . is the hermeneutic for interpreting African religiousness" (82).

As an example, consider this powerful testimony of the arrival of Christian missionaries to the Igbo in Nigeria. Okorocha, who is now an Anglican bishop in Nigeria, argues that Igbo people converted to Christianity because they saw that "the God of the missionaries appeared to have more power than the native divinities."

> My father told me that the God of the missionaries appeared to have more power than the native divinities. When they wanted to settle, we gave them land in the evil forest where the most wicked spirits lived. We expected them to die within days. But they lived on. They cleared the forest and built houses, including a house for their God and schools for those children who were foolish enough to associate with such strange people. Besides, we saw by their robust health, that they were in possession of a better quality of life. We decided to discover the secret of this power that gave them such superior quality of life. That was how my father got converted to Christianity. Before then he was a "native doctor" and "juju" worshipper. He passed his attractive and vibrant new faith on to me as you can see today. (83)

The role of spiritual powers in the life of the Igbo people was paramount. However—and this is the critical point—in their mind, the spiritual and the earthly realms were not seen as separate. Instead they are merged into one "sacrosanct whole" (76). The spiritual operates through the material, and the material reflects what takes place in the spiritual. Spirit and matter are both ends of the same pole.

If the central theme of African religiosity is salvation, and salvation is understood as the enhancement of life (*Ezi Ndu*), then it is evident that for the African communities, salvation must become visible in the here and now. As in the Americas, a this-worldly focus of history probably represents the greatest difference between Western and African notions of salvation. Whereas Western Christian soteriology often stresses the afterlife (or spiritual) dimension of salvation, African people must perceive evidence of their salvation in the here and now. "Now" must become the symbol of "tomorrow." For the Igbo people, the here-and-now aspect of salvation does not oppose the realities of salvation tomorrow (or in the afterlife). Rather, Africans seem to think in terms of salvation today and a tomorrow, "or better still—salvation tomorrow, because, and as, received today" (79). However, the here-and-now concern is by far larger than the afterlife concern. In fact, the preoccupation with the present is a projection of the African people's fear of death, representing a striking contrast with the Pauline idea that "living is Christ and dying is gain" (Phil. 1:21).

The Igbo believe "their cosmos to be populated by life-vitiating spirit forces locked in an internecine battle at the center of which is humankind" (82). Now, since this cosmic battle centers on the human community, the behavior of each individual is nothing less than the reflection of the good and bad spirits in his or her life. At a societal level, a chaotic society would be the reflection of the triumph of evil powers over good powers. Likewise, an orderly society represents the triumph of good powers. Because of this understanding, the African notion of salvation has a communal dimension—it must be, in part, a societal salvation.

Communalism as an aspect of *Ezi Ndu* has four characteristics: (1) solidarity, involving the group consciousness, which stresses both individual and communal rights—the "I" and the "we" are equally important; (2) mutuality, which implies a consciousness that "we are all equal" and no one has the right to rule over or dominate another; (3) reciprocity, which has to do with interdependence—generosity is a trait of every good and saved person; and (4) altruism, which refers to living for others and is the key motif in Igbo social philosophy.

Because life in community is vital, Africans hold in high esteem the notion of fair play and justice, which leads to an understanding of salvation as a revelation of justice in the world around them. According to Okorocha, "To the Igbo, viable life or *Ezi Ndu* hinges upon the dual concept of justice and moral probity, *Ofor na ogu*. Thus a full understanding of the idea of salvation among African peoples, especially among the Igbo, must take into account this dualistic socioreligious phenomenon" (82).

One implication, however, is that because Africans hold justice and fairness in such great esteem, they have a hard time understanding the concept of a forgiving God (78). Furthermore, this understanding leads to the idea that the gods act only on behalf of the just (there is no room for grace, so to speak). "The Igbo, in their insistence that *Chineke* must always reject evil, have no room for the justification of the unjust and the salvation of the weak" (78). For this reason, for Africans a person should embody a visible righteousness in order to attain salvation. According to Okorocha, this is the greatest weakness of the notion of salvation in Africa; it could lead to the idea that salvation is largely achieved throughout the work of humankind (19).

A Quest for a Mutually Constructive Dialogue

Lying behind these very different approaches in the West and the non-West are more fundamental issues that are worth exploring. These differences do not reflect merely different starting points or approaches, but their different histories result in radically different understandings of the nature of theological reflection. Consider the controversy surrounding Jon Sobrino, a Spanish theologian who has taught most of his life in El Salvador, as an illustration of this fundamental difference. In 2007 the Congregation for the Doctrine of the Faith (CDF) in Rome issued what it called a "notification" on the teaching of Sobrino. While it did not condemn Sobrino outright or forbid him from teaching in Catholic institutions, the notification alerted the faithful to problems that existed in the work of this influential theologian. The notification listed a number of such problems: (1) Sobrino was felt not to be in sufficient harmony with the traditional teaching of the church by suggesting that the New Testament, though it planted the seeds of this, does not offer a formal definition of Jesus's divinity; (2) Sobrino appeared to teach that Jesus may not have attributed salvific value to his death or (3) that Jesus exhibited exemplary faith in God but may not have enjoyed what Catholics call a final beatific vision of God. In his discussion of this notification, William Loewe argues that what is at stake here are differing perspectives on the way theology is done. The CDF, Loewe points out, insists that theology should be continuous with the classical faith of the church, especially as this takes the form of classic scholastic theology. Judged in this light, Sobrino's work is potentially misleading (the notification is careful not to judge the "subjective intentions" of Sobrino, only the tendency of his teaching).[26]

But Loewe thinks that Sobrino's work ought to be read from a different perspective. While over the centuries this classical and dogmatic method has been dominant, over the past generation theologians (many, like Sobrino, who work outside the West) have sought "a comprehensive genetic and dialectic account of the origin and development of the church's beliefs about Jesus with a view to bringing his revelatory and redemptive significance to bear on the present." Sobrino is to be located within this broader project of theology, which still can include "metaphysically informed reflection on the dogmatic teaching of . . . Chalcedon."

26. Loewe, "Interpreting the Notification," in Pope, *Hope and Solidarity*, 150. The notification itself is reproduced on pages 255–66. None of what we say should be interpreted to mean that Sobrino should not be subjected to critical examination. Loewe points out his own problems with Sobrino's work in the article.

Interestingly, as Loewe notes, this more contemporary project of seeking significance for the present is a movement that often unites Western and non-Western theologians (and has been a motivation for the present authors in writing this book). Consider a similar argument of a contemporary Western theologian, Colin Gunton. In the last book that he wrote before he died, this prominent British theologian argued that a fundamental flaw in Western reflection on theology was to use the principle of *being* derived, he thinks, from medieval scholastic theology rather than the more biblical category of the *action* of God.[27] The problem, Gunton thinks, is that God is too often found in a realm that is foreign or even opposed to the created world where humans live. God is more often described in terms of what is called the *via negativa*—in terms of what God is not rather than what God has done (63). He notes how even the names of God in Scripture relate more to God's saving actions in history than to God's being (130). This orientation to God's actions in and with creation, Gunton thinks, will do more to help us understand both the person and the work of Christ, and to see them as a single whole. He writes, "If, then, we consider the being of God as creator in relation to his creation, the aspect of God's holy love with which we are concerned is . . . to be construed positively" (121). And both the Son and the Spirit can be seen as God's movement toward us in love. It is significant that Gunton's thought resonates with the emphasis Beltran discerned among Filipinos. Father Beltran sees the significance of Jesus there as follows: "The Christ, as the definitive crystallization of God's self-communication in history, is in his very person, salvation and redemption. His death and resurrection signaled the end of the reign of darkness and reconciled human beings to God. . . . Sinners are reconciled to God by entering into Jesus' death . . . and making them sharers of the grace of the Holy Spirit."[28]

Christ is best understood in terms of what he shows us of God's love and the ways that we may respond in faithful living. In the words of Justo González, one of the most influential historians and theologians of our time, "Truth appears there, where the eternal unites with the historical; where God becomes flesh; where a concrete man, in a concrete situation, can say I am the Truth."[29] This is the reason, some of us would say, we must follow the historical Jesus while believing in the resurrected Christ.

---

27. Gunton, *Act and Being*. Page numbers in the text refer to this work.
28. Beltran, *Christology of the Inarticulate*, 101.
29. González, *Historia del pensamiento cristiano*, 38.

6

The Church in Global Context

The Church in a Global Context—An Overview

No theological issue will be approached more differently in a global context than that of the church. This is not hard to understand when one considers the critical role cultural and historical contexts play in shaping the church. As in other areas, Western theologians have not always been conscious of this cultural rootedness. They have grown used to looking back to the ancient traditions of the church and the various forms these take today, much in the same way that they begin with the fixed theological traditions and creedal statements—the doctrines and texts we spoke about in chapter 3. So when Western Christians think of the church, they have in mind the ancient Orthodox Churches, or the Catholic Church with its Roman seat of authority, or perhaps the local expression of their own Presbyterian or Methodist or Assemblies of God Pentecostal church down the street.

But even a brief experience outside Europe and the United States/Canada shows how limited this view has become. Consider the groups of Christians dressed in their distinctive garb dancing and singing under acacia trees in Africa. Or recall Oscar's experience of that pluralistic, multicultural group of believers in Japan. These illustrate the new pluralistic and dynamic situation that characterizes the church of Jesus Christ today. Somewhere in that mix of Nisei and Sansei believers[1] and Brazilian immigrants are probably some

---

1. Nisei believers represent the second generation of Japanese-born immigrants; Sansei are third-generation immigrants.

traditional influences in addition to Brazilian Pentecostalism, but to discover their source and role would be anything but easy. And such exploration even seems beside the point. Clearly, the Spirit of God is at work through the study and preaching of Scripture, calling people together to worship and serve, and thus the church is growing and becoming established. And this is not only to be celebrated; it must also be the starting point for our theological reflection.

This dizzying diversity challenges traditional categories used to understand the church. Consider the ancient characterization of the church enshrined in the final clause of the Nicene Creed (381): "And I believe in one holy catholic and apostolic Church." It may have been easier to imagine the church as a single and catholic (i.e., universal) entity when the church appeared virtually coexistent with the Roman Empire. But even then theologians had to take refuge in Augustine's notion of the "invisible" church to see the quarreling parts of the body of Christ as one and universal, just as they needed to see its holiness as residing not in the visible body but more substantially in the holiness of Christ, the head of the church.[2] Even if the Orthodox and Roman Catholic branches of Christendom have stressed the theological significance of the visible form of church—and its visible unity, even the beauty of its holiness—such reflections are confounded by the sheer diversity of the global Christian church. Much of this has to do with the multiple contexts in which God is calling out a people.

An important part of the Spirit's work today is taking place in those parts of the non-Western world where Christianity faces long-entrenched religious traditions. In Muslim countries, various kinds of insider movements wrestle with the possibility of following Christ while maintaining their cultural identity as Muslims and continuing their attendance at the mosque. In areas of North India, where Hindu practices are strong, some Christians have attempted to shape a Christian identity that does not reflect inherited (and mostly Western) characteristics but shares much with the surrounding Hindu culture.[3] In Southeast Asia a new generation of Christians is exploring what they call multireligious belonging so as not to become estranged from the Buddhist culture of their families and communities.

Of course, movements of this kind are controversial, especially for Western Christians. In addition, for various reasons, many groups are impossible to study or even know about. But however they might be evaluated, from all we can tell, they clearly represent an important part of what God is doing in the

2. See the helpful discussion of this repositioning of the theological reality of holiness and unity on Christ in Plantinga et al., *Introduction to Christian Theology*, 340–48.
3. See Duerksen, *Ecclesial Identities*.

world today. And if we want to reflect on the church in a global context, we must take movements of this kind into account. But how can this possibly be done?

Let us propose here one way to think about this diversity in church forms. Rather than thinking of church traditions and the newer movements as mutually exclusive or in competition with each other, why not consider them on a spectrum of understandings of the church? On the one side, let's say the right, are the traditional forms of church with their long history of development and interaction. They represent important resources and have been bearers of one or another emphasis of the Christian faith throughout history (what we have described as the dominant Western traditions). But their common characteristics are a highly formalized structure and fixed forms both of worship and of confessional statements. They may in fact be very different from each other, but their common (and mostly Western) history has led them to develop various patterns of interaction and even accommodation (think of the ecumenical movement or the various Roman Catholic–Protestant dialogues).

Then consider the more informal movements we have described as occupying the left-hand side of this spectrum. These groups have all appeared quite recently, and they share a dynamic and often unsanctioned character. If those on the right have mostly clear and jealously guarded boundaries, these groups on the left can sometimes scarcely be distinguished from the cultures where they are found.[4]

Of course all churches reflect their historical and cultural settings, and all struggle in various ways to come to terms with their settings. But the fact is, like much of Western theology that we have considered, those practicing more traditional forms of church life and teaching have lost sight of the cultural sources of their traditions. As a result, these Christians have sometimes ceased to play a meaningful role in the transformation of their culture. Meanwhile, those on the left are conscious of their need to live out their faith in particular and often oppressive cultural situations, and they wrestle with such issues every day.

Recognizing and appreciating the validity of both emergent and traditional expressions of the church, and indeed of the multiple forms in between, carries an additional advantage that furthers the aim of this book. Openness to newer, emergent forms of Christianity may make Western Christians more inquisitive and more open to the many forms of house or seeker churches that are growing up all around them in the West—those groups meeting Sunday afternoon

---

4. This spectrum recalls Ernst Troeltsch's famous distinction between church and sect, but we want to emphasize the differences in cultural accommodation.

in the local night club or in a neighbor's living room. And at the same time, those championing the freedom of informal structures might realize what they have to learn from the history of the more traditional churches—which, it should be pointed out, mostly began their lives as informal and emergent movements. Clearly, God has used many forms of community to form the body of Christ, and the Spirit continues this work in the present.

The Study of the Church in Global Context

Let us consider more closely how we might understand the church today in this way, acknowledging that church life around the world is experienced in complex, interconnected, and fluid ways much more than we in the West are ready to admit. In this chapter we hope to show how the new subjects of global missions are no longer the settled, mainline, affluent, northern European–based churches but more often the poor, unsettled, Pentecostalized, non-Western and ethnic/immigrant churches. This does not mean that the former now play no role in the making of the church—missional movements are increasingly common in mainline denominations. But it does mean that the newer churches are playing a transformational role in the remaking of Christianity as a global phenomenon; they are no longer merely recipients of Western Christianity. To put this another way, we should no longer study the Christian church today by merely looking back into the annals of the historical archives of Western Christianity. The church is alive and being shaped by non-Western Christians and the newer generations of hybrid (transoccidental) believers who live in diaspora in the West.

Lately, much work has been done in Western academic institutions to try to understand the shifting of the Christian base around the world, particularly in the fields of sociology of religion and global studies.[5] This is all for the good. But in theology we are at a disadvantage when it comes to studying migration, urbanization, globalization, and interstitiality (the in-between spaces), for these subjects have never been part of the agenda of Western Christian thought. In this sense, our approach to doing theology in a global context represents a response to such a deficit and a contribution to making the field of theological studies more holistic. The point, however, is not merely collecting data and making sense of it to justify an emerging discipline, for we would then fall prey to the rhetoric of modernity by making our "subjects of study" in reality "objects of study." In other words, we should not be centered

5. A good example of such a study is Miller and Yamamori, *Global Pentecostalism*.

only on what we in the West have called objective data and rationality, which simply respond to questions such as, How accurate is our data? and, How can we make sense of these movements in religion, and how does this information affect our disciplines? Christian theology should include these matters but go beyond them. It should be attentive to how God acts and moves the human subject, not just how human beings see God acting and moving them. The new agents of Christianity have not only ceased to be the objects of Western studies but are becoming the very subjects and key protagonists of global Christianity. These agents are on the move, traveling through the networks of global imperial power and creating alternative spaces for worship and the arts, justice and compassion, community and mission. These new agents are also shaping the conditions for the emergence of a new type of church, what we will call the "glocal church." This is a genre of churches capable of embracing traditional Christian values under globalizing conditions where poverty, injustice, cultural marginality, and different types of displacements predominate. Ironically, it is in these marginal and interstitial spaces in global cities that Christianity is flourishing and even revitalizing historical/mainline churches. This poses a question to the professional theologian and religious educator: How prepared is the typical Western-rooted theologian/educator to cope with the theoretical and practical challenges that this global phenomenon signifies? In this book we have insisted that deprovincializing and decolonializing processes in our theological elaboration are necessary lest we remain ill-equipped to deal successfully with all the cultural, ethnic, economic, and political complexities shaping the global settings that make up our churches. The discussion of the church in this chapter will further highlight the theological significance of these new settings.

A Church Case Study

Recall again the case study in Japan to which we have referred. The host church in Suzuka, Japan, where Oscar went consisted of Sansei and Nisei families whose primary languages were Spanish and Portuguese. The founding couple of this church, Peruvians by birth, migrated with their parents to Japan as adolescents and met while attending a Brazilian Pentecostal church in Suzuka. As they grew up, they had to cope with all the demands presented by a multicultural/multilingual context: the majority (Japanese) society, their Brazilian church, and their Peruvian Spanish–dominant family. This borderline experience enabled them to develop a set of paradigms and skills for coping with life and church ministry in ways that a more monocultural/monolingual individual would find difficult. In the course of time, they married and were called into ministry. In order to serve the immigrant communities in Suzuka and their Japanese neighbors, they decided to plant a multilingual church where services would be in Japanese, Spanish, and Portuguese. Although Japan is not known to be a place where Christian churches grow quickly or easily, their new church, in a period of five years, grew larger than long-established churches. Currently their church houses a number of families that identify as Peruvian-Japanese, Ecuadorian-Japanese, Bolivian-Japanese, Argentinean-Japanese, and Brazilian-Japanese. Interestingly, the church even showed notable growth among local (nonimmigrant) Japanese youth due to the networking lifestyles and evangelistic passion of their youth group. Consequently, this hybrid church plant began to surprise the traditional Protestant churches in the area by creating an intercultural and ecclesial space for immigrants and the second generations and even reaching out to residents of the area.

Moved by several contextual and ministry demands, the pastor began looking for resources and possible mentors to assist the community in figuring out how to exercise a relevant ministry in their global/local context. It was through a mutual friend that we (the pastor and Oscar) connected. Some of the concerns for this church were how to understand the emerging generation while capitalizing on their cultural mixing and their multiple identities and attributes; how to encourage the emerging generation to own their experience of worship, discipleship, and witnessing to Jesus; and how to engage in civic life constructively as an immigrant church. These and other concerns typical of hybrid and immigrant communities surfaced time and again in our conversations. Two things stood out to me (Oscar). First, though we were doing church ministry in different continents, in truth, the contextual challenges and mission were similar and deeply interconnected. Second, we belonged to a common interstitial space where experiences of similar social, cultural, and ministry challenges disclose a local-and-global (glocal) trend. This exemplified to me, once more, the ubiquitous nature of globalization and how a place like Suzuka, Japan, is transnationally connected even to Los Angeles, my home. The pastor from Suzuka and I were both doing ministry in the interstices of global society. As we talked together, the glocal project that we envisioned was to facilitate a transnational mission connection between the Suzukan church and a local church in Los Angeles. Interestingly enough, we soon identified a candidate: a Latino/a church whose immigrant pastor was Brazilian and in his youth had even worked with a Nippon-Brazilian ministry in the vicinities of São Paulo, Brazil. The world is small after all!

Understanding the Scenario for the Global Church

While it might be thought that this boundary-crossing, hybrid church is anomalous, our contention is that such situations are not only increasing in number throughout the world but also representative of the future character of the Christian church.[6] Indeed, this ambiguous, polyphonic, polyvalent, and diasporic character of the Christian community corresponds more than we may realize to the first Christian churches across the Greco-Roman world. In an effort to cope with this multifaceted character of the global city, we are using the concept of the "glocal church." The word "glocal," as we use it, alludes to the multifaceted nature of the church in a global setting. The glocal community is situated in a particular context and made of a diverse number of cultural subjects (i.e., Ecuadorian-Japanese, Bolivian-Japanese, Argentinean-Japanese) that experience life in a common space and experience each other in a way that creates a Christian bond. They see each other as local agents belonging to a particular place and community. In this sense it is still a local church. But at the same time, the community is linked to several other contexts culturally, missionally, economically, politically, and so on that extend around the world and sustain part of their local identity. This is its global identity. We call it a glocal church because the identity and communal practices of the community are not defined only by one local geography or a particular context but by many connections that simultaneously interrelate to make up the ethos of the community. The glocal church, in this sense, represents a sociocultural space that is diasporic, polyphonic, and polyvalent at its core. In order to better grasp the significance of this ecclesial representation, we must frame the conditions, logics, and corresponding biblical images that make the glocal church a pertinent and practical understanding of the Christian church for the global world.

Transnationalism as a New Condition for the Global Church

Christianity in global contexts is making a transnational shift.[7] Immigrant communities such as those of Latinos/as, Middle Easterners, Africans, and Asians are becoming mission makers and cultural transmitters as they translocate and make a life in their new contexts. Once they get established in a particular location, their homes travel with them, back and forth, thus constructing a transnational route. That is, they carry with themselves their

6. Several aspects of this section first appeared in García-Johnson, "Mission within Hybrid Cultures," in Bolger, *Gospel after Christendom*, 113–26.
7. On this see Noll, *New Shape of World Christianity*.

symbolic homeland (Aztlán) as they acculturate and territorialize in their new location.[8] Many of them can be said to transmigrate instead of simply immigrate; they are making life in between Home (their native land) and home (their new residence in diaspora).

It goes without saying that these migration movements are affecting urban environments by reshaping the landscape of city life in a wide variety of ways. As these migrations advance through the back streets of imperial-global powers (and global economies and politics), cities and others geographies are affected, generating both great opportunities and great challenges.[9] The migration impact is significant because it mirrors the effects of globalization unlike many other phenomena.[10]

Globalization has redefined life for everyone, but it is particularly influential for immigrant communities. For instance, cultural and ethnic regionalization are reengineering and coloring cities, barrios, and social and religious structures.[11] Also, information and technology are fabricating a new type of social class, or social canon, where the acquisition of wealth, status, and power is based on what Manuel Castells calls "informational capitalism."[12] This globalizing effect in particular is modifying the DNA of social life and its political ramifications. Obviously, in an information-fabricated society, those situated at the top of the informational networks are able to thrive, while those placed at the bottom, who find themselves stuck in the complexities of industrial society, are stagnant and often socially, economically, and politically invisible.

Many immigrants fall into the latter category, but against all odds they manage to survive the challenges that informational capitalism imposes on this new type of worker. They are becoming subjects of societal change and shaping their own destiny as they are forced to find alternative means for survival

8. Aztlán refers here to an "alternative geography," a space of identity performance of a sojourning community. It can also refer to a space of cultural and social resistance. See Pérez-Torres, "Alternative Geographies," in Lionnet and Shih, *Minor Transnationalism*, 318–20.

9. Davey has an informative discussion on these globalizing challenges and opportunities in *Urban Christianity and Global Order*, 28–55.

10. We acknowledge that views on globalization are controversial. Some understand globalization as a process of homogenization, relying heavily on modern historical, political, and economic theories. We, on the other hand, hold a contemporary, or hybrid, view of globalization, particularly in reference to cultural processes. Although the very definition of globalization is controversial, the general consensus points to globalizing processes in terms of technological change, reconfiguration of states, regionalization, and asymmetry. As such, globalization represents a key hermeneutical concept for the understanding of transnational missions and the local church. For an understanding of "globalization as hybridity," see Held et al., *Global Transformations*; Nederveen Pieterse, *Globalization and Culture*; Vásquez and Marquardt, *Globalizing the Sacred*; Gruzinski, *Mestizo Mind*.

11. See Arreola, *Hispanic Spaces, Latino Places*, 143–291.

12. See Castells, *Power of Identity*.

and self-deployment. For example, the thousands of new churches and small businesses established every month around the globe by immigrant communities—too often under unsustainable circumstances and without the proper legal support of the state—speak highly of the human capital and the capacity for innovation of these communities. As our case in Japan illustrates, their need is to acquire a set of life skills and networks for managing themselves within a challenging global environment. Although many of these transmigrants are found in "the back alleys of society," their marginality might represent, in some respect, an advantageous borderline space. In Castells's words, "It is in these alleys of society, whether in alternative electronic networks or in grassroots networks of communal resistance, that I have sensed the embryos of a new society, labored in the fields of history by a new identity."[13] Indeed, it is in these third or informal spaces or back alleys of society where immigrant communities and minorities are plunked down that we discover an interstitial sacred space we have referred to as the glocal church.[14]

In short, globalization in the form of their own transnationalism has affected immigrant communities in particular, but at the same time it has forced them to seek alternative spaces for survival and development. The interactivity between context and community is mutual and ongoing. Thus we argue that a new transnational situation is progressively unveiling a new ecclesial skin, a new type of Christian space that is interstitial and sacred—namely, the glocal church. Let us make no mistake here, for we are not suggesting that the glocal church is merely an ethnic church in a global city. Our contention is that the glocal church is fundamentally the church of the global citizen, a *locus theologicus* of the global city.

Again, we want to emphasize that this glocal character is true not only of immigrant congregations; it is having a major impact on mainline churches in America as well. The influence of this global connectivity is seen, for example, in the growing immigrant impact on new forms of missionary outreach and partnership, new styles of worship, and an increasing awareness of global political realities.[15] The new patterns of communication and social media we have referenced make the isolation of immigrant religion impossible. Consider the following statistics reported by Robert Wuthnow and Stephen Offutt. Immigrants make up 8 percent of active religious workers in the United States. More significant, 74 percent of Americans attend churches with immigrant

13. Ibid., 362.
14. This idea is treated in more detail in García-Johnson, *Mestizo/a Community of the Spirit*, 70–96.
15. See Wuthnow and Offutt, "Transnational Religious Connections," 209–32. The statistics that follow are from this important article.

populations. In other words, most Christians in the United States have contact with immigrant faith. Moreover, American Christians are remarkably well traveled: 1.6 million go on short-term mission trips each year, 62 percent of church members have traveled or lived abroad, and 76 percent of church members contributed to relief and humanitarian causes in 2008. This is in addition to partnership and exchanges of all kinds. The question we address here is, what difference should this make in our theological reflection on the nature of the church?

Glocality: A New Self-Understanding of the Church in Global Context

Every global city requires a glocal church (or many such churches), and every glocal church is called to articulate a redemptive praxis that corresponds to its global context. The concept of a glocal church represents a way to respond to the challenges of globalization in a post-Constantinian setting. Perhaps we need to back up in history to reroot the church in a mission-oriented narrative instead of an institutional or doctrinal-oriented one—in other words, to reflect again on the church located on the left side of the spectrum we described, where God is clearly doing something new. In many global contexts, institutional Christianity faces stiff opposition as it encounters popular tendencies oriented to informal piety, community-based practices, and postmodern and postcolonial views of God, church, and society.[16] Classical definitions of church and mission based on institutionality and dogma are being questioned. Following the logic of Harvey Cox in his book *The Future of Faith*, we might say that "belief-based structures" are being superseded by "faith-based organizations."[17] According to Cox, Christianity has gone through three quintessential stages: the Age of Faith (pre-Constantinian), the Age of the Belief (Constantinian), and the Age of the Spirit (current post-Constantinian). Cox argues that we are entering a new chapter in the history of Christianity and, while "forecasts of its decline" sound amid organized religion, the future is bright. "Christianity is growing faster than it ever has before, but mainly outside the West and in movements that accent spiritual experience, discipleship, and hope; pay scant attention to creeds; and flourish without hierarchies. We are now witnessing the beginning of a 'post-Constantinian era.' . . . I suggest we call it the 'Age of the Spirit.'"[18]

16. There are several works that support this perception, for instance, Grenz, *Primer on Postmodernism*; McGrath, *Christian Spirituality*; Cox, *Future of Faith*.

17. See Cox, *Future of Faith*, chap. 1.

18. Ibid., 8.

If this is so, we argue that the Christian vitality of the "global South" is being reflected back on the "global North" through the mediation of immigrant communities. Perhaps the big surprise to many Eurocentric Christian interpreters around the world is that the immigrant communities are now carriers of the leading energy for missions and religious transformation that has characterized the Christian church throughout its history. This suggests that the logic of church planting and mission making, along with their corresponding disciplines, is changing.

Logics behind the Glocal Church

In the history of Christian thought in the West, the tendency has been to seek the essence of Christianity, the nature of God, doctrine, and so on. But more recently, the questions have included location as a rubric of theological elaboration.[19] Beginning with Oscar and Bill's biographies in chapters 1–2, we have insisted that Christian theology in global contexts should acknowledge the politics of locality when elaborating dialogue. "The essence of Christianity" or "the truthfulness of Christian doctrine," as von Harnack and Berkhof, respectively, pointed out in their particular contexts, are not the most compelling questions for the majority world and emerging Western generations. Instead, issues such as "where Christianity begins and ends" and "what it means to be a Christian and why" are capturing the attention of global Christianity.[20] The historical products of Western Christianity, as Bill pointed out, are very important and present, in one way or another, when we practice Christian faith around the world. But the legacy of the West is being assessed, rethought, and reshaped by interpreters who are becoming conscious of their locations and becoming rerooted more and more in non-Western theological loci. And this includes Western thinkers who are attentive to dwindling church membership in the West.

We have insisted that for the dialogue among different communities to be constructive in global contexts, the interlocutors should speak in a decolonial

19. In the classical disciplines, see Greene, *Christology in Cultural Perspective*; Kärkkäinen, *Christ and Reconciliation*; Rhoads, *From Every People and Nation*.

20. Interestingly, I (Oscar) am finding a promising trend in biblical studies among noted Western theologians that can lead to recognizing the impact of coloniality and occidentalism (globalism) in hermeneutics. See Bockmuehl, *Seeing the Word*; Gorman, "What Has the Spirit Been Saying?," in Hays and Alkier, *Revelation and the Politics of Apocalyptic Interpretation*. Naturally, a decolonial trend seeking global/intercultural conversations has been present in US Latino/a biblical scholarship and other "subaltern disciplines" since the end of the last century. A book that illustrates this effort is Segovia and Boer, *Future of the Biblical Past*.

language, with a glocal-constructive intent, and with an attitude of respectful listening and learning. Consider for a moment the way a great Western theologian, Jürgen Moltmann, is engaging this type of dialogue.

> At the beginning of Christianity there were two crosses: One is a real cross, the other a symbol. One is murderous gallows of terror and oppression, the other a dream-cross of an emperor. One is for victims of violence, the other for violent conquerors. The one is full of blood and tears, the other empty. The first stands on Golgotha, and Jesus hangs on it, the other is the victorious dream of the Emperor Constantine. . . . How could the memory of a victim of injustice and violence be changed into a symbol of victorious injustice and violence?[21]

Moltmann takes a vicarious approach in interpreting the history of imperial violence and sees Jesus the Messiah and Son of God on the side of the victim. Jesus takes the place of the victim, or better, suffers with the victim, giving theological meaning to his or her suffering. In this account, imperial powers throughout the centuries reflect a "Christendom temptation" that originated during the period following the conversion of Constantine to Christianity. The recurring violence shows up again and again in human history in the experience of empire victims. Moltmann then asks, "How could the memory of a victim of injustice and violence be changed into a symbol of victorious injustice and violence?"

Moltmann places the redemptive ethos of Christianity in a Christ figure who embodies suffering and a history of oppression. Moltmann opposes the dominant trend of a "conqueror's ethics" that has occupied much of the history of Christian thought, deeds, and institutions in the West and its colonies. This redemptive paradigm finds resonance in a majority world permeated by imperial-colonial injuries and continues to live under ideological, political, and economic world-systems and the resulting inequalities, injustice, poverty, and oppression. As Moltmann stands critically against an imperialistic-Constantinian mode of Christianity, he is opening a fertile terrain for global dialogue. Though he speaks from the perspective of Western history, the majority world will see here an opening for dialogue—they know only too well the violence and oppression he speaks about.

A Pentecost Narrative of the Glocal Church

Theologians from other settings would press Moltmann to acknowledge that there are other beginnings in the history of Christianity before and after

21. Moltmann, "Cross as Military Symbol," in Trelstad, *Cross Examinations*.

Constantine, inside and outside the West. The Pentecost event as narrated in the book of Acts, for instance, can be said to point to the beginning of the Christian church and, for that matter, Christianity. This account makes clear that Christianity, from the very beginning, pushed beyond the chronology and geography of the West. This obvious fact is significant, especially for those of us who have been educated to believe that Christianity, properly speaking, began with Constantine. Clearly, the New Testament church occupied a sociocultural space that embodied a number of ethnic, theological, and leadership paradoxes due to the heterogeneous composition of the people that came to constitute it. In truth, the originating church of the book of Acts, as we read it through epistemic eyes of the transoccidental Latino people of the Americas, looks far more inviting and life-giving than the Constantinian church of Western modernity. One has only to take a quick look at the Pentecostal and Charismatic movements in Africa and the Americas to corroborate this perspective.[22] These movements demonstrate an implicit critique of Western and modern colonizing ideologies. They show that the real point of inflection and tension is not merely social and economic but the dominance of Western ways of thinking. Until one is able to disengage or delink from the epistemic dialectic of Western coloniality and modernity, one cannot offer a truly liberated and liberating option.[23] The delinking process should begin with the beginning of our Christian narrative as a people of God, namely, the Christian church and its succession in the history of humanity. Let us explore this further.

The Multiple Ways of Knowing of Glocality

The Christian church emerged in a context of significant ideological, religious, cultural, ethnic, and political turmoil. We cannot think any longer of the beginning and nature of the church in terms of a homogeneous epistemic universe. If the narrative of Pentecost as portrayed by Acts 2 is taken as a formative matrix of cultural existence for the church in a global context, we would notice how compatible and functional it is for our transoccidental approach.

The Christian phenomenon that gave birth to Christian experience and the church at Pentecost, first of all, is polyphonic and polyglot, where multiple languages are evoked simultaneously and no one language dominates. Note that the miracle of Pentecost was not only one of speaking in multiple languages (what today we call the gift of "tongues") but even more the ability of each one

22. See Balcomb, "El encuentro de cosmovisiones," 7–24.
23. See this argument articulated in Mignolo, *Desobediencia epistémica*.

to hear the word in their own mother tongue: "Each one heard them speaking in the native language of each" (Acts 2:6). We might frame this as the "gift of hearing." Note how the global was also the local; no language was privileged, and no people were marginalized. Second, the church was both popular and "global" in scope; it was not restricted to the elites of Judaism, a selected group, or one individual but available to Jerusalemites and Hellenists, men and women, insiders and outsiders, old and young, and so on. Then notice that the first formation was a vernacular and informal event; it was not restricted to the rabbis, scribes, and the like but available to proselytes and curious seekers alike. At the same time, it was a public event, not a private or merely spiritual event; it immediately reached the streets and public spaces surrounding the meeting place. Hence, I argue beyond my charismatic instincts that the greatest sociocultural miracle witnessed at Pentecost is not *glossolalia* but glocality. What comes out of the Pentecost event is not simply an exotic Jewish sect, an idealistic movement, or even a new religion named Christianity; it is all that and much more. It was a culture of cultures, a cultural development engendered by none other than the Spirit of the Triune, global God.

But Where Is God?

This brings us to the theological core of a possible global ecclesiology. From the perspective of a non-Western-initiated Christianity, the birth of the church is a Spirit-engendered glocality that is richly expressed in all its diversity. It was something God was doing, calling a people together from all the nations of the earth—a global and local event, and a personal and public experience. We want to underline the multiple logics and voices that gave a polyphonic shape to the church and to point out that Enlightenment analytic rationality can easily homogenize and neutralize this basic structure. Consider this description of the church, as it was understood during the centuries preceding the Reformation, by Catholic historian Brad Gregory: "The church, established by Jesus himself, was said to be the continuing instrument for the achievement of God's plan of salvation for the human race after Jesus's ascension that followed his crucifixion and resurrection."[24]

A corollary of this was that the church around 1500 displayed doctrinal and liturgical unity across much of Europe. Gregory stresses this underlying unity and the church as "the continuing instrument . . . of salvation" to underline his point that the unintended consequence of the Reformation was to leave

24. Gregory, *Unintended Reformation*, 83.

behind Christians with insoluble doctrinal differences, which eventually led to the secular pluralism that we see around us.

But what if in fact the Reformation, flawed though it may have been, was the initial step in recognizing the essential multiplicity within the church—a polyphonic reality that had existed from the very beginning? Consider the definition of the church given by John Calvin: "Wherever we see the word of God sincerely preached and heard, wherever we see the sacraments administered according to the institution of Christ, there we cannot have any doubt that the Church of God has some existence."[25] Here God's grace is made available through the particular practices of preaching and the administration of the sacraments. But, Calvin admits, these may take a wide variety of forms. These "marks of the church" can distinguish God's people, he goes on to note, in a wide variety of places, "so that we may safely recognize a church in every society in which [these signs] exist," and "we are never to discard it so long as these remain, though it may otherwise teem with numerous faults."

So God's work in forming the church can be understood in terms of the physical-sacramental logic of Roman Catholicism on the one hand and by the more linear logic of Protestantism on the other. Or it can appear in Eastern Orthodoxy as a mystical logic that seeks to connect the believer with the heavenly space of God and the saints. We would argue that the polyvalent matrix of glocality includes these logics but can also open the way for many other ways of understanding the Spirit-led worship of God's people. These other ways, we claim, amid their variety, find their unity in the work of the Triune God forming the body of Christ by the Spirit.

Eucharist in Transoccidental Perspective

Over the centuries Christian churches have differed on the physical means the Spirit of God uses to constitute Christ's living presence on earth. But all have agreed that the church as the physical and historical body of Christ is the privileged locus of God's presence. And within that body, as it gathers week by week, God has specified particular practices—preaching, prayer, praise, and the sacraments—as the divinely inscribed media of his presence. Let us linger for a bit in this context on the Eucharist. The doctrine of the Eucharist as developed in the Eastern-Western church and appropriated by US Latino/a theologians provides a good example of how glocality from the transoccidental perspective can embrace multiple ways for constructing theologies in global

25. Calvin, *Institutes* 4.1.9, 12.

contexts. The point of reflection we will use is the Eucharist as a means to create communion and community in the body of Christ.

The Eastern Orthodox Church and Roman Catholic Church both believe in a doctrine of transubstantiation. The difference rests on how they understand it and why. The Eastern tradition affirms that the means by which the body and blood of Jesus Christ is united with the bread and wine is a divine mystery. Their logic of equivocity allows them to embrace the doctrine of transubstantiation without having to build an a priori rational framework, hence the presence of Christ in the elements is embraced as a mystery in the act of consecration. This connotes an ontological communion (i.e., the many interconnect and reflect the One) and serves as the basis for their ecclesiology in consonance with their notion of *theōsis* (divinization).

In Roman Catholicism, the Eucharist is one of the seven sacraments. Given the sociopolitical demands imposed by its origination in the empire, the Roman Catholic Church was forced to develop a logic that justifies, in the minds of many, a theopolitical hypostasis in order to understand and project itself as an imperial church. The analogy of empire, then, became an appealing hermeneutic. The concept of the church (imperial) as the kingdom of God was fleshed out in the doctrine of the Eucharist, which came to connote a metaphysical communion (i.e., the One gives order to the many) in correspondence to the self-understanding of the church as the kingdom of God. By contrast, in mainline Protestantism, the Reformers defied the metaphysically totalizing meaning of Roman Catholicism by a kind of epistemic rupture. Luther advanced the doctrine of consubstantiation, which defied the Thomistic-Aristotelian logic of Catholicism's transubstantiation. Zwingli opted for a symbolic interpretation of the presence of Christ in the elements. And Calvin took a middle way and implied that there are both symbolic and concrete benefits in the Eucharist as represented in the consecrated elements. In mainline Protestantism, therefore, we see that the Eucharist connotes an epistemic communion that challenges the metaphysics of Roman Catholicism and focuses on *sola scriptura, sola fide, sola gratia*, and so on. The point of the matter here, from Oscar's perspective, is to understand that Western doctrines are not ideologically and politically neutral. Amerindians, women, people of color, tyrants, dictators, criminals, and saints have been unfairly excluded, injured, or favored by means of these types of doctrines in the context of the former colonies of Europe.

Are we to discard biblically relevant doctrines, like Paul's instructions on the Eucharist in 1 Corinthians 11, simply because they have been misinterpreted, miscommunicated, and manipulated for the sake of a race, culture, class, genre, ethnic group, or political party? Surely not. In this regard, US Latino/a theologians offer a path that decolonizes and at the same time reconstructs doctrines like these. Diaspora Latinos/as, due to their bicultural-borderline existence, have learned to use multi-epistemic systems (border thinking) that enable them to operate at the exteriority and interiority of modernity/coloniality when thinking theologically.[26]

For us US Latino/a theologians, the Eucharist does not function as a liturgical imperative based on a univocal-colonial rationality or an imperial analogy but instead as a polyvalent relationality. First of all, the kind of marginal location and in-betweenness that we face with respect to a majority culture that marginalizes the different other helps us understand that to participate in the Eucharist means to become a people by exercising our polyphonic and glocal memory of the crucified and resurrected Christ of the Triune God. This is a fulfillment of the biblical expectation, "Do this in remembrance of me" (1 Cor. 11:24).

Second, the Eucharist as embraced and considered through the epistemic eyes of the Latino/a people represents us while challenging the most fundamental classical tendencies in Western theologies to fixate their debates on second-order epistemic disputes (transubstantiation [Aquinas], consubstantiation [Luther], symbolism [Zwingli], virtualism [Calvin]) instead of dealing with the real subjects affecting the communion-making process in the body of Christ (racialization, colonialism, classism, sexism, militarism, globalism, exploitation, etc.) and those who participate in the body of Christ, which exists both as oppressed, neglected, and exploited, and as oppressors, exploiters, and criminals. Taking the actual participants in the eucharistic dramas seriously, we argue, follows Paul's critical advice in 1 Corinthians 11:29 to "discern the body," which clearly meant in this context to pay attention to the social needs of those present. In this sense, a focus on categorization and abstract thinking (the metaphysics of the Eucharist) represents an evasion of responsibility. In the context of globalism, powerlessness, and poverty, the context of the majority world, the Eucharist must transcend the meaning given by classical Western hermeneutics to include a border-crossing and prophetic voice that seeks to open up the tables and cross the borders imposed by antilove and antijustice imperial forces embedded in politicized communities and structures that are captives of imperial cores.

Finally, the relational sacramentality informing the eucharistic practices of the Latino/a community evokes new political and economic practices that seek to transcend Western logics (analogy and univocity) by adhering to a

26. Mignolo also acknowledges this epistemic attribute in US Latino/a thinking. See Mignolo, "Geopolitics of Sensing and Knowing."

Pentecost-based paradigmatic ecclesiology instead of a Constantinian or Enlightenment one. Again, the flourishing of the charismatic movement within non-Western Roman Catholicism and Pentecostalism, which share this biblical motif, is a sign of transoccidentality. Eschatologically and liturgically, the Eucharist in the US Latino/a Christian context takes on the prophetic meaning for which many in the West and the majority world pray and struggle. In Eliceo Pérez Álvarez's words, "The Eucharist becomes the promise that social prejudice and injustice to which our people are currently subjected will be transformed into an order of justice and human fulfillment already anticipated in Jesus Christ's presence and ministry among us."[27] The Eucharist, in this sense, is a de facto global code able to transverse all cultures, races, ethnicities, genders, and futures that—oriented by the trinitarian core—has the power to hold together the newly created transoccidental pluriverse making up the global discourse, which is the body of Christ universal.

Another way of framing this point is to reclaim Paul's image in 1 Corinthians 12:14: "Indeed, the body does not consist of one member but of many." As he goes on to describe the multiple parts of the body and the variety of roles each plays in the healthy functioning of the body knit together by love and acceptance (1 Cor. 13), he is surely recalling the founding narrative of the church where each heard and responded in their own language. For what is at stake, Paul argues in Ephesians, is the contribution of every part to the building up of the body, until all reach maturity in Christ (see Eph. 4:11–15). Paul is surely describing a glocal church when he concludes that our very diversity should lead us to have "the same care for one another. If one member suffers, all suffer together with it; if one member is honored, all rejoice together with it" (1 Cor. 12:25–26).

Conclusion

The glocal church represents an ambiguous sociocultural space, but it does not deny the genes of Christian tradition. Put another way, we might identify the glocal church as a sociocultural construct resulting from several genes or contributors: (1) the gene of tradition, which points to the many traditions that merge and carry on the ubiquitous global character of Christianity since New Testament times until our day by means of doctrines, institutions, rituals, art, and so forth; (2) the gene of cultures and ethnicities, which points to the crash of multiple races, cultures, and ethnicities that play a key role in the

27. Álvarez, "In Memory of Me," in Rodriguez and Martell-Otero, *Teología en conjunto*, 34.

production of the glocal space; (3) the gene of transcendence, which points to the historical, transcendent Spirit of God who originates Christian faith in every person and synergistically creates community and the communal self understood within the referential narrative of Pentecost.[28] When we speak of the church in these terms, we are alluding to the polygenesis of the Christian community. In other words, we are speaking of the multiple roots that contribute to the making of the church as a diverse Christian community in a diverse world through the ages.

How would this apply to our church case study with which we began? In the genome of our hybrid Japanese church, we can identify (1) some Western roots: particular liturgies, doctrines transplanted by US evangelicalism first in Brazil and then carried on to Japan by immigrant populations that founded churches there. We can also identify (2) some Latin American and Japanese cultural/ethnic roots: symbolic worlds ambiguated by their collapse and expressed by multiple languages, church organizational styles, modes of pastoral care, creative forms of evangelism, and so on. We can also identify (3) the role of the transcendent religious experience personified by the Spirit of God. Indeed, if one would ask the Suzukan-Peruvian pastors, they would quickly explain how they perceived the role of the Spirit as a guide and how, because of that, they came to adopt an intercultural identity. That is, they moved on to maintain a polyglot and pluriform vision of ministry that they received as a very gift of God.

28. For instance, the communal self finds cohesion in the memory and continuous action of the Spirit of the Triune God, who brings all the stories and identities together, affirms them, resocializes them, and optimizes them in conformity to the new humanity of Jesus Christ.

7

The Christian Hope:
Eschatology in Global Perspective

We come finally to the study of the Christian hope. Putting eschatology, or the study of the "end times"—literally the "last things"—at the end of a study of theology is misleading. It can imply that what happens at the end is a kind of postscript to other, more important events. But for Christianity, nothing could be further from the truth. For Christianity, as well as Judaism from which it arose, is an inherently eschatological faith; its view of future events is determinative for the understanding of history and indeed for life in the present. Judaism divides history into two ages—the present age and the messianic age, which is coming. Christianity inherited this view but believes that with Jesus Christ the "age to come" has already shown itself and will be fully realized when Christ returns at the end of history.

To acknowledge the centrality of eschatology is not to say the emphasis on the events of the end times has been consistent, or that different parts of the church have always shared a common understanding. In fact, here there is a gulf between Western theology and theology elsewhere that is, if anything, greater than that of any other locus of theology. And as with other loci, the divergences reflect very different social and historical situations. Consider two landmark studies of eschatology published within a few years of each other: Jürgen Moltmann's *Theology of Hope* (1967) and John Mbiti's *New*

Testament Eschatology in an African Background (1971).[1] In the one, a German theologian sought to place eschatology in the center of Christian reflection, to think about history from the perspective of the resurrection of Christ. In the other, Mbiti, a Kenyan theologian, sought to place the central New Testament teaching of Jesus's resurrection in the context of African beliefs and practices with respect to ancestors. Moltmann was facing a thoroughly secularized Western tradition of progress that expected the future would always be better but had lost any sense of God's role in this; Mbiti came from a deeply religious environment in which faith in God was assumed but that had no view of the future or the end of history. For both, the New Testament views of resurrection and new creation were countercultural, but they addressed the culture from very different directions.

Let's consider the Western perspective first. Moltmann's description of the future orientation common in Western societies is itself a testimony to the deep, long-term influence of the Judeo-Christian tradition on the West, even if this debt is often unacknowledged—a point Moltmann himself makes. But as he also notes, this optimism about the future, when he wrote his book, had come to be framed in terms of economic and social progress. Moltmann's discussion seeks to rethink the whole of Christian theology from the perspective that in the resurrection of Christ, the end of history has become present; the new creation is not simply a future event but has by the Spirit become a present reality. But to make his case, he had to address the secularization of the Christian hope that characterizes Western civilization. In the first chapter he addresses the two temptations that Western theology faces because of this unique situation. The one is to focus entirely on the transcendence of both God and the human subject as the primary locus for God's work; the other is to see history itself and its progress as the indirect revelation of God's future. The book is a major corrective to both of these tendencies. Moltmann wants to argue for a "passion for the possible." As he describes this, "For our knowledge and comprehension of reality, and our reflections on it, [this passion] means at least this: that in the medium of hope our theological concepts become not judgments which nail down reality to what it is, but anticipations which show reality its prospects and its future possibilities."[2] In the third chapter, "The Resurrection and the Future of Jesus Christ," Moltmann goes on to describe the grounds for this hope in the God of promise who is revealed in the coming of Jesus Christ. Because of the resurrection of this Christ, the Christian hope has taken on a unique

---

1. Moltmann, *Theology of Hope*, and Mbiti, *New Testament Eschatology*.
2. Moltmann, *Theology of Hope*, 35.

and specific character. The Christian is able to "recognize" in this event the future that God has in mind for the world.

Moltmann's work can be said to represent a major turn in Western theology, what might be termed the eschatological turn. Moltmann and others have elaborated on and drawn out the implication of this emphasis not only for theology but also for the environment, culture, and politics.[3] This turn toward the study of the end of history is correlated with a strong emphasis on the new creation that Christ has initiated as a redemptive transformation of *this* order rather than a gnostic view of salvation as a deliverance from the world and its subsequent annihilation. N. T. Wright has addressed the focus, especially strong in conservative circles, on transcendence in his insistence that the new world begun by Jesus's resurrection, the goal of God's redemptive work, is a transformation of the body and of creation and not a denial or destruction of them.[4] Richard Bauckham has drawn out the political implications of the presence of God's reign in Christ's resurrection. Christ was for John's Revelation, Bauckham notes, the one who was, who is, and who is to come. The achievement of God's eschatological rule over the world is God's coming. But since this has already come about in Jesus Christ, Bauckham points out, the future element in the book of Revelation has been supplanted by a call to worship and thanksgiving that this reign has already begun.[5] But God's ultimate rule has another, more important implication, one with increasing relevance for the present challenges to global peace. The goal of creation is theocentric, and human life is meant to be oriented to worship of the Creator. This divine rule, Bauckham argues, "delegitimizes" all human autocracy and relativizes all human power.[6] God directs history, then, not as a superhuman being but as the "source, ground and goal of all creaturely existence" who makes all things new (Rev. 21:5).[7]

To connect this with our previous argument on the church, this means that the people of God should be seen as an "eschatological community." That is, through the Spirit, their worship of God and their life of discipleship anticipate and embody the reign of Christ that will be fully seen and realized only at the end of history. It is a community that lives out of this future, sharing with God's people of all ages and places in the eternal praise of God that John sees in the book of Revelation.

---

3. Among the important studies, see Wainwright, *Eucharist and Eschatology*; Fergusson and Sarot, *Future as God's Gift*; Moltmann et al., *Future of Hope*; and Ladd, *Gospel of the Kingdom*.
4. See Wright, *Surprised by Hope*.
5. Bauckham, *Theology of the Book of Revelation*, 29–30.
6. Ibid., 44–45.
7. Ibid., 45.

Western Christians understand this in different ways and with varying emphases on the order and importance of the events of the end—the resurrection, the return of Christ, the last judgment, and the eternal state. But what is important for our purposes is to take note of the way these emphases often respond to a particular historical and cultural setting. Moltmann's eschatological focus and the centrality of God's space and time cannot be understood apart from the secularized understanding of progress that prevailed in the West when he wrote his book. To be sure, he had his hands on central themes of biblical teaching, but these themes had particular relevance for the situation of the church of his day. But what about God's people who live in very different settings? How might they understand God's promises about the end of history?

African Eschatology

Whereas Moltmann's groundbreaking work led to a virtual torrent of work on eschatology in the West, John Mbiti's work, though equally significant in many ways, stands out as one of the very few works that specifically address eschatology outside the West. This surprising fact calls for comment. Why is a focus on eschatology apparently absent in much non-Western theology? As we will note, especially in Africa and Asia, Western eschatology had a great, and not always positive, influence. But indigenous reflection on God's future, like that of Mbiti, is rare.[8] Why is this?

One apparent reason is discussed in detail in Mbiti's book.[9] Among the Akamba tribe, which Mbiti describes (and to which he belongs), the primary focus is on the formation and preservation of the human community. The cycle of this process moves horizontally from "birth, through initiation, marriage, procreation to death and entry into the community of the departed" (7). As is clear from the order of these events, time moves from the present into the past. From his analysis of language and mythology, Mbiti concludes that for the Akamba (and, he thinks, many African tribal groups), time moves backward. He argues that "people look more to the 'past' for the orientation of their being than to anything that might yet come into human history" (24–25). Though he admits this is changing because of the influence of modernization and missionary teaching, he concludes that the Akamba have no idea of a distant future or of the end of the world (31).

8. In his fine article "Eschatology" in the *Global Dictionary of Theology*, Roland Chia is not able to point to a single non-Western thinker or source that discusses eschatology.
9. Mbiti, *New Testament Eschatology*. Page numbers in the text refer to this work.

Mbiti's insistence that Africans know nothing about the future has caused some discussion, but his central claim is hard to dispute: there seems to be nothing in African religiosity that parallels the Christian teaching about the future.[10] Here, then, is one reason some non-Western settings show little interest in events at the end of history: their cultural perspective apparently gives them no framework in which to place such a discussion. In the case of the Akamba, Mbiti is asking, how does one describe God's promises in a language with little or no future orientation? To the biblical claim that Jesus brings the promises of the future into realization, Mbiti concludes that though "the Resurrection must constitute the uniqueness of the Christian hope of the hereafter," nothing in the African situation provides them with a handle to understand this (185). Whatever we make of the criticisms that have been subsequently leveled at his argument, Mbiti's insistence that a careful examination of language and mythology is a necessary starting point for indigenous theological reflection was as necessary as it was revolutionary.

In fact, Mbiti's book began a conversation—as often with anthropologists as with theologians—that has opened up entirely new ways of thinking about theology, one that interestingly belies the claim that African frameworks cannot comprehend eschatology.[11] Two theological developments with respect to discussion of the future might be put forward to illustrate these new ways of doing theology in an African setting: first, the centrality of ancestors, and second, the rethinking of the role of Christ that this has stimulated. Presenting these themes might help us see that the so-called absence of eschatology has more to do with the uniqueness of the conversation in this setting (and its contrast with the West) than any real deficit.

First, consider the anthropocentric view of the human community that prevails in African indigenous thinking. The focus and practices of religion have always highlighted the community—family, tribe and clan, and the ongoing need for communion with those who have died. Traditional practices of offerings and sacrifices have typically sought to facilitate this ongoing communion as a means of assuring the continuing health and stability of the community. But as Bénézet Bujo points out in an important study, "Communion with the ancestors has both an eschatological and a salvation dimension. Salvation is the concern of both the living and the dead members of society, for all affect

10. This connects to a more general claim that Mbiti makes at the very beginning of his book: "We do not know much about the theological issues precipitated by the presence of the Christian faith in an African setting" (ibid., 1).

11. For a review of the conversation about Mbiti's arguments, see Gehmen, *Doing African Christian Theology*, 64–71.

each other and depend on each other."[12] If this is so, Bujo claims, then even if African thinking has no eschatology strictly speaking, the fact that African communities consider their ancestors and indeed all of nature as "pointing sacramentally to God"—on their way to a fulfillment that can only be found in God—indicates they have a powerful if implicit awareness of eschatology.

Mbiti had anticipated the claim Bujo develops by describing the inherent sacramental understanding of the human community and nature in Akamba culture. If traditional religion allowed them to understand their sacrifices and offerings as connecting them sacramentally to their ancestors, Mbiti proposes that the Akamba could easily understand baptism as a sacrament of inaugurated eschatology that implements the "act of salvation" and the Eucharist as a foretaste of the messianic banquet.[13] His point is that the concrete, this-worldly orientation of Akamba culture could in fact allow them to understand the community of God's people, the church, as an "eschatological field" in which the end is realized in the here and now.

Even this brief discussion helps us see that an indigenous perspective can sometimes provide alternative ways to frame biblical themes, pathways that are often invisible to outsiders. Note as well how Bujo and Mbiti closely intertwine the concepts of salvation and eschatology in their arguments. Both salvation and eschatology must be tied to the flourishing of the human community, and both are tied to the role of ancestors. Ancestors, as Ngarndeye Bako points out in a recent dissertation, are central to the mythmaking of African communities, and so neither salvation nor eschatology could be fully understood apart from them.[14] But none of this was evident in the teaching that John Mbiti had received growing up. The premillennial focus of missionaries from African Inland Churches (AIC), in which Mbiti was raised, had insisted on proposing dates for the return of Christ and, in the process, overlooked entirely the sacramental potential of the Akamba worldview. This teaching not only imposed an incomprehensible linear understanding of the future but missed out on ways in which biblical themes could be illumined by indigenous terms.[15]

---

12. Bujo, *African Theology in Its Social Context*, 24. See also n. 16 on this page for Bujo's elaboration of this point and the quotation that follows.

13. Mbiti, *New Testament Eschatology*, 101. See 101–7 for his full discussion. The term "eschatological field" is found on p. 107.

14. Bako, "Eschatology in African Folk Religions," 144. He surveys the important discussion of ancestors begun by Mbiti and developed by Nyamiti.

15. Mbiti, *New Testament Eschatology*, 55–57. Mbiti notes their focus was on a minor and debatable aspect of Christian eschatology, not on its central polarities in Christ. He illustrates this by showing the inconsistent ways terms were translated into Kikamba in the AIC hymns and catechisms.

But, second, there is an even more important implication of this more indigenous approach to eschatology: the rethinking that this stimulated about
the role of Christ. If ancestors are central to the community's mythmaking,
and if the integrity and health of the human community is the central preoccupation, then Christ's role as ancestor provides a way of deepening the
Christian understanding of both salvation and eschatology. Since we have
focused on Christ in an earlier chapter, we do not need to develop this in any
detail, but the role of Christ as key to understanding African eschatology
needs special emphasis. The Pauline teaching that Christ brings the age to
come into view is of course central to New Testament eschatology. But as
J. V. Taylor points out, for Africans the role of Christ as the second Adam,
the last and final ancestor, has such profound impact that it overshadows all
other aspects of the gospel. When Paul says in Romans that in Adam all die,
he communicates something many readers miss. But as Taylor points out,
Africans understand what it means to be "in the first ancestor." So when Paul
says that in Christ all shall be made alive, they can envision Christ as the first
ancestor "in order to reconstitute the whole organism upon himself as the
second Adam."[16] Taylor goes on: "Now in Christ the word is whispered that
God is inextricably involved in man. The whole family of mankind is his
creation and child." If this is so, then it is not hard for Africans to understand
the crucifixion and resurrection of Christ as eschatological events—indeed,
they might understand these in a way that Western thinkers cannot. Christ
embodies, Bako notes, "all the qualities and virtues that the African ascribes
to his or her ancestors."[17] So understanding Jesus as the "last ancestor and
sole mediator" takes on particular resonance. As the mediator of a better
covenant, Jesus fulfills and yet transcends the role ancestors play in connecting the people to both the past and the future. None of this appears to deal
with eschatology as it is understood in the West; but growing from pressing
existential questions, it addresses not only the future that Christ has brought
into view but also the deep-seated longings of African culture.

The Americas

We have considered one reason that eschatology as a theological issue seems
to be missing outside the West: the apparent inability of some indigenous
languages to speak about the future. This difficulty, we found, was more

16. Taylor, *Primal Vision*, 118. The following quotation is from p. 114.
17. Bako, "Eschatology in African Folk Religions," 150. See also p. 137 for what follows.
His argument here makes generous use of the work of Kwame Bediako.

apparent than real, for all references to the future, if they are to communicate anything at all, must be framed in terms of the present and the past, that is, in terms of the narrative a people tells about itself. For Africans (and indeed for some Asian cultures), relationship with ancestors provides such terms and opens a familiar narrative. Now we will present the eschatological case for the Americas.

In many places in Latin America, the daily challenge to survive in a context of violence and poverty makes it difficult to imagine a better future. How can a people who have suffered so much at the hands of foreign conquerors and who continue to experience grinding poverty imagine something better? Félix Palazzi, in his discussion of Jon Sobrino's theology, frames this difficulty in these terms: How does one understand any future, indeed any way of thinking about human dignity in the present, amid the daily struggle to survive? How do we announce any meaningful "irruption of eschatology" within the framework of *this* history?[18]

As Oscar has often reminded us in these pages, the theological difficulty here is to understand *this history*, one that is so foreign to most Western Christians, as a place where God is at work, as a *locus theologicus*. This may be especially difficult in Latin American discussions of eschatology. As Willie Jennings has pointed out, the ideology of conquest brought with it an implicit understanding of eschatology as the end of history. What the conquest brought to Latin America, he argues, was theorized as a new creation, a creation ex nihilo. Jennings summarizes the character of this project in Latin America as follows: "Detached from the land, oblivious to the ongoing decimation of native ecologies, deeply suspicious of native religious practices, and most important, enclosed within Iberian whiteness, the performance of Christian theology would produce a new, deformed, and deforming intellectual circuit."[19]

Unaware of their own dependency on indigenous (European) narratives, eschatology, for both Catholic and Protestant missionaries, was often portrayed in terms of a break with the past. But if God's project involves a break with the past, what do we make, theologically, of a present that presses in on us with such painful immediacy? What hope can we find in these circumstances? In a powerful description of the Christian understanding of hope, Salvadorean theologian Jon Sobrino puts forth one possible answer: announcing the presence of the reign of God in Jesus Christ.[20] But Sobrino insists the hope Christ brings is not a generalized hope for some utopia—like that of Plato or

---

18. Palazzi, "Hope and the Kingdom of God," in Pope, *Hope and Solidarity*, 131.
19. Jennings, *Christian Imagination*, 81–82.
20. Sobrino, *Fuera de los pobres*, 135–37.

Thomas More, which do not really exist. It is a specific hope that addresses the particular suffering of the poor. The liberation that Christ brings does not open up some ideal world "but is more modest, though more human and more necessary and urgent: that *a just and dignified life for the poor comes into being*, such that the very real cruelty and its suffering does not have the last word."[21] This hope arises from a particular experience of the biblical God who sees those who suffer, hears their cries, and through various historical events and signs loves and defends them. This gives believers strength to oppose all that Sobrino calls the "anti-kingdom."

Félix Palazzi sees this ability to oppose injustice as central to the understanding of eschatology in his Central American context.[22] Without eschatology, he notes, there is no force to transform the present. This impulse reflects both the exodus and the covenant God made with Israel, as well as the end of history revealed in Jesus Christ. For these are both ethical and eschatological realities. They are "eschatological because the ethical dynamism that such a social praxis generates tends toward its definitive realization and its ultimate consummation in the future of God." Again, this is not a general hope or the encouragement to do justice but a specific historical praxis that was revealed in the concrete life of Jesus. This leads Palazzi to propose that "history is related to eschatology as the historical Jesus is related to the resurrected Christ."[23] Though this resurrection life will only be fully realized at the end of history, it is already to be seen in Christ—God has already become part of history, *this* history. Hope then becomes a radical dynamic that allows the poor to struggle against the anti-kingdom with what Palazzi calls an eschatological praxis that leads to conversion. He concludes, "The salvific project of God has to be announced as what is good and positive in what is already present, though minimally, in history."[24]

Though framed in terms of the Catholic tradition of conversion and salvation, here is a constructive response to a particular setting that interprets God's eschatological project in Christ for Latin America, and specifically for the poor who struggle to survive in the underside of history. Earlier in the book cited above, Sobrino has some strong words to say about the inequalities that exist between the world of the poor and the West, and about the role of the United States in allowing this injustice. Here, above all, we need to heed the call for a transoccidentalism—a theological reflection that is freed from dependency on first-world power and influence. Sobrino calls on Americans to

21. Ibid., 137. Emphasis in the original.
22. Palazzi, "Hope and the Kingdom of God," 132–35. The quotation is from p. 133.
23. Ibid., 135.
24. Ibid., 140.

disentangle their eschatology from their sense of national "manifest destiny," "which justifies itself," Sobrino contends, "as an empire that feels sent to the world as a missionary of the wealth god (*divinidad-riqueza*) and expects to be thanked as a generous benefactor."[25] Such wielding of power, Sobrino thinks (citing Ignacio Ellacuría, one of the martyred Jesuits in El Salvador in 1989), does nothing to bring hope to the world—it more often brings fear.

Here is the reason eschatology, as it has been framed in the West, *appears* to be absent in Latin American theology: the discussion of eschatology that the situation in Latin America elicits is simply not audible to Western theologians, not because it comes from a foreign place or because it is spoken in a foreign language, but because the words it speaks are painful and difficult for us to hear. Much as my (Bill's) family had to come to terms not only with the situation of deep poverty we encountered in the Philippines during the 1970s but also with our collusion with the processes that brought about these excruciating injustices, we find Latin American discussions of eschatology challenging to our theological identity. Sobrino and others in Latin America are reminding us that this challenge is, in part at least, eschatological: What does Jesus's announcement of the presence of the kingdom mean for this ever-increasing inequality between the rich nations and the poor?

So Western theologians have not recognized a vibrant eschatology in Latin America. But similarly, for their part, Latino/a theologians have difficulty tuning into Western discussions of eschatology. As we have noted frequently, one of the main criticisms of Latinamericanist theologians against Western theology focused on the dichotomous language embedded in the conception of history and human redemption as recounted by traditional/classic theology. They did not recognize themselves in this narrative. The subject of human history and its redemption understood in a linear-progressive way belongs to the essence of Western eschatology. In the context of the Americas, this narrative was heard in terms of the logic not of progress but of a colonial civilizing mission and the subsequent "evangelization" that took place on the continent. Clearly, since the beginning of Christianity in the Americas, the West articulated a particular version of eschatology, the redemption of human history by means of the sharing of the gospel and the spreading of Panamericanism and the doctrine of development and modernization. Historically, politically, and economically, colonies appeared to exist to enable the flourishing of Europe and, later on, the United States. The popular imagination rarely had any

25. Sobrino, *Fuera de los pobres*, 30. "Queda justificado como imperio, se siente enviado al mundo como misionero de la divinidad-riqueza y piensa que se lo deben agradecer como generoso benefactor."

sense of its own history, and even when the political independence of the new republics of the Americas became a reality, the intellectual and ideological independence was delayed and, in some cases, never fully accomplished. On top of this, the Americas inherited the liberal-versus-conservative imaginary, leaving the vast evangelical public with little understanding of their own history and the history of the world. In such a setting, how could a biblical view of the future be developed?

Liberation theology emerged, in part, as a corrective to over-Westernized eschatologies based on two histories (transcendence/immanence), but even this did not fully delink itself from the European view of history as progress. After the fruitful times of the 1960s and 1970s, however—with the Latin American literary flowering and the appearance of more fully developed Latin American Liberation theologies—one thing became clear for Latino/a eschatology: the utopian biblical imagination of the continent would avoid mimicking Western linear thinking.

In Western eschatology the categories "time" and "history" are future and linear; they constitute the main framework by which the West has come to develop its doctrine of human progress. Meanwhile, communities in the majority world (and the diaspora) think and live eschatologically and sacramentally based on a hope that focuses on the present and aims at the flourishing of the community. The eschatological sense of community subsumes both ancestry and progeny; hence, human flourishing implies recovering the dignity of ancestors and caring for the well-being of their families. Hope implies a future but not in the deterministic and progressive way the West has come to understand it. The pioneering work of Justo González, *Mañana: Christian Theology from a Hispanic Perspective*, can serve as an illustration. *Mañana*, which translates into English as "tomorrow," is an eschatological notion developed from the perspective of life in the Holy Spirit.[26] Interestingly, González develops this understanding as he exegetes what it means to be spiritual in the Pauline sense. He resists the dichotomy of "spirit and matter," which has traditionally fueled the two-history view in the Western imagination. He finds that Paul's understanding of "being spiritual" does not result in an antithesis to "matter" but to the "old nature." Consequently, being spiritual has to do with having a new life and experiencing the power of the Spirit, who "intervenes to make things become what they are not."[27]

---

26. For an eschatological utilization of González's concept of *mañana*, see Pedraja, *Teología*, 187, and Escobar, *Changing Tides*, 147.

27. González, *Mañana*, 160.

In my (Oscar's) work *The Mestizo/a Community of the Spirit*, I elaborate three ways to understand eschatology from a US Latino/a context based on González's concept of *Mañana*.[28] I begin by acknowledging that the mestizo/a body of Christ (Latino/a church) is a product of paradoxes and ambiguities. On the one hand, the mestizo/a body of Christ is a hub of mixing with the oppressor and cohabitating with the exploiter, while on the other hand, it is a place of self-discovery. This means being enriched by the fluidity of other cultural identities and encountering a common intersection for surviving, hoping, and believing in the possibility of a better future. The practice of everyday life (*cotidiano*) in such a chaotic borderline existence, I argue, is only possible under the *aleteo del Espíritu* ("fluttering of the Spirit"). *Mañana* is essentially an eschatological understanding of the church based on the Spirit of Christ in historical perspective. *Mañana* is the story of the mestizo/a community of Christ moving toward God's promised future in today's challenging context by the *aleteo del Espíritu*. In the first place, *mañana* is radical living based on "a radical hope that the future will be transformed to bring justice, liberation, and life."[29] Here the Christian imagination—*mañana* thought—shows creativity and theological utopism, for, as González puts it, *mañana* means "radical questioning of the present by the future as envisioned by God." In the second place, *mañana* based on radical hope is communicated in the vernacular as a celebration of life—*mañana* talk. The concept of resurrection is ubiquitous in the language of the people. There is a sense among Latinos/as that *siempre hay un mañana* ("there is always a tomorrow"). In the third place, *mañana* should not be understood as laziness or irresponsibility, for, González argues, *mañana* "is much more than tomorrow."[30] The Latino theologian Luis Pedraja builds on González's *mañana* eschatology and brings about a Spanish adage to illustrate a *mañana* "walk": *Que será, será* ("Whatever will be, will be").[31] Pedraja suggests that this popular Spanish phrase "is a statement of faith" rather than a fatalistic or procrastinating attitude of the Latino/a people. In other words, *Que será, será* acknowledges the Spirit as a source of possibility and creativity, of faith and hope. In this regard, Pedraja proposes, "*Que será, será* might serve theology as an eschatological maxim, calling us to trust God with the future and work to make the reign of God a reality in the present."[32]

Here is a constructive Latin American take on an eschatology that is both rooted in the context of its unique history and conversant with the best of

---

28. García-Johnson, *Mestizo/a Community of the Spirit*, 120–25.
29. Pedraja, *Teología*, 188.
30. González, *Mañana*, 164.
31. Pedraja, *Teología*, 201.
32. Ibid., 202.

Western theology. But there is a further constructive aspect to a majority-world perspective on eschatology that needs to be noted and developed—indeed developed much more than we will be able to do here. The situation of underdevelopment in Latin America, and indeed in Africa and parts of Asia, raises questions that theologians in these places have interpreted in eschatological terms. We have seen already that Latin American theologians want to apply the Christian hope to the ethical dynamic that challenges idols of the anti-kingdom—what Palazzi calls "historical eschatology," which brings about a struggle against injustice and a "resurrection of the suffering innocent."[33]

This way of framing the Christian response to the good news of the gospel offers the possibility of reflecting on community development and work among the poor in fresh ways. Here may be an additional reason that "eschatology" as it is known in the West often appears absent in non-Western theology. Their preoccupation is with what Jesse Mugambi, a Kenyan theologian, calls "social reconstruction."[34] Mugambi argues that African theology has been overly preoccupied with theological anthropology—something that our earlier discussion in this chapter illustrates. He calls for African theologians to move beyond this to understand the liberation that Christ brings in terms of a new theological paradigm, namely, social reconstruction. Liberation was useful as long as foreign powers held sway, but now that Africans control their own destiny, Mugambi argues that the paradigm of social reconstruction should replace that of liberation. This means that the leadership of church councils as well as government agencies needs to understand its role in practical terms—that is, the realization of the transformation that the gospel embodies in communities. The model will no longer be one of Moses leading his people out of Egypt but of Nehemiah seeking to rebuild the walls of Jerusalem.[35]

While Western readers may not recognize this process as eschatological, for an African theologian like Mugambi, this process of social transformation is what eschatology must mean for Africa today if it will have any meaning at all. This is why a critical component of his reconstruction is theological: it moves away from a theology that spiritualizes the human condition to one that engages with this in the holistic terms the gospel provides. Such reconstruction, he thinks, may be the "springboard for revitalization of African political and social life."[36]

33. Palazzi, "Hope and the Kingdom of God," 139.
34. Mugambi, *Christian Theology and Social Reconstruction.*
35. Ibid., 58–59.
36. Ibid., 37.

Daniel Groody has sought to put this in the perspective of global spirituality.[37] He sums up the Catholic social teaching that supports this as following the God of life, a praxis that provides both an ethical and theological foundation for global transformation. His summary of the aspects of this teaching includes the analysis of social reality that realizes the gratuity of God (that all is a gift), orders society toward the common good, affirms the dignity of the human person, exercises the preferential option for the poor, and involves all people in the creation of a new social order.[38] Earlier, Groody had cited Ignacio Ellacuría's insistence that this process must be grounded in the historical reality of the poor. For among the poor, Ellacuría believed, one finds more theological density. There you will find not only the suffering and pain of people but also the God of life. Because of this, one might see in these places the reality of the gospel in a way invisible elsewhere.[39]

Together these comments suggest that what is called "community development" in the West has deep eschatological relevance. Justo González has called the church a "*mañana* people"—a future-oriented community.[40] The ability to question prevailing norms and seek a new order, he notes, is the driving force of political and social action. Seeking justice and opposing the idols of the anti-kingdom is eschatological work, even if this is not immediately apparent to outside observers. And it is work in which God is already engaged in the communities of the poor. The call of the gospel, so these theologians claim, is to join God there and engage in work that both illustrates and embodies an eschatological vision.

Some Eschatological Voices in Asia

We turn now to briefly consider eschatology in an Asian context. This sprawling continent, where most of the world's people reside and where Christianity is mostly a minority religion, resists any theological generalization. But it is safe to say one major challenge to Christianity is embodied in the encounter with long-standing and deeply entrenched religious traditions—Buddhism, Hinduism, Confucianism, and Islam. Aside from Islam, all these traditions see reality as an interdependent whole (monism). One might frame this fundamental challenge for Christian theology as follows: How can one understand this cosmic unity in the light of the gospel? In one sense, of course, the idea

37. Groody, *Globalization, Spirituality, and Justice.*
38. Ibid., 100–115.
39. Ibid., 25.
40. González, *Mañana*, 164.

of a personal God who creates and sustains the world disrupts the notion of a single reality. As Kosuke Koyama has argued, the idea of God entering history has shaken the Asian worldview at its very foundations. He writes, "History has never been so profoundly penetrated and enlightened because of God's respectful approach to history."[41] It is respectful, Koyama thinks, because God did not enter history to "handle it" but to inquire of the human creature, "Where are you?" So it was disruptive in its very gentleness in Christ, the true light lighting everyone (John 1:9).

One might characterize the conversations about eschatology in Asia as the struggle to define this disruption: Is it a radical break, as it often was in Latin America, or does it rather, as Koyama implies, penetrate to the foundation of the order of things? To place this in terms of transoccidentalism, must the introduction of the gospel imply imposing a foreign (i.e., Western) worldview, or might it mean allowing the leaven of the gospel and the presence of a personal and living God to permeate (and thus transform) the existing view?

There is no question that the usual introduction of eschatology into Asia, at least among evangelical Protestants, implied a radical break with the past, a kind of ending of history as we know it. Among many of the first wave of evangelical missionaries—before the war in Korea and China, and afterward in Southeast Asia—an expectation of the immanent return of Christ was foundational to Christian spirituality. And this was also true for the Pentecostal missionaries who made up an increasingly large portion of Western missionaries.[42] Indeed, many of the early missionaries were products, directly or indirectly, of the deeper life movement and the Pentecostal revivals. These revivals were mostly sparked, Wonsuk Ma claims, by the proposition that Jesus is coming soon. Most evangelical missionaries shared a premillennial orientation and the resulting eschatological urgency that it was necessary to reach a lost world before Christ's return and the judgment that would follow.

Interesting here is the virtual identification of eschatology with the return of Christ and the events surrounding this not only as a centerpiece of their spirituality but as a motivation to mission, which has been the case among evangelicals in many parts of the world. But it is not hard to see that this focus on a horizontal reading of history sits uneasily alongside the monistic and integrated understanding of reality that is so pervasive in Asia. Perhaps this is one reason that the urgency about Christ's return slowly but steadily disappeared in places like the Philippines and was replaced by a concern for

---

41. Koyama, *No Handle on the Cross*, 13.
42. On these developments, see Ma, "Pentecostal Eschatology," 95–112.

life in this world, for miracles in the here and now, and even for social and environmental issues.[43]

But the question we have raised lingers in the mind: How might the invasion of the "end" (or the telos) of history in Jesus Christ be framed in such a way that it addresses fundamental concerns arising in this vast continent? Can irruption be seen rather as a penetration? This is the approach that Simon Chan takes in his recent work on grassroots theology in Asia.[44] Interestingly, he sees the key to a viable eschatology in Asia to be a fresh reflection on ancestor veneration (AV), which is pervasive. Chan thinks the "failure to address AV in a satisfactory manner has been a major hindrance to the acceptance of Christianity in Asia" (72). Pentecostal theology, he thinks, has partially addressed this concern by its focus on Jesus as healer, which can imply a healing not only of physical ailments but also of relationships. It can even include what Chan calls "cosmic healing" (108). But the more promising approach, he thinks, is through a reconsideration of the classic Christian understanding of the communion of the saints (*communio sanctorum*). Traditionally this has involved a belief in the unity and communion of God's people, living and dead, as this is made possible by their incorporation into the body of Christ— a belief that Protestants have often resisted for various reasons. Chan argues that this notion of communion not only is central to Christian eschatology but also potentially connects in vital ways to the Asian understanding of AV. In classic Christian teaching, Chan notes, "full communion is an embodied communion that is consummated at the final resurrection of the body" as this is symbolized by the marriage supper of the Lamb or a eucharistic meal (189). Chan thinks AV anticipates this Christian teaching by positing a communion of persons that transcends space and time. Why cannot Christian thinking about communion in the body of Christ extend not only diachronically over time but synchronically into the deep structure of the human community?

Note how this construal of a fundamental doctrine of Christianity is being rethought in the light of this very different cultural context. The focus on diachronic eschatology of course fits well with the linear sense of time that is widespread in the West, and it does comprehend important aspects of the biblical teaching of end-time events. But why not consider eschatology in its depth dimension so as to address the deep-seated concern for family solidarity that prevails in Asia? Chan notes that Paul in Colossians 1:20 implies that "Christ who reconciles all things in heaven and on earth is the foundation of

---

43. This is the argument of Ma in ibid., 100–104. He argues that the need is to recover a "healthy eschatology with the Pentecostal theology of empowerment" to equip Pentecostals to be a significant missionary force in the coming decades (110).

44. Chan, *Grassroots Asian Theology*. Page numbers in the text refer to this work.

communion between saints on earth and in heaven" (133). Why not rethink this in the light of AV?

The question of AV is not an abstract issue for many Christians in Asia but a living and often painful concern. And the Christian emphasis on "irruption" and breaking with traditional structures has sometimes alienated Christians across Asia from their families and larger communities. Chan's discussion is a pioneering and hopeful sign that reflection sparked by this unique cultural challenge may issue in fresh theological reflection on the relation between the living and the dead and the ongoing communion that might exist.[45] Chan describes the way indigenous Christian movements in Japan, for example, have actually introduced services in which pictures of deceased family members are brought forward and placed on the Communion table while living family members receive Communion on behalf of these deceased members. Though controversial for many, such practices may spur more traditional churches to reconsider the biblical reasons for their current customs.

Notice that the process occurring replicates what we have seen in other settings. The responsibility to take seriously the facts on the ground, the assumptions and traditions that animate a community, has not simply ushered in a rethinking of Christian practice but also initiated reflection on biblical teaching that explores new interpretations. The process has meant we have learned something about what God is doing that we did not know before. As always in Christian history, the process of mutual listening and rereading of Scripture has taken Christians some steps further along in the process of their growing up into Christ in all things (Eph. 4:15–16).

Conclusion

Obviously there are large parts of the teaching of eschatology that we have not touched on in this chapter—for instance, the reign of Christ on earth ("the millennium"), the scope of the resurrection, the nature of the new creation that God will bring from heaven, the last judgment, and the final state of both the righteous and the wicked. Our purpose has not been to survey all these areas but to show how the very different settings in which the gospel has been received have reflected on biblical teaching about the end and goal of history.

But one thing has become clear in this brief sampling of eschatological reflection: each cultural setting offers both limitations and possibilities with respect

45. Chan's discussion is especially helpful in describing in some detail the ongoing conversations between Protestants and Catholics on these issues and the rapprochement and mutual learning that is resulting.

to comprehending the earth-shattering events associated with God's entrance into human history and how that will one day be fully realized when God will be all in all. First, consider the limitations that human cultures erect to a clear understanding of God's purposes. We have noted the limitation (otherness) of language and cultural expectation that exists in Africa, where it is simply not possible for Africans to conceive of or even verbalize some of the teaching that Scripture contains about the future. We have seen that in many places of the world, the limitations and strictures posed by poverty, lack of education, or access to medical facilities challenge traditional Western ways of thinking about the end. How might God's future be framed amid the daily struggle to survive? Is such a prospect escapist or, worse, simply irrelevant to the challenges life offers? And what about the challenges offered by monistic philosophical frameworks that see all of life as an interdependent and evolving unity? How can God's entrance into human history be framed in such a setting? And this does not even begin to address the challenges provided by the secularism and materialism in which Western Christians seek to understand God.

All of these limitations speak of a common human problem: as finite and sinful humans, we simply cannot imagine on our own what God has in mind for the world. Indeed, we cannot work out why God has created the world in the first place. This of course is not a new problem. When it came to understanding Christ's life and work in the first century, the Greeks found the idea of eternity invading time to be simple nonsense; the Jews found the appearance of God in human form to be a stumbling block. So Paul concluded, in words relevant in fresh ways today, "Since, in the wisdom of God, the world did not know God through wisdom, God decided, through the foolishness of our proclamation [of the gospel], to save those who believe" (1 Cor. 1:21).

Eschatology, in a fundamental sense, involves otherness, the ability to imagine the world in ways that no human culture on its own can conceive. This is why the most important qualification we can bring to interpreting the images of Scripture is a fresh, Spirit-filled imagination. As both Jürgen Moltmann and Jon Sobrino have reminded us in this chapter, it is the unique role of Christian hope to nourish this new imagination about the future. The images and stories of Revelation, for example, are not meant to be decoded like a map of buried treasure but experienced by a new imagination that the Spirit makes possible. It gives us the ability to look out on the world with fresh eyes. For, Paul reminds us, "'what no eye has seen, nor ear heard, nor the human heart conceived, what God has prepared for those who love him'—these things God has revealed to us through the Spirit" (1 Cor. 2:9–10).

This is why, when Jesus stood with Mary and Martha at the tomb of Lazarus, he did not just announce that he was the resurrection and the life and that those believing in him would never die. He went on to pointedly ask them—and us!—"Do you believe this?" That is, can you imagine this? Can you imagine a world in which resurrection, not death, has the last word?

But we should not leave things here. For the multiple cultures of the world do not only offer obstacles to our understanding; they also provide windows—new possibilities for thinking about biblical teaching. This is because the relationships and practices they treasure all reflect something of the manifold goodness and abundance that God has placed in the created order. What these people have made of creation, though often marred by sin, has also produced wonders that bring additional glory to God. So it is not surprising that reflection on ancestors, poverty and development, or the interrelationship of all things should provide windows through which we can see something new about God's truth. For this reason it can all be critically engaged, as Paul tells Timothy, with thanksgiving to God, disciplined by the Word of God and by prayer (1 Tim. 4:5), so that it might all be used to sharpen our communal Christian imagination to hear and see what John calls to our attention.

> "See, the home of God is among mortals.
> He will dwell with them;
> they will be his peoples,
> and God himself will be with them;
> he will wipe every tear from their eyes.
> Death will be no more;
> mourning and crying and pain will be no more,
> for the first things have passed away."

And the one who was seated on the throne said, "See, I am making all things news." (Rev. 21:3–5)

Appendix

The Historical Traditions of the Church

The Early Church and the Formation of Eastern Orthodoxy

According to Acts 2, the Christian church from the very beginning had to deal with people from "every nation under heaven" (2:5). At the start, however, these were all devout Jews. So the church started its life by the Holy Spirit being poured out on faithful Jewish believers from many places in the world. Soon, however, the apostles realized that God intended this good news to be for gentiles as well as Jews, and they set about determining how Christ and the gospel could be described in this new, expanded setting. The first letter of Paul to the Corinthians, for example, can be understood as an initial attempt to explain what faith in Christ might mean for a gentile audience. As Andrew Walls points out, the most urgent problems were not doctrinal but practical—how do I behave as a Christian in this or that situation?[1] Newly minted gentile Christians first needed to know whether, for example, it was right to accept an invitation to dinner when the menu included meat offered to idols. And it was in the context of questions like this—what should I *do?*—that Paul explained the new wisdom represented by Christ's life and death—thus helping them know how they should *think* about these things in the light of Christ. Inevitably, then, it was the Greco-Roman culture and its philosophical and cultural heritage that became the setting in which Christianity first took shape.

1. Walls, "Rise of Global Theologies," in Greenman and Green, *Global Theology in Evangelical Perspective*, 22–26.

Consider the great christological conversations in the third and fourth centuries. To be sure, there were influences from Syriac and North African cultures on all these early conversations. Athanasius, perhaps because he was a bishop from Alexandria (in Egypt), understood the accents of Eastern thought and, later, those of British Christians. He was thus able to lead Western theologians in defining the nature of Christ and the Trinity in ways that both responded to these influences and held as closely as possible to biblical language. Clearly, the Nicene Creed (AD 325/381) was a product of decades of reflection and conversation from many parts of the church, but it was the Western church, as it was then constituted, that came together to develop the definitive christological and trinitarian formulas. Similarly, practices that emerged during these early centuries determined what books would become part of the canon of the New Testament.

More to the point, it was these early conversations that began to coalesce in the sixth and seventh centuries into what came to be known as the Orthodox tradition of theology—also known as Eastern Orthodoxy—which gradually distinguished itself from the Western church (even though geographically both entities arose in Western Europe and Asia Minor). This tradition lays a strong claim to reflecting the original heritage of the Christian church, basing its theology entirely on the first seven ecumenical councils—from the First Council of Nicaea (325) to the Second Council of Nicaea (787). Although there were growing differences and some tensions between the Western and Eastern branches of the church, especially over the role of images and relics, the final split took place in 1054. Orthodox believers see this split and the sixteenth-century Protestant Reformation as unfortunate tears in the fabric of what was the original—and, to their minds, the best-preserved—form of the church represented by the early councils.

This tradition has figured less prominently in the global spread of Christianity than others we explore, but in some places, notably in Africa, it represents an important and long-term presence—for example, the Egyptian and Ethiopian Coptic Churches. Though rooted in all the earliest councils, Orthodoxy finds its definitive theological expression in the Second Council of Nicaea led by John of Damascus. Here in particular, icons—two-dimensional images of saints as well as of Mary and Christ—were affirmed as expressive of the reality of Christ's incarnation in human form. Their continued role (and presence) in the liturgy was also affirmed.

Based on the theological insights of the second-century theologian Irenaeus, Orthodoxy focuses on the way the Christian life, and the liturgy in particular, recapitulates the life of the first Adam as this has been renewed by Christ, the second Adam. In the fourth century, Athanasius argued famously that Christ became human so that we, through our life of prayer and devotion, might become like God. This life of prayer is central for Orthodox theology, and it is embodied specifically in the liturgy, where believers are progressively formed into the likeness of Christ. In all important respects Orthodox theology is a liturgical theology. It finds it highest expression in the liturgy's richly developed images and practices, which are to form and shape not only the believer but also the very life of the world, as Alexander Schmemann explains in his book *For the Life of the World*.[2]

The Medieval Church and the Roman Catholic Tradition

After the patristic period of the church, the next important period of theological development was the High Middle Ages. During the period from 1100 to 1300, theologians like Bernard of Clairvaux, Anselm of Canterbury, and Thomas Aquinas developed fresh understandings of the Christian faith. These thinkers clearly responded to the philosophical and cultural concerns of their day, but the results were so substantial that they continue to influence Western theology to this day. More important, they provided foundational understandings of a tradition that came to be known as Roman Catholicism. Like its Orthodox sibling, the Roman Catholic Church was also founded on the classical heritage of Greco-Roman culture and philosophy, which not only is foundational for Catholic theological reflection but also conditions its appeals to Scripture—Catholics are drawn to see their liturgy, for example, as rooted in Old Testament worship.

Despite this common heritage with Orthodoxy, particular theological emphases and liturgical practices developed during the high medieval period that not only became characteristic of the Roman Church but also continue to influence Christianity in all its forms. Indeed, whether Protestants admit it or not, in many ways the theology of the great medieval thinkers, from Augustine to Aquinas, has come to define the Christian faith much more fundamentally than the Orthodox tradition has.

The Roman Catholic tradition has placed great emphasis on what it calls the *theologia perennis*, a common understanding of the faith grounded in the teaching office of the magisterium—the teaching of the popes and bishops— that is believed to be unchanging. After Vatican II (1961–65), however, the Catholic Church has aggressively attempted to contextualize its preaching and teaching as it has spread into the diverse cultures of the world.

2. Schmemann, *For the Life of the World*.

Throughout the church's history, certain teachings have become central to Catholic teaching. Primary among these is the conviction that the Catholic Church expresses the continuing reality of the incarnation of Christ. The church, as Karl Rahner has put it, is the fundamental sacrament.[3] It embodies not simply the apostolic teaching of the truth of Scripture but also the very real presence of Christ in the world, and it represents the divinely authorized mediation of this through the sacraments. For the Catholic Church, then, the continuing work of God in the world is represented in and by the church, though the reality of the incarnation also means this "presence" can be glimpsed in the larger culture as well—providing Catholics with what Andrew Greeley has called a "sacramental imagination."[4]

The church is constituted by the priests, bishops, and pope, who along with baptized believers make up what Vatican II called the "pilgrim people of God." The sacrament of ordination by the bishop expresses and continues the apostolic tradition that is rooted in Christ's earthly ministry. For Catholics, this apostolic authority means that God continues to speak in and through the church. The Scriptures of course play a central role in the thinking and teaching of the church (again, especially since Vatican II), but this teaching must be consistent with the magisterium. This leads Catholic scholars to frequently quote papal encyclicals alongside their references to Scripture and other theologians.

Just as the Catholic Church mediates the correct understanding of Scripture, it also mediates salvation in a way that is unique to this tradition. Salvation is tied to the church and the authorized apostolic ministration of the sacraments. This apostolic ministry mediates the saving grace that has been made available to the world in Jesus Christ. Though claiming an unchanging nature, the Catholic tradition has in fact experienced periods of renewal in the mendicant movements and the mystics of the medieval period to the Counter-Reformation of the sixteenth century (which sought to respond to the corruption that led to the Protestant Reformation), right up to the renewal sparked by Vatican II in the last century. Because of its long historical heritage and its rich theological and liturgical resources, the Catholic Church continues to exert a wide-ranging and truly global influence.

The Reformation and the Reformed (and Evangelical) Tradition

Equally important for theological reflection today are the developments represented by the Reformation of the sixteenth century. It is not possible to

3. Rahner, *The Church and the Sacraments.*
4. Greeley, *The Catholic Imagination.*

understand contemporary forms of Christianity, even those emerging around the world, apart from the events of that century. Especially in theology, which is our primary concern, the recovery of biblical notions of justification and grace by Luther and Calvin have been critical to theological developments since then—for all Christians and not just for Protestants. Resisting the domination of the pope and bishops and their misreading of Scripture in the medieval period, Luther and Calvin called the church back to the centrality of the gospel message. And as careful students of the patristic and medieval theologians, they were able to recover the evangelical notes in these earlier theologies as well.

This tradition has exerted a dominant influence on all subsequent Protestant traditions. Luther might be said to have founded an alternative tradition to this, but this has had less influence on the development of evangelical theology and on its missionary presence around the world. (Even in Lutheran-dominated areas of Europe, one can see a much more Reformed imagination at work than Luther himself would have liked.) Some form of Reformed thought has been the dominant influence on the missionary movement, which, insofar as it has displayed a theological grounding at all, may be loosely termed "Calvinist."

Characteristic of this tradition is a strong sense of God's sovereignty in life and faith. Often this led to a recognition that God must draw people to faith (election) and a related confidence in creation and the structures of government and society to order this. In its more evangelical form, this tradition has placed a strong emphasis on the need for a personal faith in Christ as the means of salvation, which was derived from the Reformation watchwords *solus Christus* and *sola fide*—"Christ alone" and "by faith alone." In the American context, evangelicals have developed this emphasis on personal faith under the influence of the Pietist movement in Europe and later the American revivals of the eighteenth and nineteenth centuries.

Finally, the Reformed and evangelical tradition has placed a strong emphasis on the authority of Scripture for faith and life. In the more conservative forms of the tradition, Scripture takes on a regulative authority not only for living the Christian life but for the development of worship forms as well—the regulative principle of worship, which holds that Scripture expressly commands all that believers do in their worship life together.

Radical Reformation and the Anabaptist Tradition

During the sixteenth century, there were those who thought the major Reformers did not go far enough in purifying the church and returning it to the

New Testament model. Menno Simons and Michael Sattler forged a more radical reformation that was continued in what came to be known as the "peace churches," especially the Mennonites and Moravians. Their emphasis was on a gathered church rather than one allied with the dominant political powers, as the major Reformers stipulated. The true church, they believed, was not simply those baptized in a parish but those whose lives and witness gave evidence of being transformed. These were often "rebaptized" as adults, thus giving rise to their name "ana-baptists" (those baptized again).

This tradition has had a strong missionary presence throughout the world. Anabaptists developed a strong sense of living their faith over against the official powers of the state, which enforces its power by the sword (that is, by violence). Thus Anabaptists famously refuse military or political service as an expression of their commitment to peace. This faith is nurtured by a strong sense that the Christian life means following Jesus in one's everyday life, especially in the sense of taking the way of the cross. Their sense of a costly discipleship often led Anabaptists to form alliances with various forms of evangelicalism for whom personal faith and discipleship were similarly important. Finally, this tradition has a strong emphasis on the community of believers, a people gathered out of the world and engaging in a countercultural witness. They share with other Reformation groups a strong sense of the authority of Scripture, and they are drawn most centrally to the teachings of Christ.

The Modern Pentecostal Tradition

The newest theological tradition, and arguably the most widely influential in the non-Western world, is the Pentecostal tradition. Influenced by and continuing the holiness tradition of John Wesley and nurtured by indigenous spiritualities, this movement has its historical origin in the early twentieth-century revivals in America and Europe. This tradition is characterized by a strong emphasis on the immediate working of the Holy Spirit. Its worship thus emphasizes various gifts of the Spirit—prophesying, speaking in tongues, and ministries of healing—giving it a lively and dynamic character. The focus on the gifts of the Spirit, often experienced through what is called the "baptism in the Holy Spirit," has often provided its members with a strong sense of personal empowerment. This has often led even poor congregations to have a lively expectation of God's intervention on their behalf. This expectancy and the resulting empowerment of individuals has given the movement a social impact often out of proportion to its numbers, and it has sometimes led to an overemphasis on God's promises of prosperity. This has led to the spread of the "health and wealth gospel" in many places of Africa and Latin America. The Pentecostal tradition sees its rise as a reconstitution of the earth-shaking events recorded in the book of Acts, and members often refer to this book in their worship and devotional life.

Bibliography

Alves, Rubem. "Apuntes para un programa de reconstrucción en la teología." *Cristianismo y sociedad* 7, no. 2 (1969).

Amaya Amador, Ramón. *Prisión verde*. Tegucigalpa: Universidad Nacional Autónoma de Honduras, 1988.

Anderson, Allan H. "Types and Butterflies: African Initiated Churches and European Typologies." *International Bulletin of Missionary Research* 25, no. 3 (2001): 107–13.

Arreola, Daniel D. *Hispanic Spaces, Latino Places: Community and Cultural Diversity in Contemporary America*. Austin: University of Texas Press, 2004.

Asad, Talal. *Genealogies of Religion: Discipline and Reasons of Power in Christianity and Islam*. Baltimore: Johns Hopkins University Press, 1993.

Augustine. *On Christian Teaching*. Translated by R. P. H. Green. Oxford World's Classics. Oxford: Oxford University Press, 1999.

Bako, Ngarndeye. "Eschatology in African Folk Religions." ThD diss., University of South Africa, 2009.

Balcomb, Anthony. "African Evangelical Theology." In *Global Dictionary of Theology: A Resource for the Worldwide Church*, edited by W. Dyrness and V. M. Kärkkäinen. Downers Grove, IL: IVP Academic, 2008.

———. "El encuentro de cosmovisiones: Premoderna, moderna y posmoderna." *Vida y pensamiento* 28, no. 1 (2008): 7–28.

Barrett, David B. *Schism and Renewal in Africa: An Analysis of Six Thousand Contemporary Religious Movements*. Nairobi: Oxford University Press, 1968.

Barrett, Justin L. *Cognitive Science, Religion, and Theology: From Human Minds to Divine Minds.* West Conshohocken, PA: Templeton Press, 2011.

Barth, Karl. *Church Dogmatics* III/1. Translated by G. W. Bromiley and T. F. Torrance. Edinburgh: T&T Clark, 1958.

―――. *Dogmatics in Outline.* New York: Harper & Brothers, 1959.

―――. *Evangelical Theology: An Introduction.* Grand Rapids: Eerdmans, 1979.

Bauckham, Richard. *The Theology of the Book of Revelation.* Cambridge: Cambridge University Press, 1993.

Bediako, Kwame. "Africa and Christian Identity: Recovering an Ancient Story." *Princeton Seminary Bulletin* 25 (2004): 153–61.

―――. *Christianity in Africa: The Renewal of a Non-Western Religion.* Edinburgh: Edinburgh University Press, 1995.

―――. "Identity and integration : An Enquiry into the Nature and Problems of Theological Indigenization in Selected Early Hellenistic and Modern African Christian Writers." PhD diss., University of Aberdeen, 1983.

―――. *Theology and Identity: The Impact of Culture upon Christian Thought in the Second Century and in Modern Africa.* Oxford: Regnum, 1992.

Beltran, Benigno P. *The Christology of the Inarticulate: An Inquiry into the Filipino Understanding of Jesus the Christ.* Manila: Divine Word, 1987.

Bhabha, Homi K. *Nuevas minorías, nuevos derechos: Notas sobre los cosmopolitismos vernáculos.* Translated by Hugo Salas. Buenos Aires: Siglo Veintiuno Editores, 2013.

Bilson, Thomas. *The True Difference betweene Christian Subjection and Unchristian Rebellion.* Oxford: Joseph Barnes, 1585.

Bloxham, Donald. *The Final Solution: A Genocide.* Oxford: Oxford University Press, 2012.

Bockmuehl, Markus. *Seeing the Word: Refocusing New Testament Study.* Grand Rapids: Baker Academic, 2006.

Boer, Roland, and Fernando F. Segovia. *The Future of the Biblical Past: Envisioning Biblical Studies in a Global Key.* Atlanta: Society of Biblical Literature, 2012.

Boerma, Conrad. *The Rich, the Poor—and the Bible.* Philadelphia: Westminster, 1979.

Boff, Leonardo. *Holy Trinity, Perfect Community.* Maryknoll, NY: Orbis, 2000.

―――. *Jesus Christ Liberator: A Critical Christology for Our Time.* 9th ed. Maryknoll, NY: Orbis, 1994.

———. *La cruz nuestra de cada día: Manantial de vida y resurrección*. Translated by Bernardo Guízas. Mexico City: Dabar, 2004.

Borthwick, Paul. *Western Christians in Global Mission: What's the Role of the North American Church?* Downers Grove, IL: InterVarsity, 2012.

Branson, Mark Lau, and René C. Padilla. *Conflict and Context: Hermeneutics in the Americas*. Grand Rapids: Eerdmans, 1986.

Brown, Peter. "Recovering Submerged Worlds." *New York Review of Books*. July 11, 2013, http://www.nybooks.com/articles/archives/2013/jul/11/re covering-submerged-worlds/.

———. *Through the Eye of a Needle: Wealth, the Fall of Rome, and the Making of Christianity in the West, 350–550 AD*. Princeton: Princeton University Press, 2012.

Bujo, Bénézet. *African Theology in Its Social Context*. Maryknoll, NY: Orbis, 1992.

Burkhart, Louise M. "The Cult of the Virgin of Guadalupe in Mexico." In *South and Meso-American Native Spirituality: From the Cult of the Feathered Serpent to the Theology of Liberation*, edited by Gary H. Gossen and Miguel León Portilla. New York: Crossroad, 1993.

Callanta, Ruth S. "A Transformational Strategy: Toward Filling the Hungry with Good Things." In *The Church and Poverty in Asia*, edited by Lee Wanak and Bina Agong. Mandaluyong City: OMF, 2008.

Calvin, John. *Institutes of the Christian Religion*. Edited by John T. McNeill. Translated by Ford Lewis Battles. Library of Christian Classics. Philadelphia: Westminster, 1960.

Casalis, Georges. "Jesús: ni vencido ni monarca celestial." In *Jesús: ni vencido ni monarca celestial*, edited by José Míguez Bonino. Buenos Aires: Tierra Nueva, 1977.

Castells, Manuel. *The Information Age: Economy, Society, and Culture*. Malden, MA: Wiley-Blackwell, 2010.

———. *The Power of Identity*. Malden, MA: Blackwell, 1997.

Castro-Gómez, Santiago, and Eduardo Mendieta, eds. *Teorías sin disciplina: Latinoamericanismo, poscolonialidad y globalización en debate*. Mexico City: Miguel Ángel Porrúa, 1998.

Chambers, Robert. *Rural Development: Putting the Last First*. London: Longman, 1984.

Chan, Simon. *Grassroots Asian Theology: Thinking the Faith from the Ground Up*. Downers Grove, IL: IVP Academic, 2014.

Chia, Roland. "Eschatology." In *Global Dictionary of Theology: A Resource for the Worldwide Church*, edited by William A. Dyrness and Veli-Matti Kärkkäinen. Downers Grove, IL: IVP Academic, 2008.

Columbus, Christopher. *Los cuatro viajes: Testamento el libro de bolsillo*. Translated by Consuelo Varela. Madrid: Alianza, 1986.

Coote, Robert T., and John R. W. Stott. *Down to Earth: Studies in Christianity and Culture*. Grand Rapids: Eerdmans, 1980.

Cox, Harvey. *The Future of Faith*. New York: HarperOne, 2009.

Davey, Andrew. *Urban Christianity and Global Order: Theological Resources for an Urban Future*. Peabody, MA: Hendrickson, 2002.

De Acosta, José, Jane E. Mangan, Walter Mignolo, and Frances M. López-Morillas. *Natural and Moral History of the Indies*. Durham, NC: Duke University Press, 2002.

Díaz del Castillo, Bernal, Genaro García, and Alfred Percival Maudslay. *The True History of the Conquest of New Spain*. London: Hakluyt Society, 1910.

Dickson, Kwesi A. *Theology in Africa*. London: Darton, Longman and Todd, 1984.

Duerksen, Darren. *Ecclesial Identities in a Multi-Faith Context: Jesus Truth-Gatherings (Yeshu Satsangs) among Hindus and Sikhs in Northwest India*. Eugene, OR: Pickwick, forthcoming.

Duffy, Eamon. *Saints, Sacrilege and Sedition: Religion and Conflict in the Tudor Reformations*. London: Bloomsbury, 2012.

Dussel, Enrique D., and Alan Neely. *A History of the Church in Latin America: Colonialism to Liberation (1492–1979)*. Grand Rapids: Eerdmans, 1981.

———. "Transmodernity and Interculturality: An Interpretation from the Perspective of Philosophy of Liberation." http://enriquedussel.com/txt/Transmodernity%20and%20Interculturality.pdf.

———. "World-System and 'Trans-Modernity.'" *Nepantla: Views from the South* 3, no. 2 (2002): 221–44.

Dyrness, William A. *How Does America Hear the Gospel?* Grand Rapids: Eerdmans, 1989.

———. *Learning about Theology from the Third World*. Grand Rapids: Zondervan, 1990.

———. *Reformed Theology and Visual Culture: The Protestant Imagination from Calvin to Edwards*. Cambridge: Cambridge University Press, 2004.

Dyrness, William A., and Veli-Matti Kärkkäinen, eds. *Global Dictionary of Theology: A Resource for the Worldwide Church*. Downers Grove, IL: IVP Academic, 2008.

Edwards, Paul. *The Encyclopedia of Philosophy*. New York: Macmillan, 1967.

Effa, Allan L. "Releasing the Trigger: The Nigerian Factor in Global Christianity." *International Bulletin of Missionary Research* 37, no. 4 (2013): 214–18.

Engel, James F., and William A. Dyrness. *Changing the Mind of Missions: Where Have We Gone Wrong?* Downers Grove, IL: InterVarsity, 2000.

Escobar, Samuel. *Changing Tides: Latin America and World Mission Today*. Maryknoll, NY: Orbis, 2002.

———. *En busca de cristo en América latina*. Buenos Aires: Kairos, 2013.

Espín, Orlando O. *Grace and Humanness: Theological Reflections because of Culture*. Maryknoll, NY: Orbis, 2007.

Feliciano, Juan. "Suffering: A Hispanic Epistemology." *Journal of Hispanic/Latino Theology* 2, no. 1 (1994): 41–50.

Fergusson, David, and Marcel Sarot. *The Future as God's Gift: Explorations in Christian Eschatology*. Edinburgh: T&T Clark, 2000.

Fernández Retamar, Roberto. "Nuestra América y occidente." *Casa de las Américas* 98 (1976): 36–57.

Fraijó, Manuel. *Fragmentos de esperanza*. Spain: Verbo Divino, 1992.

Fulljames, Peter. *God and Creation in Intercultural Perspective: Dialogue between the Theologies of Barth, Dickson, Pobee, Nyamiti and Pannenberg*. Frankfurt: Peter Lang, 1993.

Gadamer, Hans-Georg. *Truth and Method*. Translated and edited by Garrett Barden and John Cumming. New York: Seabury, 1975.

García-Johnson, Oscar. "Eucaristía de comunión: Sacramento de la iglesia glocal." *Vida y pensamiento* 33, no. 1 (2013): 125–59.

———. *Mestizo/a Community of the Spirit: A Postmodern Latino/a Ecclesiology*. Eugene, OR: Pickwick, 2009.

———. "Mission within Hybrid Cultures: Transnationality and the Glocal Church." In *The Gospel after Christendom: New Voices, New Cultures, New Expressions*, edited by Ryan K. Bolger. Grand Rapids: Baker Academic, 2012.

Geertz, Clifford. *The Interpretation of Cultures: Selected Essays*. New York: Basic Books, 1973.

Goizueta, Roberto S. *Caminemos con Jesús: Toward a Hispanic/Latino Theology of Accompaniment.* Maryknoll, NY: Orbis, 1995.

———. *Liberation, Method, and Dialogue: Enrique Dussel and North American Theological Discourse.* Atlanta: Scholars Press, 1988.

———. *We Are a People! Initiatives in Hispanic American Theology.* Minneapolis: Fortress, 1992.

González, Juan. *Harvest of Empire: A History of Latinos in America.* New York: Penguin, 2011.

González, Justo L. *Historia del pensamiento cristiano.* Barcelona: Clie, 2010.

———. *Mañana: Christian Theology from a Hispanic Perspective.* Nashville: Abingdon, 1990.

González Faus, José Ignacio. *La humanidad nueva: Ensayo de cristología.* 8th ed. Santander: Sal Terrae, 2000.

Gorman, Michael J. "What Has the Spirit Been Saying? Theological and Hermeneutical Reflections on the Reception/Impact History of the Book of Revelation." In *Revelation and the Politics of Apocalyptic Interpretation,* edited by Richard B. Hays and Stefan Alkier. Waco: Baylor University Press, 2012.

Greeley, Andrew. *The Catholic Imagination.* Berkeley: University of California Press, 2004.

Green, Joel B. *Practicing Theological Interpretation: Engaging Biblical Texts for Faith and Formation.* Grand Rapids: Baker Academic, 2011.

Greene, Colin J. D. *Christology in Cultural Perspective: Marking Out the Horizons.* Grand Rapids: Eerdmans, 2003.

Greenman, Jeffrey P. "Learning and Teaching Global Theologies." In *Global Theology in Evangelical Perspective: Exploring the Contextual Nature of Theology and Mission,* edited by Jeffrey P. Greenman and Gene L. Green. Downers Grove, IL: IVP Academic, 2012.

Gregory, Brad S. *The Unintended Reformation: How a Religious Revolution Secularized Society.* Cambridge, MA: Belknap Press of Harvard University Press, 2012.

Grenz, Stanley J. *A Primer on Postmodernism.* Grand Rapids: Eerdmans, 1996.

Groody, Daniel G. *Globalization, Spirituality, and Justice: Navigating the Path to Peace.* Maryknoll, NY: Orbis, 2007.

Gruzinski, Serge. *The Mestizo Mind: The Intellectual Dynamics of Colonization and Globalization.* Translated by Deke Dusinberre. New York: Routledge, 2002.

Gunton, Colin E. *Act and Being: Towards a Theology of the Divine Attributes.* Grand Rapids: Eerdmans, 2002.

———. *The Promise of Trinitarian Theology.* Edinburgh: T&T Clark, 1991.

———. *The Triune Creator: A Historical and Systematic Study.* Grand Rapids: Eerdmans, 1998.

Gutiérrez, Gustavo. *Hablar de Dios desde el sufrimiento del inocente: Una reflexión sobre el libro de Job.* 2nd ed. Salamanca: Sígueme, 1988.

———. *A Theology of Liberation: History, Politics, and Salvation.* Maryknoll, NY: Orbis, 1973.

Held, David, Anthony McGrew, David Goldblatt, and Jonathan Perraton. *Global Transformations: Politics, Economics and Culture.* Stanford, CA: Stanford University Press, 1999.

Henry, O. *Cabbages and Kings.* Digireads.com (2011).

Hille, Rolf. "European Theology." In *Global Dictionary of Theology: A Resource for the Worldwide Church,* edited by W. Dyrness and V. M. Kärkkäinen. Downers Grove, IL: IVP Academic, 2008.

Horne, Gerald. *The Deepest South: The United States, Brazil, and the African Slave Trade.* New York: New York University Press, 2007.

Isasi-Díaz, Ada María, and Eduardo Mendieta. *Decolonizing Epistemologies: Latina/o Theology and Philosophy.* New York: Fordham University Press, 2012.

Jenkins, Philip. *The Next Christendom: The Coming of Global Christianity.* Oxford: Oxford University Press, 2002.

Jennings, Willie James. *The Christian Imagination: Theology and the Origins of Race.* New Haven: Yale University Press, 2010.

Jenson, Robert W. *Systematic Theology.* Vol. 1, *The Triune God.* New York: Oxford University Press, 1997.

Kalu, Ogbu. *African Pentecostalism: An Introduction.* Oxford: Oxford University Press, 2008.

Kärkkäinen, Veli-Matti. *Christ and Reconciliation: A Constructive Christian Theology for the Pluralistic World.* Grand Rapids: Eerdmans, 2013.

Katongole, Emmanuel. *The Sacrifice of Africa: A Political Theology for Africa.* Grand Rapids: Eerdmans, 2011.

Keener, Craig S., and M. Daniel Carroll R. *Global Voices: Reading the Bible in the Majority World.* Peabody, MA: Hendrickson, 2013.

Kelly, J. N. D. *Early Christian Creeds.* 3rd ed. London: Longman, 1972.

Kitamori, Kazo. *Theology of the Pain of God.* Richmond: John Knox, 1965.

Koyama, Kosuke. *No Handle on the Cross: An Asian Meditation on the Crucified Mind*. Maryknoll, NY: Orbis, 1977.

————. *Water Buffalo Theology*. Maryknoll, NY: Orbis, 1974.

Kwok Pui-lan. *Postcolonial Imagination and Feminist Theology*. Louisville: Westminster John Knox, 2005.

LaCugna, Catherine Mowry. *God for Us: The Trinity and Christian Life*. San Francisco: HarperSanFrancisco, 1991.

Ladd, George E. *The Gospel of the Kingdom*. Grand Rapids: Eerdmans, 1990.

Lores, Rúben. "El destino manifiesto y la empresa misionera." *Vida y pensamiento* 7, nos. 1–2 (1987): 13–30.

Ma, Wonsuk. "Pentecostal Eschatology." *Asian Journal of Pentecostal Studies* 12, no. 1 (2009): 95–112.

Mackay, John Alexander. *The Other Spanish Christ: A Study in the Spiritual History of Spain and South America*. New York: Macmillan, 1933.

Martí, José. *Nuestra América*. Venezuela: Fundación Biblioteca Ayacucho, 2005.

Martínez, Juan F. "'Outside the Gate': Evangelicalism and Latino Protestant Theology." In *Global Theology in Evangelical Perspective: Exploring the Contextual Nature of Theology and Mission*, edited by Jeffrey P. Greenman and Gene L. Green. Downers Grove, IL: IVP Academic, 2012.

Mbiti, John S. *African Religions and Philosophy*. London: Heinemann, 1969.

————. *New Testament Eschatology in an African Background: A Study of the Encounter between New Testament Theology and African Traditional Concepts*. London: Oxford University Press, 1971.

McGrath, Alister E. *Christian Spirituality: An Introduction*. Oxford: Blackwell, 1999.

Menocal, Maria Rosa. *The Ornament of the World: How Muslims, Jews, and Christians Created a Culture of Tolerance in Medieval Spain*. Boston: Back Bay, 2002.

Mignolo, Walter. "Decolonizing Western Epistemology/Building Decolonial Epistemology." In *Decolonizing Epistemologies: Latino/a Theology and Philosophy*, edited by Ada María Isasi-Díaz and Eduardo Mendieta. New York: Fordham University Press, 2012.

————. *Desobediencia epistémica: Retórica de la modernidad, lógica de la colonialidad y gramática de la descolonización*. Buenos Aires: Del Signo, 2010.

————. "Epistemic Disobedience and the Decolonial Option: A Manifesto." *Transmodernity* 1, no. 2 (2011): 44–66.

————. "Geopolitics of Sensing and Knowing: On (De)coloniality, Border Thinking and Epistemic Disobedience." *Postcolonial Studies* 14, no. 3 (2011): 273–83.

————. "Postcolonialismo: El argumento desde América latina." In *Teorías sin disciplina: Latinoamericanismo, poscolonialidad y globalización en debate*, edited by Santiago Castro-Gómez and Eduardo Mendieta. Mexico City: Miguel Ángel Porrúa, 1998.

Míguez Bonino, José. *Doing Theology in a Revolutionary Situation*. Philadelphia: Fortress, 1975.

————. *Faces of Latin American Protestantism: 1993 Carnahan Lectures*. Grand Rapids: Eerdmans, 1997.

Miller, Donald E., and Tetsunao Yamamori. *Global Pentecostalism: The New Face of Christian Social Engagement*. Berkeley: University of California Press, 2007.

Moffett, Samuel H. *A History of Christianity in Asia*. Vol. 1, *Beginnings to 1500*. San Francisco: HarperSanFrancisco, 1991.

————. *A History of Christianity in Asia*. Vol. 2, *1500 to 1900*. Maryknoll, NY: Orbis, 2005.

Moltmann, Jürgen. "The Cross as Military Symbol for Sacrifice." In *Cross Examinations: Readings on the Meaning of the Cross Today*, edited by Marit. A. Trelstad. Minneapolis: Fortress, 2006.

————. *The Crucified God: The Cross of Christ as the Foundation and Criticism of Christian Theology*. Translated by R. A. Wilson and John Bowden. London: SCM, 1973.

————. *Theology of Hope: On the Ground and the Implications of a Christian Eschatology*. New York: Harper & Row, 1967.

Moltmann, Jürgen, with Harvey Cox et al. *The Future of Hope: Theology as Eschatology*. Edited by Frederick Herzog. New York: Herder and Herder, 1970.

Morimoto, Anri. "Contextualised and Cumulative: Tradition, Orthodoxy and Identity from the Perspective of Asian Theology." *Studies in World Christianity* 15, no. 1 (2009): 65–80.

Morris, Rosalind C., and Gayatri Chakravorty Spivak. *Can the Subaltern Speak? Reflections on the History of an Idea*. New York: Columbia University Press, 2010.

Mugambi, J. N. Kanyua. *Christian Theology and Social Reconstruction*. Nairobi: Acton, 2003.

Myers, Bryant L. *Walking with the Poor: Principles and Practices of Transformational Development*. Maryknoll, NY: Orbis, 1999.

Nederveen Pieterse, Jan. *Globalization and Culture: Global Mélange.* Lanham, MD: Rowman & Littlefield, 2004.

Nelson, Derek R. Introduction to *Theologians in Their Own Words.* Edited by Joshua M. Moritz and Ted Peters. Minneapolis: Fortress, 2013.

Noll, Mark A. *The New Shape of World Christianity: How American Experience Reflects Global Faith.* Downers Grove, IL: IVP Academic, 2009.

Nyamiti, Charles. *African Tradition and the Christian God.* Eldoret: Gaba, 1970.

——. *Christ as Our Ancestor: Christology from an African Perspective.* Gweru: Mambo, 1984.

O'Connor, Flannery. *Mystery and Manners: Occasional Prose.* Edited by Sally Fitzgerald and Robert Fitzgerald. New York: Farrar, Straus & Giroux, 1962.

Okorocha, Cyril. "The Meaning of Salvation: An African Perspective." In *Emerging Voices in Global Christian Theology,* edited by William A. Dyrness. Grand Rapids: Zondervan, 1994.

Padilla, C. René. *Mission between the Times: Essays.* Grand Rapids: Eerdmans, 1985.

——. "Toward a Contextual Christology from Latin America." In *Conflict and Context: Hermeneutics in the Americas,* edited by Mark Lau Branson and C. René Padilla. Grand Rapids: Eerdmans, 1986.

Palazzi, Félix. "Hope and the Kingdom of God." In *Hope and Solidarity: Jon Sobrino's Challenge to Christian Theology,* edited by Stephen J. Pope. Maryknoll, NY: Orbis, 2008.

Pedraja, Luis G. *Teología: An Introduction to Hispanic Theology.* Nashville: Abingdon, 2003.

Pérez Álvarez, Eliceo. "In Memory of Me: Hispanic/Latino Christology beyond Borders." In *Teología en conjunto: A Collaborative Hispanic Protestant Theology,* edited by José David Rodriguez and Loida I. Martell-Otero. Louisville: Westminster John Knox, 1997.

Pérez-Torres, Rafael. "Alternative Geographies and the Melancholy of Meztisaje." In *Minor Transnationalism,* edited by Françoise Lionnet and Shu-mei Shih. Durham, NC: Duke University Press, 2005.

Plantinga, Richard J., Thomas R. Thompson, and Matthew D. Lundberg. *An Introduction to Christian Theology.* Cambridge: Cambridge University Press, 2010.

Pobee, John S. *Toward an African Theology.* Nashville: Abingdon, 1979.

Pope, Stephen J. *Hope and Solidarity: Jon Sobrino's Challenge to Christian Theology.* Maryknoll, NY: Orbis, 2008.

Rahner, Karl. *The Church and the Sacraments*. New York: Herder and Herder, 1963.

———. *The Trinity*. Translated by Joseph Donceel. New York: Herder and Herder, 1970.

Rhoads, David M. *From Every People and Nation: The Book of Revelation in Intercultural Perspective*. Minneapolis: Fortress, 2005.

Ringma, Charles. "Liberation Theologians Speak to Evangelicals: A Theology and Praxis of Serving the Poor." In *The Church and Poverty in Asia*, edited by Lee Wanak and Bina Agong. Mandaluyong City: OMF, 2008.

Rivera-Pagán, Luis. *Evangelización y violencia: La conquista de América*. San Juan: Cemi, 1991.

Said, Edward W. *Orientalism*. New York: Vintage, 1979.

Sanneh, Lamin O. *Translating the Message: The Missionary Impact on Culture*. Maryknoll, NY: Orbis, 1989.

Schmemann, Alexander. *For the Life of the World: Sacraments and Orthodoxy*. Crestwood, NY: St. Vladimir's Seminary Press, 1973.

Schreiter, Robert J. *The New Catholicity: Theology between the Global and the Local*. Maryknoll, NY: Orbis, 1997.

Shaw, Mark. "Robert Wuthnow and World Christianity: A Response to *Boundless Faith*." *International Bulletin of Missionary Research* 36, no. 4 (October 2012): 179–84.

Silva Gotay, Samuel. *El pensamiento cristiano revolucionario en América latina y el caribe: Implicaciones de la teología de la liberación para la sociología de la religión*. 3rd ed. Río Piedras, Puerto Rico: Huracán, 1989.

Smith, Adam. *The Wealth of Nations*. New York: Collier, 1902.

Smith, Christian, and Melinda Lundquist Denton. *Soul Searching: The Religious and Spiritual Lives of American Teenagers*. Oxford: Oxford University Press, 2005.

Sobrino, Jon. *Christology at the Crossroads: A Latin American Approach*. Maryknoll, NY: Orbis, 1978.

———. *Fuera de los pobres no hay salvación*. San Salvador: UCA Editores, 2008.

Stinton, Diane, ed. *African Theology on the Way: Current Conversations* London: SPCK, 2010.

Strong, Josiah. *Our Country*. New York: Baker and Taylor, 1885.

Sweet, Leonard I. *AquaChurch*. Loveland, CO: Group, 1999.

Tamez, Elsa. *Bible of the Oppressed*. Maryknoll, NY: Orbis, 1982.

———. "Reliving Our Histories: Racial and Cultural Revelations of God." In *New Visions for the Americas: Religious Engagement and Social Transformation*, edited by David B. Batstone. Minneapolis: Fortress, 1993.

Tanner, Kathryn. *Theories of Culture: A New Agenda for Theology*. Minneapolis: Fortress, 1997.

Taylor, Charles. *A Secular Age*. Cambridge, MA: Belknap Press of Harvard University Press, 2007.

Taylor, John V. *The Primal Vision: Christian Presence amid African Religion*. London: SCM, 1965.

Torres, Sergio, and Virginia Fabella. *The Emergent Gospel: Theology from the Underside of History*. Maryknoll, NY: Orbis, 1978.

Vasconcelos, José. *La raza cósmica: Misión de la raza iberoamericana*. Buenos Aires: Espasa-Calpe, 1948.

Vásquez, Manuel A., and Marie F. Marquardt. *Globalizing the Sacred: Religion across the Americas*. New Brunswick, NJ: Rutgers University Press, 2003.

Wainwright, Geoffrey. *Eucharist and Eschatology*. New York: Oxford University Press, 1981.

Walls, Andrew. "The Rise of Global Theologies." In *Global Theology in Evangelical Perspective: Exploring the Contextual Nature of Theology and Mission*, edited by Jeffrey P. Greenman and Gene L. Green. Downers Grove, IL: IVP Academic, 2012.

Wanak, Lee, and Bina Agong. *The Church and Poverty in Asia*. Mandaluyong City: OMF, 2008.

Wandel, Lee Palmer. *The Reformation: Toward a New History*. Cambridge: Cambridge University Press, 2012.

Woodberry, Robert D. "The Missionary Roots of Liberal Democracy." *American Political Science Review* 102, no. 2 (2012): 244–74.

Wright, N. T. *Jesus and the Victory of God*. Minneapolis: Fortress, 1996.

———. *Surprised by Hope: Rethinking Heaven, the Resurrection, and the Mission of the Church*. New York: HarperOne, 2008.

Wuthnow, Robert. *Boundless Faith: The Global Outreach of American Churches*. Berkeley: University of California Press, 2009.

Wuthnow, Robert, and Stephen Offutt. "Transnational Religious Connections." *Sociology of Religion* 69, no. 2 (2008): 209–32.

Zizioulas, Jean. *Being as Communion: Studies in Personhood and the Church*. Crestwood, NY: St. Vladimir's Seminary Press, 1985.

Index